NATO 2.0

Also by Sarwar A. Kashmeri

America and Europe After 9/11 and Iraq:
The Great Divide, Revised and Updated Edition

Related Titles from Potomac Books

Diplomacy Lessons: Realism for an Unloved Superpower
—John Brady Kiesling

Divided America on the World Stage:
Broken Government and Foreign Policy
—Howard J. Wiarda

Flawed Diplomacy:
The United Nations & the War on Terrorism
—Victor D. Comras

NATO 2.0

Reboot or Delete?

Sarwar A. Kashmeri

Foreword by AMB. ROBERT E. HUNTER

Potomac Books, Inc.
Washington, D.C.

Library of Congress Cataloging-in-Publication Data
Kashmeri, Sarwar A.
  NATO 2.0 : reboot or delete? / Sarwar A. Kashmeri ; foreword by Robert E. Hunter.
     p. cm.
  Includes bibliographical references and index.
  ISBN 978-1-59797-664-0 (hardcover : alk. paper)
  1. North Atlantic Treaty Organization. I. Title.
  JZ5930.K38 2011
  355'.031091821–dc22

                                            2010054080

Printed in the United States of America on acid-free paper that meets the American National Standards Institute Z39-48 Standard.

Potomac Books, Inc.
22841 Quicksilver Drive
Dulles, Virginia 20166

First Edition

10 9 8 7 6 5 4 3 2 1

To my dear wife, Deborah Ellis,
whose love keeps me inspired,

and to her five sheep and Jenny May, the donkey,
who put it all into perspective

Contents

Foreword

For more than sixty years, the North Atlantic Treaty Organization (NATO) has been the premier international military security institution. Indeed, it is common to say that NATO is the most successful alliance in history.

But what of NATO in the future, or "going forward," in contemporary slang? Geopolitical developments now under way will inevitably impact the future of NATO and the willingness of governments—and people—both to see it as having continuing value and to invest in its capabilities. At one level, there is a growing division among many of the allies about the locus of the threat and challenge to individual nations and to the alliance as a whole. To overgeneralize, most European countries focus on the continent itself, both on "problems still unresolved," especially the future of Russia, and on new problems that have emerged, including potential (and actual) threats to the delivery of energy and to the security of cyberspace. By contrast, the United States is focused less on matters of European security—where it sees most of the work as done—and more on the Middle East and Southwest Asia, including Iraq, Iran, Afghanistan, and Pakistan, along with attendant threats from terrorism. This is not to say that European states are not also cognizant of potential threats to their own security emanating from this part of the world, just that there is a difference of emphasis and, hence, a difference of commitment to be engaged and to invest resources. Thus, there is no overall agreed basis for common assessment of security threats to all members of the alliance—certainly not similar to the situation in the Cold War—or, even when there is such agreement, of the proper means of responding.

At another level, the nature of security itself has changed remarkably since the end of the Cold War, especially with the disappearance of the central preoccupation with a single threat, that from the Soviet Union (and associated communism). For one thing, far more attention is being paid to domestic issues of security, including the health of economies and the environment, and in the classic area of dealing with external threats there is more preoccupation, varying from state to state, with homeland security and, as noted for some countries, new concerns regarding energy and cyberspace. For another thing, even in classic areas of security, the nature of challenges is requiring a mixture of responses. As has been made clear in Bosnia, Kosovo, Iraq after the initial 2003 invasion, and now in Afghanistan, in such conflicts military power and presence are only one requirement. Of significant, if not in some cases equal, importance are nonmilitary instruments of power and influence. Thus, in Afghanistan it has become a truism that the military efforts of the International Security Assistance Force (ISAF) have to be buttressed with the promotion of good governance and major progress in reconstruction and development.

These observations clearly point to a major conclusion: NATO, as basically a military (or political-military) institution, does not necessarily dispose of the capabilities—or the experience and temperament—best suited to meet nonmilitary requirements, and, all things being equal, it would not be wise to develop those capabilities within NATO as opposed to relying on individual nations or one or another institution. And among those other institutions, the European Union (EU) stands out. Not only does it bring together just the European states—thus, in its calculation of security issues, taking the perspective of European interests—but it also can dispose, directly or through mobilizing the efforts of nations, of a wide range of nonmilitary capabilities precisely in the disciplines so much needed notably in Afghanistan today. Further, through its Common Security and Defense Policy (CSDP), the EU can undertake activities in security where the two non-European NATO members, the United States and Canada, would prefer not to be engaged, for example, in parts of Africa, as evident in some actions already taken by the CSDP.

It would thus seem natural, therefore, that NATO and the EU—through the CSDP—would work closely together. But such is not the case. Indeed, in the early part of the post–Cold War period, the two institutions—then NATO and the Western European Union—largely held aloof from each other and engaged in a kind of competition, as much about form as about substance, including about which of the two institutions would have primacy. It was possible to argue, indeed, that NATO and the EU are two institutions living in the same city (Brussels) but on different planets.

Much of that relationship has now changed, as the United States, for its part, and some of the more independent members of the EU, for their part—notably France—have come to understand that more unites the perspectives of NATO and the EU than divides them, or at least this should be so. This realization also comes at a time when spending on military forces, at least in almost all of Europe (and Canada), have been falling considerably and when the need has arisen for integrating civilian with military efforts. The issue then naturally becomes how to get NATO and the EU (in the CSDP) to work together. This matter is not a simple question, but answer it we must. All of us on both sides of the Atlantic, whatever our allegiances or preferences in terms of the primacy of one institution or another, must answer the question together. Indeed, it is now crucial, in order to command the attention and the support of governments and people, on both sides of the Atlantic for common security efforts, that primacy needs to be put on devising a new transatlantic compact—a new Atlantic Charter, as it were—and only then on parceling out tasks to nations, to NATO, to the EU, and to the two institutions working together.

Fortunately, we have in hand a recipe book for undertaking this important work both of analyzing the basics of NATO's potential future and of advancing NATO-EU cooperation. This task is set forth in this volume, *NATO 2.0: Reboot or Delete?*, and it brilliantly succeeds. Its author, Sarwar A. Kashmeri, is a nonresident senior fellow with the Atlantic Council's International Security Program. In *NATO 2.0*, he brings together a wealth of information, a clear grasp of history, a deep understanding of both the inner and outer workings of NATO and the European Union, and especially the requirements that both must meet—singly and especially together—to have relevance as security institutions for the future. The blueprint for moving forward is here, especially in NATO-CSDP relations. Further, if this book can help the two institutions, finally, to make the great leap forward to seeing their futures as necessarily intertwined and thus be willing to work together, effectively, as never before, it will have more than proved its worth.

Robert E. Hunter
RAND Corporation
June 15, 2010

Acknowledgments

The trouble with creating an acknowledgments section is that one invariably forgets to recognize the help of a valued source without whom the book would be the poorer. So, let me apologize in advance to anyone whose name does not appear here. Now, I will try to settle my accounts.

First and foremost, I thank my interlocutors, the political and military leaders, and NATO experts who took time from their busy schedules to speak with me. They are listed at the end of this section, and I want them to know how grateful I am for their contribution.

I am especially grateful to Lt. Gen. Brent Scowcroft and Senator Chuck Hagel for their support and encouragement. Both are extraordinarily gifted Americans, and I am lucky to have had their guidance during the writing of this book.

It is a pleasure to acknowledge the help of the Atlantic Council of the United States. Damon Wilson, director of the council's International Security Program, was particularly helpful. Besides introducing me to a number of officials in the North Atlantic Treaty Organization (NATO), Damon helped me understand what took place within the secretary-general's office in NATO on September 11, 2001. I wound up starting my book with that firsthand account. Dr. Frances G. Burwell, the council's Director of Transatlantic Relations and Studies, served as another valuable resource. The Atlantic Council is a powerful force in preserving and enhancing the close ties between America and Europe, a sentiment to which I have long subscribed.

The other organization to which I owe a great deal of thanks is the Foreign Policy Association (FPA), where I have been a longtime fellow. Noel Lateef, its president and chief executive officer, is both a personal friend and valued counselor. Fast approaching its centenary, the FPA is an extraordinarily effective, nonpartisan organization dedicated to informing the American public about the world and the conduct of U.S. foreign policy.

The views expressed in this book are mine alone and do not represent the opinions of either the Atlantic Council of the United States or the FPA.

Special thanks go to Christopher Matthews, the helpful and knowledgeable press officer at the European Union's Mission to the United Nations in New York, Stavros Petropoulos, the press counselor of the Council of the European Union in Brussels, and Col. Paul Van Der Heijden, NATO's permanent liaison to the United Nations in New York, for their kind help in opening doors and making sure I was well briefed. My friend Anna Typrowicz copyedited the manuscript before it went to the publisher. She is the toughest and most thorough of copyeditors, for which I am eternally grateful. A special thanks also go to Allison Miller, who transcribed all the interviews.

My brother, Zuhair Kashmeri, the well-known Canadian journalist and author, makes good writing look easy. He does it in his sleep. Whenever I needed a creative boost, I called Zuhair. So thanks, brother.

Every writer should be lucky enough to find an agent like Sally van Haitsma. She personally takes each proposal from her charges and insists on sharp, fast-moving prose with substance as well as imagery. She guided me throughout the creation of this book. Thanks for your guidance, Sally.

And I was lucky to team up again with Hilary Claggett, a senior editor at Potomac Books, Inc., and editor of my first book. Hilary recognized the value of this book and insisted it go to Potomac. For that I am grateful. Kathryn Owens, production editor, and her team at Potomac, especially Vicki Chamlee, hammered the draft into a book and made it look effortless. Amro Naddy, assistant editor, adapted table 5, thankfully paying no attention to those who said it could not be done.

Finally, to those whose names appear below, you are the reason I was able to understand NATO and the European Union's Common Security and Defense Policy (CSDP). More important, you encouraged me to think beyond the subject of the book, to the strategic vision that underlies both NATO and the CSDP, and the enormously important Euro-Atlantic alliance. I hope the book does justice to the time you took to speak with me.

INTERLOCUTORS FOR *NATO 2.0: REBOOT OR DELETE?*
(in alphabetical order)

From the United States

- Andrew Bacevich, professor of international relations, Boston University
- Erik Bleich, associate professor of political science, Middlebury College, Vermont
- Arnaud de Borchgrave, director and senior adviser, Transnational Threats Project, Center for Strategic and International Studies
- R. Nicholas Burns, Professor of the Practice of Diplomacy and International Politics, Harvard Kennedy School; former assistant secretary of state; and former ambassador to NATO
- Soner Cagapty, senior fellow and director of the Turkish Research Program, Washington Institute for Near East Policy
- Tim Cornett, colonel, USA; commander, Standing Joint Force Headquarters, U.S. Southern Command
- Bantz J. Craddock, general, USA (Ret.); former NATO Supreme Allied Commander Europe
- Larry Goodson, director and associate professor of Middle East studies, U.S. Army War College, Carlisle, Pennsylvania
- Robert Gosende, associate vice chancellor for international programs, State University of New York; former ambassador to Somalia
- Marc Grossman, vice chairman, the Cohen Group; former ambassador to Turkey and Pakistan
- Chuck Hagel, former senator; cochairman of the president's Intelligence Advisory Board; chairman of the Atlantic Council of the United States
- James Hoge, editor, *Foreign Affairs* magazine

- Noel Lateef, president and CEO, Foreign Policy Association
- Leo G. Michel, senior research fellow, Institute for National Strategic Studies, National Defense University
- Victoria Nuland, former ambassador to NATO
- Michael C. Ryan, colonel, U.S. Mission to the European Union
- Brent Scowcroft, lieutenant general, USA (Ret.); former national security adviser; CEO of the Scowcroft Group
- Stan Sloan, visiting scholar, Middlebury College, Vermont
- Tom Twetten, retired deputy director for operations, Central Intelligence Agency
- Charles Van Bebber, colonel, USA; director of European studies, U.S. Army War College, Carlisle, Pennsylvania
- Damon Wilson, vice president and director, International Security Program, Atlantic Council of the United States

From Canada
- James Appathurai, NATO spokesman, Strategic Director of Press Office
- Christopher J. R. Davis, lieutenant general, CMM, CD; Canadian military representative to NATO
- Elizabeth Race, deputy defence policy adviser, Canadian Joint Delegation to NATO

From Turkey
- H. Tarik Oguzlu, assistant professor, Ankara University
- Ersin Onunduran, professor of international relations, Ankara University

From the European Union
- Stéphane Abrial, general, Supreme Allied Commander for Transformation, NATO
- Jan Alhadeff, EU Crisis Management Planning Directorate
- Jurgen Bornemann, lieutenant general; director general, NATO, International Military Staff
- Patrick Chevallereau, captain, French navy; executive assistant, Supreme Allied Commander Transformation, NATO
- Giampaolo Di Paola, admiral; chairman, NATO Military Committee

- Carlos Fernández-Arias Minuesa, ambassador; chairman, European Union Political and Military Committee
- Mark C. Fischer, Transatlantic Center, German Marshall Fund of the United States (Brussels)
- Jeremy Greenstock, Sir, GCMG; former U.K. ambassador to the United Nations
- Shada Islam, senior program executive, European Policy Studies (Brussels)
- Karl-Heinz Lather, general, German Army; chief of staff, Supreme Headquarters Allied Powers in Europe, NATO (Casteau, Belgium)
- David Leakey, lieutenant general, CMG, CBE; director general, European Union Military Staff
- Antonio Missiroli, director of studies, European Policy Studies, Brussels
- Patrick Nash, lieutenant general; former commander, European Union Force in Chad and the Central African Republic
- Patrick de Rousiers, lieutenant general, French air force; French military representative to the European Union Military Committee and the NATO Military Committee
- Pedro Serrano, ambassador and acting head of the European Union's delegation to the United Nations
- Håkan Syren, general; chairman, European Union Military Committee
- Andrzej Towpik, ambassador of Poland to the United Nations
- Sverker Ulving, colonel; minister counselor, European Union Military Staff; military liaison officer to the United Nations
- Fernando Valenzuela, ambassador of Spain to Russia
- Stefani Weiss, director, Europe's Future/Shaping Global Future, Brussels Office—Bertelsmann Stiftung
- Dick Zandee, head, Planning and Policy Unit, European Defense Agency

From Russia
- Dmitri Rogozin, ambassador to NATO

These one-on-one conversations refined my ideas and conclusions. Where appropriate, direct quotations from these conversations are used to illuminate my narrative. When one of these interlocutors is quoted in this book without a citation, the reader can assume it is a direct quote from one of our conversations.

There is no question that my interlocutors were enormously helpful and a source of firsthand information. They inspired me. But the conclusions I came to are entirely my own, and it would be a mistake to link them to any particular interlocutor.

NATO, like any other bureaucracy that has developed for more than half a century, is not easy to describe. To simplify the narrative and keep it on message, I have chosen to bypass some of NATO's elements such as its Partnership for Peace (PfP) projects. I also chose not to spend time on the dozens of departments and programs that are embedded within the alliance such as the Military Committee Meteorological Group and the NATO Frequency Management subcommittee. Additionally, I decided to not drill into NATO arcana such as the differences among the NATO Standardisation Organisation, the NATO Committee for Standardisation, the Office for NATO Standardisation, and NATO Standardization Agency.

While reading the chapter on NATO's organization, the reader should keep in mind that at the Lisbon NATO Summit, held during November 2010, a decision was made to dismantle scores of committees from the NATO bureaucracy, slash a number of headquarters and commands, and reduce NATO's headcount by a few thousand (from some 14,000). A decision on where in the organization these cuts will fall had not been made as this book went to press.

The European Union's Common Security and Defense Policy (CSDP) is an important part of this book's narrative. It used to be called the European Security and Defense Policy (ESDP) until the Lisbon Treaty took effect on December 1, 2009. To avoid going back and forth between ESDP and CSDP, I use CSDP throughout the book.

I intend to update and continue to comment on this book's subject matter after publication. These observations together with ongoing news about the book will be posted on its website: www.2nato2.com.

Introduction

On an overnight visit to one of the U.S. Navy's aircraft carriers, I found myself seated at dinner between two senior naval officers whose ages differed by around eighteen years. During dinner I asked the older officer what he thought about the North Atlantic Treaty Organization (NATO). His answer was an emphatic endorsement. "It is and will continue to be the most powerful alliance for safeguarding the world," he said. Later, during a conversation with the younger officer, I asked the same question. His answer was equally forthright but dramatically different from that of his comrade in arms. "I remain to be convinced that NATO serves a useful purpose anymore," he told me.

I am often asked why I decided to write a book on NATO. That conversation on the high seas, in one of the most powerful warships in the world, answers the question more clearly and succinctly than I ever could. The answers from the two naval officers stripped the protective shield that surrounds any discussion of NATO and boiled the argument down to its essentials. If two senior members of America's armed forces could have such divergent opinions about the greatest military alliance in history, does anyone really understand why, twenty years after the end of the Cold War, NATO still exists and what its main purpose is?

The confusion illuminated by the naval officers is even more pronounced among Americans outside the military. "You mean NATO is still around?" an incredulous investment banker in New York recently asked me. The dean of a well-known private college in Boston confidently assured me that she was quite certain NATO was not a military force anymore and was "probably just humanitarian assistance staffs." A retired college professor from Arizona asked if I was sure, absolutely sure, that NATO troops were serving in Afghanistan.

How, I wondered, could there be so much confusion about a military alliance that is supposed to be at the core of the relationship between America and Europe? Given what I was finding out about NATO from my conversations, the transatlantic alliance ought to be in tatters. But this situation is clearly not the case.

The United States and the European Union between them represent some eight hundred million people who produce almost two-thirds of the world's economic activity. They invest more in one another and hire more of each other's citizens to work in their companies than any two entities in the world. And from a range of issues spanning art, culture, history, and academia, the transatlantic relationship has seldom appeared stronger.

What is true I found out, while doing research for my earlier book, *America and Europe after 9/11 and Iraq: The Great Divide,* is that there has been a steady deterioration in the political and security aspects of the transatlantic relationship. This divide deepened since 2001 as the American military pursued actions after 9/11 that the Europeans believe were taken without adequate regard for the core agreement of the NATO alliance, which requires unanimity among members and conformance with international law as represented by the Security Council of the United Nations.

My earlier book argued that the divide is structural and would not repair itself simply through a change in personalities. This observation has certainly been borne out by the flow of events. Neither the change in American administrations nor the change in a number of EU countries' leaders has done much to bridge the divide, even though the rhetoric has become far more civil.

As I researched this book I came to realize that instead of being a force for transatlantic unity and geopolitical stability, as it is supposed to be, NATO has become the reverse. The alliance is increasingly a force that works against transatlantic unity and geopolitical stability. And, as I shall demonstrate, NATO's professed, indeed required, assurances of protection for its members are promises it can no longer keep. Left dangling in this state and as its internal tensions continue to damage the already frayed transatlantic ties, NATO risks becoming irrelevant to the security needs of the European-Atlantic area.

NATO's downward trajectory is in contrast to the upward sweep of the European Union's increasingly successful Common Security and Defense Policy (CSDP).

The alliance's lackluster performance in Afghanistan has left an impression in North America that the Europeans have no desire to engage in military action anymore. Many Americans believe that the process of creating the European Union has left Europeans with the feeling that every geopolitical problem can be resolved with patience, negotiations, and compromise. In other words, the Europeans have become pacifists.

Nothing could be further from the truth. Over the last decade the European Union has sent out twenty-seven CSDP military and civilian missions around the world. Most of them were small deployments, but they also included the first naval deployment by the European Union and a powerful military force sent to Africa.

The European Union's naval deployment to the Horn of Africa protects shipping against Somali pirates and is twice the size of a similar NATO force that also operates off Somalia. The military mission was sent to Chad in the center of Africa. Twenty-three EU member states were joined by Russia, Albania, and Croatia to mobilize over ten thousand troops for the African mission. As seen in chapter 5, during the nineteen-month mission to Africa, the European Union's military force fought three engagements against insurgents, deployed and used European special forces, and handled complex logistics required to send and maintain military forces in a landlocked country thousands of miles from Europe.

I spent two weeks in Brussels meeting with key leaders of the CSDP to find out more about the European Union's military arm. I subsequently had two conversations with Lt. Gen. Patrick Nash, the Irish operations commander of the Chad mission.

As a result of this research I have developed a far more nuanced understanding of the European approach to crisis management. Instead of a military-centric approach, the European Union relies on multidimensional missions that can be tailored to the needs of a crisis by using a toolbox of military, diplomatic, police, human rights, and development aid resources.

As of August 7, 2010, a new EU department, the European External Action Service (EEAS), took over responsibility for these missions. Uniquely, this department combines the European Union's military arm, its diplomatic service, and its development aid programs into a powerful crisis management tool. This arrangement would be akin to combining the U.S. Departments of Defense and State under one secretary. It is a novel and far more effective approach to winning hearts and minds in the conflicts projected for the twenty-first century.

The CSDP, the European Union's military arm, is still relatively young. The total military staff in Brussels numbers around two hundred as compared to some fourteen thousand permanent positions in NATO. But the CSDP has wind in its sails while NATO's sails are stalling. The CSDP has a sense of where it is headed while NATO is still grappling with its relevance after the end of the Cold War. The Europeans appear solidly behind the CSDP while their commitment to NATO appears half hearted, as demonstrated by the largest NATO allies, which are quitting the fighting in Afghanistan and heading home. Crucially, both the CSDP and NATO are feeling the impact of the global economic downturn.

Another thing to keep in mind is, contrary to popular belief, NATO does not have a standing military force. Both NATO and the CSDP generate forces for a mission by dipping into the same pool of European military resources that include some 2 million army, navy, and air force personnel; 5,000 military aircraft; and 3,500 helicopters. The combined military budgets of the twenty-seven European Union members, of some 210 billion euros (approximately $360 billion), fund the military assets from which both NATO and the CSDP can draw resources. It is a budget that is now under considerable strain given the financial downturn and quickly disappearing support from European publics for the seemingly interminable Afghan war.

Recognizing that today's threats will be considerably different from those encountered during the Cold War, NATO has begun to transform itself from a defensive military organization to one geared to crisis management missions. But the European Union, through the CSDP, already has this base covered. It is ready, willing, and able to handle the crisis management missions that NATO is trying to transform itself to execute.

What NATO has is an integrated military command and control structure that the alliance has perfected over its sixty-year life span. The CSDP will surely need these capabilities as it expands its role to include European territorial defense, and outgrows the ad hoc military headquarters system that controls the European Union's deployments.

It is also clear from recent speeches delivered by Secretary of State Hillary Rodham Clinton and Defense Secretary Robert Gates, and from the deliberation at the NATO Summit meeting in Lisbon, November 19–20, 2010, that NATO will have to significantly trim its bureaucracy and become much more cost effective and relevant. Maintaining hundreds of committees, a bureaucracy of some fourteen thousand people, and multiple military commands is no longer feasible given the deep and continuing global economic downturn.

In this emerging picture of two organizations with overlapping objectives and financial constraints lies a window of opportunity.

Press most Europeans and you will find they still believe NATO is their ultimate security blanket. It is this historical trust in the NATO brand that provides an opportunity for leaders on both sides of the Atlantic to synchronize again the strategic visions of Europe and North America and to revitalize the transatlantic security relationship.

If the CSDP and NATO were businesses, I would propose sending in a top-flight investment bank to recommend a range of alternatives, from undergoing a full merger to combining significant parts of their businesses. I realize neither the CSDP nor NATO is a business and that there are political hurdles to any kind of combination, as demonstrated by the two organizations' inability to formally collaborate on anything major. But the task may not be as daunting as it sounds.

As the Paris-based EU Institute for Security Studies has pointed out, four countries in Europe—Britain, France, Germany, and Italy—provide roughly 70 percent of the European Union's defense spending. (Britain and France alone provide 45 percent.) Add two more countries—the Netherlands and Spain—and the six account for 80 percent of the European Union's defense spending. All are members of the European Union, which passed the Lisbon Treaty in 2009 and set up the EEAS. Its head, the High Representative of the Union for Foreign and Security Policy, is a potentially powerful position that was created to present a unified European security and foreign policy to the world.

The United States and Canada should encourage these six European Union countries to use their clout and leadership within the European Union and empower High Representative Catherine Ashton to begin working with the American secretary of state or the American secretary of defense, and the Canadian defense minister, on a project to develop the road map to bridge NATO and the CSDP. During the project the allies would be forced to consider the broader political divide between America and Europe and to take steps to forge a strategic consensus that recalibrates the transatlantic security relationship for the new century. A newly energized European-American security relationship would strengthen and further promote the growth of the wider transatlantic alliance, which is, I believe, the real prize and the key to global security and financial stability.

I recognize that the NATO's new mission statement, adopted at its Summit meeting in Lisbon (see appendix E) rededicates the alliance to the protection of its members. And it commits the alliance to handling new threats such as cyberattacks, nuclear proliferation, terrorism, and ballistic missile defense while developing a civilian-military crisis management capability.

It is difficult to understand how NATO will be able to pay for all these new capabilities as it slashes its budget and workforce. For example, the alliance believes the development of a Europe-wide anti-ballistic missile shield will cost its members around $200 million over ten years, or around $770,000 per member per year. But a more realistic estimate for the shield was provided by *The Telegraph* on November 24, 2010. The respected British newspaper estimated the cost at around $58 billion.[1] Will European states come up with this level of funding for the project as their budgets are being slashed? I think not.

NATO cannot survive simply by dreaming its way out of reality. In its original version, that I call NATO 1.0, the alliance could exist as a successful stand alone military alliance. For the threats and economics of the twenty-first century, its viability requires NATO to reboot and transform itself into NATO 2.0 by bridging itself to the EU's CSDP.

It would be a pity to let NATO fade away because we may then have to reinvent it someday. And that will not be easy.

Abbreviations

ACT	Allied Command Transformation, one of two operating commands. Charged with keeping NATO's capabilities and equipment at the cutting edge, and located in Norfolk, Virginia
ANA	Afghan National Army
AWACS	Airborne Warning and Control System
BiH	Bosnia and Herzegovina
CAR	Central African Republic
CFSP	Common Foreign and Security Policy
CONOPS	Concept of Operations
CSDP	Common Security and Defense Policy, previously called the ESDP
EC	European Commission
EDA	European Defense Agency
ESDP	European Security and Defense Policy; this phrase was replaced by CSDP on December 1, 2009, with the passage of the Lisbon Treaty
ESS	European Security Strategy
EUFOR	European Union Force
EUFOR Tchad/RCA	European Union Force in Chad and the Central African Republic
EUJUST	European Union Rule of Law Mission
EUJUST LEX/Iraq	European Union Integrated Rule of Law Mission for Iraq

EUJUST Themis   European Union Rule of Law Mission in Georgia

EULEX Kosovo   European Union Rule of Law Mission in Kosovo

EUMC   European Union Military Committee, directs all EU military activities and provides the Political and Security Committee (PSC) with advice and recommendations on military matters. Composed of the defense chiefs of all twenty-seven EU states. *See* NATO MC

EUMM   European Union Monitoring Mission

EUMM Georgia   European Union Monitoring Mission in Georgia

EUMS   Military Staff of the European Union, performs strategic planning for all EU-led operations

EUPM/BiH   European Union Police Mission (Bosnia and Herzegovina)

EUPOL   European Union Police Mission

FYROM   Former Yugoslav Republic of Macedonia

HR   High Representative

ISAF   International Security Assistance Force (Afghanistan)

MSC (HOA)   Maritime Security Center (Horn of Africa)

NAC   North Atlantic Council, NATO's top decision-making body

NATO   North American Treaty Organization, the West's military alliance, headquartered in Brussels

NATO MC   NATO's Military Committee, NATO's highest military authority is composed of the chiefs of defense of all twenty-eight member countries. Reports to the NAC. *See* EUMC

NAVFOR   European Union's naval force in the Horn of Africa

PSC   Political and Security Committee (European Union); the EU's military arm, CSDP, reports to the PSC

SACEUR   Supreme Allied Commander, Europe. Runs NATO's Operations Command from Brussels. *See also* SACT

SACT   Supreme Allied Commander Transformation. Runs NATO's transformation command from Norfolk. *See also* ACT and SACEUR

SHAPE   Supreme Headquarters Allied Powers, Europe, located in Casteau, Belgium, and serves as the headquarters of NATO's military organization

TEU   Treaty on European Union

CHAPTER ONE

Fault Lines

NATO has been the world's most successful military alliance. But what do we do with it now?

—*Lt. Gen. Brent Scowcroft, U.S. Air Force (Ret.)*

Damon Wilson, deputy director of the private office of Secretary-General Lord Robertson at the headquarters of the North Atlantic Treaty Organization (NATO) in Brussels, will never forget the frustration he felt when he saw the hijacked United Airlines Flight 175 fly into the South Tower of the World Trade Center in New York City. It was 3:03 p.m. in Brussels on September 11, 2001, which had started out as a quiet, uneventful day. Wilson remembers that Lord Robertson was in and out of the office, attending a sequence of meetings, as his personal staff attended to the myriad details that continuously find their way to NATO's chief executive officer.

News that something highly unusual was taking place in New York had begun to filter into the office immediately after the North Tower of the World Trade Center was hit by the hijacked American Airlines Flight 11 some twenty minutes earlier. That is when Wilson and the rest of the staff moved into the private conference room attached to the secretary-general's office and switched on the large television monitor.

Lord Robertson's office of the sprawling military alliance of the then-nineteen countries comprised a surprisingly small and tightly knit group (the alliance has since expanded to twenty-eight countries). Besides Wilson, there was John Day, director of the Private Office; Edgar Buckley, the assistant secretary-general; and Steve Stern, the office director. All Americans, they were glued to the unfolding horror of terrorist attacks on New York and Washington.

Wilson remembers being in shock as he watched the towers collapse in a huge pall of smoke: "I have a lot of friends in Washington and New York, so I was immediately trying to get through to family members and close personal colleagues in government. It was very difficult to get any connections and I remember feeling this sense of hopelessness . . . so far away from home . . . your country being attacked . . . what is to be done?"

NATO has a well-oiled crisis management and security plan that had already been activated. Throughout Europe, NATO offices, military posts, and command centers added layers of security and went into emergency operating mode. And in the secretary-general's office, the initial feeling of shock gave way to needing to respond in some way. As Wilson recalls, "Here we were, sitting at NATO, the headquarters of a *military* alliance, whose leader has just been attacked. What can NATO do?"

And then a message popped up on Wilson's computer screen: "NATO should invoke Article 5 of the NATO Treaty!"

Article 5 of the alliance's 1949 founding treaty is the pivot around which NATO's power and mission revolves. It is the heart of the NATO alliance. This "one for all and all for one" declaration promises that an attack on any NATO member will be considered an attack on all its members. Never previously invoked, even in the darkest days of the Cold War with the Soviet Union, here finally was the opportunity for NATO to demonstrate its power, continuing relevance, and decision-making machinery. It was time for NATO to stand shoulder to shoulder with one of its members and give notice that in its response to the terrorist attacks in New York and Washington, the United States would not fight alone. It would have the combined might of all the members of the North Atlantic Treaty Organization fighting with it. But would the allies take this momentous step?

On the other side of the NATO headquarters building, R. Nicholas (Nick) Burns, the American ambassador to NATO, was asking himself the same question. Burns recalls being at lunch when his driver brought word that an aircraft had crashed into one of the World Trade Center buildings: "We thought it was an accident or something. But by the end of the lunch, as other information streamed in, we knew that a horrific crime had been committed."

As the American delegation tried to put the pieces together and figure out who had perpetrated this horrific act, Burns recalled a telephone call from David Wright, the Canadian ambassador to NATO. Wright believed the Americans should request an invocation of Article 5, and he felt there was a good chance the allies would get on board.

"I was the newcomer to NATO, having just arrived there," Burns told me. "And Wright was the dean of NATO's diplomatic corps, having served there the longest, so we decided to go for it." Burns called Condoleezza Rice, the U.S. national security adviser, to make sure the Bush administration agreed with the plan. "Condi told me she would brief the president and the cabinet, but felt we should go ahead because it would be a huge psychological boost for the American people if they got up in the morning and found out that all eighteen NATO allies had thrown their support behind the United States. And that's what we did."

So many things were happening at once that afternoon that he cannot be sure, but Wilson believes it was Stern, the office director, who thought up the idea of invoking Article 5 in the secretary-general's office. "When I and the other members of the office saw Stern's message on the screen, we knew that was what the response had to be, and it galvanized us into action," Wilson said.

Lord Robertson, to his credit, immediately recognized the enormous importance of NATO showing solidarity with the United States in its hour of peril and need. "He showed real leadership," Wilson said, "because we knew it would be virtually impossible to get through the normal State Department–Defense Department–White House chain of command in this emergency. If it was going to be done, Lord Robertson would have to drive it, and he did." Wilson, of course, had no way of knowing that Rice and Burns had already short-circuited the chain of command.

Later that evening, at a meeting of all the NATO ambassadors, Burns would formally table America's request to invoke Article 5, with a request that the ambassadors return with a decision the next day.

Decisions in NATO are made by consensus in the North Atlantic Council (NAC). The NAC (pronounced "knack" by everyone in the alliance) is the alliance's top decision-making body, and it includes ambassadors from every member nation. Each of them would have to consult his or her respective nation's leader before giving approval to the unprecedented step of invoking Article 5 for the first time. Lord Robertson and his staff hit the telephones to start building consensus and ensure every NATO country agreed with the Article 5 decision. The secretary-general set up an emergency meeting of the NAC for the evening of September 12, with a press conference to follow.

Wilson remembers the whirlwind of activity in the secretary-general's office that followed: "We were on the phone to London, Germany, Paris, getting hold of presidents, prime ministers, defense ministers, anyone and everyone, to make sure each country's representative would have the authority to say yes to the Article 5 decision."

Suddenly, out of nowhere, a bottleneck occurred. The Belgian government could not agree to join the decision. "It was potentially a catastrophe in the making," Wilson told me. "The Belgian cabinet was locked in fierce debate and could not agree on a course of action." Finally, Robertson stepped in; telephoned Guy Verhofstadt, the prime minister of Belgium; and insisted that the prime minister take his call in the middle of the cabinet's debate. Robertson forcefully reminded the Belgians that NATO was founded to help protect countries like theirs from Russian troops rolling over them, and that now Belgium was refusing to stand by the United States, it was breaking unanimity on invoking Article 5. It was disgraceful, the secretary-general told the Belgian cabinet. The pressure worked. "And we got the Belgians to shut down the debate and green-light the decision for the NAC meeting the next day," Wilson said.

After its meeting on September 12, the NAC began to draft its decision to invoke Article 5. It declared that in its time of need, "America can rely on its eighteen Allies in North America and Europe for assistance and support. NATO solidarity remains the essence of our Alliance. Our message to the people of the United States is that we are with you. Our message to those who perpetrated these unspeakable crimes is equally clear: you will not get away with it."[1] After half a century of NATO's planning to respond to just such a moment, the gears of its military machine meshed into action, through the mechanism of Article 5 of its founding treaty.

As the press release was being finalized for the world's media, there arose another unexpected bottleneck. NATO's lawyers had discovered a legal technicality that needed to be resolved before this weighty clause could be invoked. The lawyers insisted that Article 5 only applied to aggression from outside the borders of the NATO countries, and pending a confirmation that an outside force was responsible for the attacks on the United States, NATO could not invoke the mutual defense clause. Robertson's press announcement would have to be postponed.

But NATO members believed it was far too important to show both their outrage at the terrorist acts committed against the United States and the solidarity with America to hold up the press conference. They would invoke Article 5 conditionally, pending confirmation of the source of the attacks. And so they did. NATO's first ever Article 5 declaration bowed to the alliance's lawyers with a sentence that read, "If it is determined that this attack was directed from abroad against the United States, it shall be regarded as an action covered by Article 5 of the Washington Treaty."[2]

Don Murray, reporting for the Canadian Broadcasting Corporation, summed up the mood after the Article 5 announcement. "It won't just be the United States looking to avenge Tuesday's terror attacks, behind the United States will be the eighteen other member nations of the North Atlantic Treaty Organization. . . . NATO members now consider an attack against one of them to be an attack against all of them."[3]

It was a milestone in NATO's history. NATO's decision was laden with existential consequences for the alliance that were not then apparent. But on that fateful day, September 12, 2001, NATO stepped up and acted in the best tradition of the transatlantic alliance.

The CBC's Don Murray did comment on the considerable historical irony of NATO's first use of Article 5. "Originally, Article 5 was designed to bring the United States to the aid of Europe if it was attacked by the Soviet Empire," he reported, "instead as the American President talks about the first war of the twenty-first century, the Article is being invoked to bring Europe to the aid of the United States."[4]

Within days the United States had found out that the 9/11 attacks were committed by members of the global terrorist organization al Qaeda, which was headquartered in Afghanistan and acting under the protection of the Taliban regime. That discovery sealed the deal with NATO, and on October 2, 2001, at a special press conference, NATO secretary-general Lord Robertson announced that since it had been determined that the attacks had been directed from abroad, they were regarded as an action covered by Article 5 of the Washington Treaty. He was careful to point out "at present, it was premature to speculate on what military action would be taken by the alliance, be it individually or collectively." But lest there be any doubt about the alliance's commitment, Robertson went on to "reiterate that the United States of America can rely on the full support of its eighteen NATO allies in the campaign against terrorism."[5]

On October 9, 2001, NATO operationalized Article 5 by agreeing to a number of specific actions in support of the United States and other allies. These stipulations included the provision of blanket overflight clearances for their aircraft, enhanced intelligence sharing and cooperation, increased security for their facilities on European territory, and their continued access to ports and airfields on the territory of NATO nations for refueling and for operations against terrorism.

That day, the first of five NATO airborne warning and control system (AWACS) aircraft began deploying to the United States. They freed up American aircraft for the war against al Qaeda and the Taliban in Afghanistan.[6]

Warships from nine NATO countries pooled together into the Standing Naval Force Mediterranean (STANAVFORMED) and steamed out to new battle stations in the eastern Mediterranean Sea. The naval squadron provided a perfect example of how NATO combines assets from member countries, under the alliance's integrated military command structure, to meet its defense responsibilities: STANAVFORMED's flagship HMS *Chatham*, a frigate from the U.K. navy, led the German frigate FGS *Bayern*, Greek destroyer HS *Formion*, Italian frigate ITS *Aliseo*, Dutch frigate HN-LMS *Van Nes*, Spanish frigate SPS *Santa Maria*, Turkish frigate TCG *Gire-*

sun, American frigate USS *Elrod*, and an auxiliary oiler from Germany, FGS *Rhoen*.[7]

In the history of NATO, the concept of Article 5 takes center stage. The economy and industry in most of continental Europe had been destroyed during World War II. Even the economy of Britain, part of the allied victory team, was on its knees. In this weakened position Western Europe faced an existential threat from an aggressive Soviet Union that had begun to subjugate countries on its border and absorb them into the Soviet Empire.

NATO was created to harness America's might to help defend Western Europe against the Soviet Empire's hostile ambitions. Article 5 raised the bar for any Soviet invasion of Europe to a virtually unscalable level. In unambiguous terms, Article 5 warned any would-be aggressor that NATO would consider an attack on any NATO member as though it was an attack on every member. An attack on tiny Luxembourg, for instance, would be treated as an attack on the territory of Germany, Britain, or the United States.

Article 5 directly connected America's power and resources to the defense of Europe and was the fulcrum on which NATO would execute its defensive mission. It was the deterrent threat embodied in NATO's Article 5, backed up by American power, that had ensured the Cold War remained cold.

The awesome industrial power of the United States and NATO's Article 5 checkmated the aggressive designs of the Soviet Union. The Soviets simply could not risk picking a war with the United States. In the end, thanks to the threat of Article 5 and structural weaknesses within the Soviet Union, the communist state collapsed without NATO ever having fired a shot.

That Article 5 had never been used during the Cold War is why NATO's invoking it after 9/11 had so much symbolism for the Euro-Atlantic countries. Just the act of invoking Article 5 sent a clear signal to the world that ten years after the collapse of the Soviet Union the transatlantic alliance was still relevant and in good shape. The Europeans were ready to stand shoulder to shoulder with their American cousins. France's popular daily, *Le Monde*, summed it up for the world in its editorial on September 12,

2001. "In this tragic moment, when words seem so inadequate to express the shock people feel, the first thing that comes to mind is this: We are all Americans!" the newspaper proclaimed.[8]

What NATO did not then know was that in its flurry of activity to invoke Article 5, it had already reached the limits of what it could do to help the United States. The supply of adrenaline that 9/11 had injected into NATO's veins had just about run its course. America would soon make clear that it had no interest in using NATO to dispense justice on the 9/11 perpetrators. All that trouble NATO's members had gone through to invoke Article 5 within a day of 9/11 had been for naught.

Three weeks later when the United States went to war in Afghanistan, it did so alone. NATO's offer to execute an Article 5 action and send NATO forces to avenge the attack on a NATO member was cavalierly dismissed by the United States. Paul Wolfowitz, U.S. deputy secretary of defense, attended a NAC meeting in September and brusquely told America's allies that thanks, but no thanks; that it would be too hard to integrate the alliance's forces; and that America was going into Afghanistan by itself. "We had a disastrous NAC," Wilson said to me.

But there was more to come. Wolfowitz's boss, Donald Rumsfeld, the American defense secretary, went to the NAC meeting in December 2001. Answering Robertson's plea to let America's NATO allies help the United States and to go into Afghanistan as an allied force, Rumsfeld briskly announced that it really was not necessary. He said America was going to be out of Afghanistan in three months, or by March of the following year. To add insult to injury, Rumsfeld said there might be a need for NATO to help America clean up after the fighting.

Robertson literally almost fell out his chair, Wilson recalls. "What unbelievable hubris," Wilson remembers thinking to himself at the meeting. "Here we were in December of 2001, the Taliban had just been routed, and the defense secretary of the United States was saying American forces would be home by March of 2002."

The message from the United States to its NATO allies could not have been clearer: while it appreciated the alliance's offers of support and was grateful for the small naval flotilla in the Mediterranean and the AWACS airplanes, when there was real fighting to be done, America would go it alone. Going to war together with its allies, America judged, would be more of a hindrance than a help. This was an incredible statement, considering that the alliance had been practicing to wage battle together as an integrated force for fifty-two years.

It was as though the famous motto of the Three Musketeers—"one for all and all for one"—had counted for naught. At the first sign of danger the allies' leader, their d'Artagnan, had waved to his fellow swordsmen and left to do battle by himself.

It was a revealing glimpse into the real state of the transatlantic military alliance on which the members had spent billions of dollars and untold amounts of political capital. If NATO's first ever invocation of Article 5 had suddenly yanked the military alliance back from obscurity and planted it in the world's media headlines, America's dismissal of the alliance as unworkable sent a clear public message that America no longer considered NATO to be its premier platform for fighting today's wars.

A fault line was now visible in NATO's steely exterior. It was to widen in the lead-up to America's invasion of Iraq two years later, when it was NATO that would repay the compliment. Despite repeated pleas from its leader, the alliance would refuse to support America and did not go to war in Iraq.

During the debate in the United Nations (UN) on the reasons for invading Iraq, differences appeared within NATO's ranks about the justification for invading a sovereign country. Meanwhile, the European members of NATO were startled to discover that Defense Secretary Rumsfeld believed there really were two Europes, an old Europe and a new Europe.

The "new Europe," as he defined it, comprised NATO members that agreed with the United States that the invasion of Iraq, a sovereign country, could proceed without the authorization of the United Nations or consensus among NATO members. All that was necessary, Rumsfeld believed, was for America to say it was the right thing to do.

The "old Europe," Rumsfeld explained, was represented by all the ancient, rusty European nations that lived in the backwaters of geopolitics. Its members cared more for UN mandates and NATO consensus than for following the United States into war without any ifs, ands, or buts.

And so it came to pass, two years after overlooking NATO and invading Afghanistan by itself, the United States ignored the United Nations and the advice of many of its NATO partners and invaded Iraq. Even the fact that some of NATO's largest and most important members, such as Germany and France, had serious misgivings about the justification for the invasion had not influenced America's decision.

In the end NATO decided not to participate in the Iraq War. The United States went ahead with the campaign, using individual NATO members that had decided to join the invasion. The open split in the alliance's ranks was yet another sobering reminder about NATO's fall from grace.

But the emerging fault lines kept spreading. Part of America's invasion strategy involved pouring troops into Iraq through Turkey, one of NATO's oldest and most reliable members. The trouble was, no one on the invasion team had bothered to consult the Turks about using their country to invade one of its neighbors. It had simply not occurred to anyone to pave the way with the Turkish government and to seek permission first from the Turkish parliament. The American military planners assumed that a military request from another NATO member, especially the United States, would never be turned down.

It was the wrong assumption to make.

Rebuffing the heavy-handed pressure to accept America's war plans, the Turkish parliament denied the use of Turkish soil for the invasion.[9] Another fault line had opened up in NATO. But it was only a visible part of numerous related issues with potentially dangerous implications for NATO and the wider transatlantic alliance.

Turkey is a republic in which the vast majority of citizens are Muslims. The governing party, now reelected twice, is openly Islamist, meaning it draws its inspiration from the teachings of the Prophet Muhammad. However, Islam is not—and under Turkey's secular constitution, cannot be—the official state religion. Turkey serves as a powerful model for Muslim countries of the Middle East. After all, for six hundred years, the Ottoman Empire was the largest in the world, and its ruler was the caliph of the world's Muslims. The Ottoman Empire is now long gone, but Turkey is the inheritor of that history and its cachet. Its very name has a special meaning for Muslims around the world.

Turkey is in the process of joining the European Union (EU). It was invited to join the European Union in 1999, but lately the Europeans have been sending strong signals that they are rethinking their invitation to Turkey. Why? Because the countries opposed to membership (especially France and Germany) claim Turkey is "not suited for EU membership."[10] The change in opinion used to be phrased more subtly, but it has lately become much more overt. If Turkey is refused membership into the European Union, how will this decision play out in the halls of NATO? The Turks, who are good enough to put their lives on the line for NATO, might ask why they are not good enough to join the European Union. Will another fault line appear in NATO's structure?

And what about the growing number of Europeans of Turkish descent? How will they react to NATO's long war in Muslim lands? Europe, as we shall see in chapter 6, has around three million Turkish immigrants,[11] and as this voting constituency increases in importance, Europe's elected officials will need to give its sensitivities growing attention. What might the impact of this constituency be on the alliance's future?

NATO was created for the purpose of defending its members against armed attack. In the 1990s, under strong pressure from the United States, NATO decided to become involved in Bosnia and Kosovo, the alliance's first military missions outside the territory of NATO members. Although controversial, these missions did succeed in restoring stability to NATO's backyard. More important, the missions in Bosnia and Kosovo helped NATO take the first steps in recognizing that it could move beyond its historical defensive mission and become a force for offensive military interventions beyond its members' borders. NATO formally adopted this out-of-area role in 1999 and made it a part of its new strategic concept, a mission statement that the alliance recalibrates every ten years.

The adoption of its out-of-area role is what ultimately led NATO into Afghanistan, where the alliance now leads the International Security Assistance Force (ISAF), which the United Nations set up to stabilize Afghanistan. NATO asked for and received command of the ISAF in 2003. It is the alliance's first attempt at deploying troops thousands of miles away from Europe, and it is not going well. NATO has struggled to perform the Afghanistan mission, revealing serious structural problems that were largely invisible during NATO's Cold War period. In spite of the bravery and sacrifice shown by individual soldiers from NATO countries, the performance of the alliance as a whole has been far from inspiring. "Most European nations are spending less on defense than they promised and are avoiding the main battles in Afghanistan," said Nicholas Burns, the former American ambassador to NATO and now a professor at Harvard.[12] Afghanistan may yet be the end of NATO's global crisis management aspirations.

As an illustration, on September 5, 2009, two fuel trucks hijacked by the Taliban were stuck knee-deep in mud four miles south of Kunduz. From his intelligence sources, Col. Georg Klein, commanding officer of NATO's German troops deployed in Afghanistan, knew that in a matter of hours the Taliban would convert the trucks into gigantic bombs capable of blowing up thousands of troops under his command. For now, fortuitously, the trucks were mired in the river.

At his direction, a U.S. Air Force F-15E strike fighter circling the tankers relayed live video feed, and on their glowing screens Colonel Klein and his officers could see the trucks surrounded by scores of people. The colonel's intelligence on the ground confirmed they were Taliban, trying to free the trucks. Trusting his battlefield instincts and his intelligence, Colonel Klein ordered the jet fighter to attack. Within seconds a precision-guided, five-hundred-pound bomb hit each truck.

The resulting firestorm could be seen for miles. The trucks and the dots disappeared from the colonel's radar screen. It was an awesome demonstration of modern war and NATO's interoperability—that is, the ability of troops from many countries to act as one integrated fighting machine. What the colonel could not see then was another firestorm that would hit him broadside within hours. This one would come from his own country.

Among the 125 people killed by the bombs were dozens of civilians. As NATO began an investigation into the colonel's bombing decision, prosecutors in Potsdam—the headquarters for the German army—began their own investigation to determine whether Colonel Klein should be charged with homicide. Under German law its forces can only be deployed for peacekeeping. America might be at war in Afghanistan, but Germany is not. The German colonel had violated the condition under which German troops were sent to Afghanistan. Colonel Klein had forgotten that he could parade with a NATO army but not fight with it.

Germany is not the only country that sets strict conditions on its NATO troops. Half of the allied forces in Afghanistan operate under restricted battlefield conditions. Gen. Dwight Eisenhower stormed the beaches of Normandy in 1944 with an allied army that followed his every command. In Afghanistan, however, American commanders have to consult a checklist for each mission to figure out which allied soldiers may be called on to fight.

NATO's internal disagreements have also introduced an element of instability into Euro-Atlantic relations. Within days of the Kunduz air strike, German ambassadors fanned out in important NATO and European Union member states to stop fellow NATO nations from criticizing the controversial air strike. The disagreement between NATO members played out publicly and embarrassingly in media reports.

A former spokesman for the German foreign ministry, Jens Ploetner, told the *Financial Times* in Berlin that in the face of public criticism by its NATO partners, Germany's ambassadors in important NATO and EU member states had launched diplomatic protests with those countries' governments. The errant members were quick to retort, "What should a minister say if such an attack kills 80 and there are civilians among them? Nothing?" The German government also confirmed reports that it would send its own investigation team to accompany the NATO probe into the air strike. A defense ministry spokesman, Thomas Raabe, denied that the team would try to correct NATO's review of what actually happened in Kunduz. "You don't need to correct anything when there's nothing to be corrected," he said at a press conference.[13]

Against this backdrop of a misfiring alliance, the people in NATO countries have become increasingly skeptical about the nine-year-old war in Afghanistan. Fierce opposition to NATO's request to extend the deployment of two thousand Dutch troops beyond 2010 led to the collapse of the Dutch government on February 19, 2010, dooming the fourth largest Allied troop commitment in Afghanistan. Even as NATO secretary-general Anders Fogh Rasmussen promises that the alliance will be in Afghanistan for as long as it takes, over 60 percent of America's NATO allies now want their forces in Afghanistan severely reduced or removed altogether.

At the November 2010 NATO Summit in Lisbon, under strong pressure from the United States and Rasmussen, NATO agreed to prolong its Afghanistan involvement until 2014. But the extension applies to NATO training resources, not battle forces. Many of NATO's largest troop contributors will pull their forces out long before then.

The truth, which remains buried under shining uniforms and grand military titles, is that NATO today is increasingly dysfunctional, a shadow of what it used to be during the Cold War when it was rightly called the world's most formidable military alliance. Today NATO is "faltering. It's being hollowed out and not performing up to par," Burns said.[14] It's no wonder, then, that the alliance's dreams of adopting an out-of-area mission are withering in the mountains of Afghanistan.

Colonel Klein had inadvertently cracked open a window into the house of NATO. And in 2009 the view inside was not pretty. With Western economies in financial freefall and as more people understand its diminished status, how long can NATO dodge tough questions from the taxpayer? The issue is especially pressing considering the younger European generation, for whom the phrases "Cold War" and "Soviet Union" are a distant memory, is now witnessing the successful evolution of the European Union's own military arm, the Common Security and Defense Policy (CSDP).

The CSDP was established in 1999 and in spite of its infancy sent shock waves through the NATO establishment. Alarm bells went off in the United States about the newcomer into the Euro-Atlantic security mix, and NATO circled the wagons and fenced off its turf.

As chapter 5 recounts, the European Union, under American pressure, agreed to strict rules about when and how it could use the CSDP to deploy missions. NATO had first rights of refusal on security missions, and the CSDP was prohibited from setting up its own planning and control staffs, lest it go off on its own and become an even more serious competitor to the older organization. The paranoia at NATO was so intense that when the CSDP deployed a small French peacekeeping mission to the Congo, without consulting NATO and under the EU flag, it caused the alliance to panic and cancel another well-publicized collaborative mission between the two organizations.

Nevertheless, even though it is not the smoothest of relationships, the CSDP and NATO have now coexisted for over a decade. During this time, even though the CSDP is far smaller with relatively minimal funding, it has made significant progress. For example, a CSDP naval flotilla that is twice the size of NATO's patrols the coast of Somalia to offer protection against pirates. It has already deployed twenty-four missions over its short lifetime, including a military mission of thirty-seven hundred persons to Chad, in the center of Africa, thousands of miles from Brussels—a powerful demonstration of the CSDP's ability to deploy and sustain military forces at considerable distances. The introduction of the CSDP into the European security landscape has added yet another element of uncertainty to NATO's future.

Most members of NATO are also part of the European Union, and that duality results in another fault line. The European Union has brought European nations together into an ever-closer political, financial, and economic union. But the same members act as separate countries within NATO and have to unintegrate themselves for NATO decision making. This arrangement of forcing the EU states to disconnect themselves when wearing their NATO hats is the only way America can maintain control of NATO. Otherwise, the EU block would always outvote it.[15] Can this state of affairs in which Europe cannot fully control its foreign and security policies survive for long?

For a number of reasons the clock is running out on these archaic arrangements in which two security establishments vie for primacy to provide security for the Euro-Atlantic alliance. First, unlike NATO's only foray outside Europe, none of the CSDP's missions—whether deployed to Africa, the Middle East, or Asia—have encountered the skepticism and disillusionment in Europe that NATO has engendered by its Afghan deployment. True, the Afghan mission *is* vastly different in size from the CSDP missions, but in terms of cohesion, public support, lack of infighting, and results, the EU missions stand as a stark contrast to NATO's only deployment outside Europe. Second, America's leadership of NATO took a big hit after its perceived unilateral approach to the Iraq War, its attempts to divide Europeans and disregard the United Nations, as well as the subsequent revelations of secret prisons and accusations of torture. Europeans seem less interested in taking directions from America now.

Last, faced with the global financial meltdown and the deepest economic recession since 1929, the United States has begun to review its huge and growing global commitments. "Set thine house in order," Andrew Bacevich of Boston University advises America while quoting from the Bible.[16] This sentiment would find its way into President Barack Obama's speech delivered on November 25, 2009, at the United States Military Academy at West Point. "As President, I refuse to set goals that go beyond our responsibility, our means, or our interests," he said. "Our prosperity provides a foundation for our power. It pays for our military. It underwrites our diplomacy. It taps the potential of our people, and allows investment in new industry."[17]

The day of reconciling objectives to reality is near for the Euro-Atlantic allies. And in the process it is inconceivable that the need for the permanent existence of two separate security organizations in Europe, with potential duplication of resources and assets, will not be questioned.

It will not be sufficient, in my opinion, to simply say that NATO has kept Europe and North America safe for sixty years and so should continue. After all, NATO's threat for most of those sixty years—the Soviet Union—is no more. And the broken and shattered Europe of the 1940s is now the European Union, arguably the most successful geopolitical project of the last century. The European Union rightly feels it needs a diplomatic and security arm of its own. CSDP, the EU's security arm, was set up in 1999. The Lisbon Treaty of December 1, 2009, added the EU's diplomatic corps—the European External Action Service (EEAS)—and brought the two under the responsibility of one EU official, the High Representative for Foreign Policy. This would be a potential game changer in global geopolitics.

The European Union is not exempt from the laws of economics. Though the role the Europeans envisaged for the CSDP is more limited in scope, the financial and manpower pressures weigh also on the European Union's plans. Paradoxically, shrinking European defense budgets can only strengthen the EU's plans under the CSDP. Witness the recent decision by France and Britain to combine operations of their aircraft carrier and nuclear programs. This is one of many such cost-sharing arrangements now under way among Britain, France, Germany, Italy, and Holland, not to mention other EU countries.

The Lisbon Treaty gives even greater powers to the CSDP to deploy military missions that combine the military elements of a mission with nation-building. Finally, a significant differentiator between NATO and the CSDP is that the CSDP is part of a political entity—namely, the European Union. That situation gives it a diplomatic clout on the world stage that NATO, a military alliance, cannot match. This authority will continue to grow as the European Union does and makes its presence increasingly felt in the corridors of power around the world.

So where does this development leave NATO? I will address this question throughout the book.

In spite of its fault lines, NATO has a number of tested and ready-to-use competencies. One of these, the ability to quickly organize and respond to a humanitarian crisis thousand of miles from its headquarters, was on full display during NATO's speedy response to the calamitous earthquake that hit Pakistan on October 8, 2005. Over eighty thousand people were killed in the tragedy that was located in an inhospitable mountainous region. Another three million were left without food or water. NATO responded to the disaster within three days after the Pakistani government asked for help and did a magnificent job saving lives, rebuilding, and tending to the wounded.

Air bridges were set up from Germany and Turkey to ferry relief goods and supplies. Under Spanish command, NATO's boots on the ground included Spanish and Polish engineer units; an Italian heavy construction equipment unit; British engineers who specialized in high-altitude relief work; a NATO field hospital led by the Dutch army and staffed with Czech, French, Portuguese, and British personnel; one Spanish and three Lithuanian water purification teams; and two civil-military cooperation teams from Slovenia and France. Ultimately a thousand NATO personnel and over two hundred medical specialists worked in Pakistan during the operation.[18]

Such complex operations do not just happen. They require training, field deployment exercises, detailed contingency planning, and an officer corps that is able to work easily with units from a number of countries. It becomes a NATO core competency because of its multinational membership.

NATO also has an enviable record when it comes to creating networks of military officers from dozens of countries, establishing standardized operating procedures, providing collaborative training and deployment exercises, and sharing intelligence. Armies from Canada to Estonia develop field instructions using standard NATO forms to ensure that multinational forces that might have to be deployed together can operate together. NATO's Allied Command Transformation, based in Norfolk, Virginia, has become the alliance's network to absorb lessons learned, improve equipment and procedures, and respond to commanders in the field as they seek practical solutions to battlefield problems.

"I have attended many NATO-organized meetings, and they are full of knowledgeable, important people, diplomats, political leaders, military officers," one of Turkey's best-known foreign policy professionals, Ersin Onunduran of Istanbul University, told me. "Everybody talks about common problems, shares knowledge, discusses deficiencies. I would say if NATO did not exist they would have to invent one."

As the German Marshall Fund of the United States has documented over and over again, citizens of Europe and of North America continue to have warm feelings for NATO as the embodiment of the transatlantic security relationship. In the latest edition of the fund's annual publication, NATO was seen as essential by 59 percent of respondents in the European Union and 60 percent of Americans. But the report flagged a disturbing trend: "While there was majority support for NATO this year, looking at long term trends, support for NATO has decreased over the years."[19]

The question about NATO's future is ultimately linked to the health of the wider transatlantic alliance that encompasses the dense network of business, cultural, emotional, and security links between Europe and the United States.

The wider transatlantic alliance is more necessary than ever in a rapidly changing and interconnected world, with dramatically different security threats and emerging challenges from countries that will soon become global economic behemoths. These new power centers may or may not share the entire spectrum of liberal beliefs in democracy, human rights, and the place of the individual in society that underpin the values and principles of America and European countries. Nor should they, seeing that each comes to the world stage inspired by its own history and experience. It is as guides, mentors, and influencers that the United States and Europe can help smooth the rise and integration of these developing economic and political powerhouses by sharing their own experiences.

German chancellor Angela Merkel spoke eloquently about this continuing relevance of, and need for, the transatlantic alliance in Washington, D.C., during the summer of 2009:

> For me, the special feature of this transatlantic partnership is our sharing of the same fundamental values, meaning we do not have to endlessly debate our interpretation of human rights and respect for the dignity of the person. Our common ground is the sharing of these fundamental values—something that goes for every partnership between German Federal Chancellors and American Presidents, and likewise for partnerships all the way down to the level of members of parliament and local politicians in the states of the Union and the German Länder. The dignity of every individual human being is our benchmark.[20]

It is for this overriding reason, as NATO is still an important part of the structure that holds the transatlantic alliance together, that the alliance must reinvent itself to serve the needs of a new millennium. It is an imperative for leaders in North America and Europe. But this transformation will not be achieved unless the wider public, on both sides of the Atlantic, understands what ails NATO today and agrees on steps to recalibrate the alliance for the twenty-first century.

I contend that one cannot recalibrate NATO today without acknowledging that the Europeans are well on their way to managing their own foreign and security policy by themselves. NATO must also recognize that, in the future, it will add value to the Euro-Atlantic security equation only in situations that require the European Union to act in collaboration with North America, that is, for threats of a magnitude that the Europeans cannot handle on their own. Without NATO recognizing these realities and grafting itself to the European Union's CSDP to remain relevant, its future is far from assured.

Explaining NATO's storied past, its present predicament, and setting the stage for NATO 2.0, a recalibrated alliance for the twenty-first century is the purpose for which this book was written.

CHAPTER TWO

NATO:
The Nuts and Bolts

> Well, we are very glad that Russia is so close to NATO.
> —*Aleksander Kwasniewski, former president of Poland*

The year 1988, one year before NATO celebrated its fortieth anniversary, marked a unique milestone in the alliance's history. NATO did something it had never done before and hired Michael Stopford, who had spent two years burnishing Coca-Cola's image, to re-create NATO's fizz and apply the tools of Madison Avenue to reinforce NATO's continuing importance to an increasingly disinterested and skeptical public. Stopford joined NATO as the deputy assistant secretary-general for strategic communication services. He had his work cut out for him.

Unlike NATO, Coca-Cola has never lost touch with what it is, a tasty thirst quencher, recognized the world over. NATO, meanwhile, over its lifetime, had become an amorphous, hard-to-describe alliance of Western countries that believed NATO could be a world cop, reduce carbon emissions, rebuild nations, defend European borders, prevent money laundering and piracy, serve as a defense research and technology lab, and preserve Western values.

NATO's grab bag self-image has had a predictable result: no one is really sure what NATO, now an alliance of twenty-eight countries, is all about. Not surprising, between 2002 and 2007, the number of those who believed NATO was still essential for security declined by 19 percent in Germany, 12 percent in Britain, 13 percent in Italy, and 8 percent in Poland. Meanwhile, an internal document from NATO noted that the populations of member countries had only vague ideas about the alliance's purpose and policies.[1]

By contrast, in 1949, when NATO was formed, its reason for existing was crystal clear. In fact, its purpose could be—and was—described in one sentence: "NATO was created to keep the Russians out, the Americans in, and the Germans down," said Lord Ismay, NATO's first secretary-general. In that one sentence Ismay had succeeded in explaining the three main reasons NATO was created and in defining its mission.

Any attempt at invading Europe by its then archenemy, the Soviet Union, would be met with NATO's formidable military forces. Also, recognizing that the United States had a habit of disappearing after wars were won, NATO would ensure America's continued presence in Europe. In addition, European wars usually had one common denominator, Germany. By enfolding Germany in the alliance's embrace, both the Europeans and the Americans felt the country's power could be harnessed for the West's common good, as opposed to being the trigger for repeated European wars.

NATO was one of a number of global institutions set up through the far-sighted leadership of post–World War II America and Europe to ensure peace, security, and growing prosperity throughout the world. These institutions included the United Nations, the World Trade Organization (or the General Agreement on Tariffs and Trade, as it was then called), the World Bank, the International Monetary Fund, and NATO.

As crucial as the other institutions were to the unprecedented wave of prosperity that would soon sweep the Western world, it was NATO that ensured the steady march of the "free world" out of the chaos and destruction generated by World War II. NATO provided the security umbrella, confidence, and stability that the war-weakened European nations needed to rebuild themselves and shed their economic wounds.

The Soviet Union played a significant part in the Western alliance that destroyed the Nazi war machine. After the war ended, however, the Soviet Union increasingly distanced itself from Britain, France, and the United States while forcibly incorporating its neighbors into a new communist empire. Within a year of the war's end in May 1945, Russia's Communist leaders had gobbled up its Eastern European, Central European, and Baltic neighbors. The Soviet Empire had now reached the boundaries of Western Europe. As Sir Winston Churchill, Britain's wartime prime minister, so eloquently put it,

> From Stettin in the Baltic to Trieste in the Adriatic an iron curtain has descended across the Continent. Behind that line lie all the capitals of the ancient states of Central and Eastern Europe. Warsaw, Berlin, Prague, Vienna, Budapest, Belgrade, Bucharest and Sofia; all these famous cities and the populations around them lie in what I must call the Soviet sphere, and all are subject, in one form or another, not only to Soviet influence but to a very high and in some cases increasing measure of control from Moscow.[2]

The Soviets now stood eyeball to eyeball with the Western Europeans. It was commonly assumed that, sooner rather than later, the Communists' march westward would continue. Using coercion, intimidation, and outright force, the Soviets would march into the Western European countries and add them to their burgeoning empire. Given the impoverished and weakened condition of Western Europe, there was little that these proud nations could do to defend themselves. They knew their real defense against Soviet domination lay across the Atlantic. Somehow America had to become the guarantor of Europe's security.

With this aim in mind, Britain, France, and the three Benelux countries—Belgium, the Netherlands, and Luxembourg—signed the Treaty of Brussels in March 1948, establishing a defensive alliance to demonstrate to the Americans that Europe was serious about taking steps to defend itself against a communist onslaught. The signatories' weakened state, however, meant the pact would be powerless to fight a Soviet invasion of Western Europe without American might. And in the autumn of 1948 the five members of the Brussels Treaty invited the United States and Canada to formally join them in creating a transatlantic security pact.

The Brussels Treaty was the genesis of the North Atlantic Treaty Organization. It came into being on April 4, 1949, in Washington when twelve countries signed the North Atlantic Treaty. Norway, Denmark, Iceland, Italy, and Portugal joined Britain, France, the Benelux countries, Canada, and the United States in the ceremony to create NATO. The treaty is a model of brevity and clarity and is reproduced in its entirety in appendix A.

It is interesting to note that Portugal, one of the founding members of NATO, was then ruled by a dictatorship that the Portuguese military kept in power. This fact is conveniently forgotten when discussions arise today about letting Russia join NATO. Moreover, they are always cut short with the argument that its membership would change the nature of the alliance, as NATO after all is an alliance of democratic countries. Clearly, NATO's founders had no such qualms.

The second point worth noting, as a cursory glance at appendix A will show, is the close connection the signatories of the North Atlantic Treaty established between NATO and the United Nations. This detail is another fact not generally known or is conveniently overlooked these days.

The first line of the treaty begins, "The Parties to this Treaty reaffirm their faith in the purposes and principles of the Charter of the United Nations." Then, Article 1 states, "The Parties undertake, as set forth in the Charter of the United Nations, to settle any international dispute in which they may be involved by peaceful means in such a manner that international peace and security and justice are not endangered. . . ." Article 7 acknowledges the "primary responsibility of the [UN] Security Council for the maintenance of international peace and security."

The connection with the United Nations brings into focus why most European members of NATO could never let the alliance join America's 2003 invasion of Iraq. The Europeans consider the United Nations to be at the center of world order; so without the Security Council's approval, the American invasion of Iraq was deemed illegal.

As Gordon Rayner's column explained in the *Daily Telegraph* of November 27, 2009, "Britain and the US were . . . unable to get a second UN resolution directly authorizing war after they argued that Saddam was not co-operating with the inspectors and was simply playing for time. The lack of a second resolution has led many critics of military action to argue that the invasion was illegal under international law."[3]

The reverse was true with Afghanistan. The European members of NATO have sent troops to Afghanistan under a NATO flag because the United Nations specifically authorized the creation of the International Security and Assistance Force. A UN mandate provides the legal authority for European troops to be in Afghanistan.[4] I will return to this point later because it has an impact on future NATO operations.

The final point worth highlighting is the absence of Germany from the list of NATO's twelve founding members. Before Germany could play a role in Europe's defense, it had to be allowed to rearm. It had taken the combined might of the United States, Soviet Union, Britain, and a host of other allies to defeat Germany's powerful war machine. NATO was founded just four years after the defeat of Nazi Germany, and the Europeans were understandably sensitive about allowing the Germans to reestablish their armed forces. France, especially, was not convinced that NATO would be able to contain a reconstituted Wehrmacht, or German defense force.[5]

At this point France came up the idea of organizing a West European army, which would be created by merging West European armed forces under a European minister of defense. This arrangement was an early manifestation of the French-led vision of an ever-tighter integration of Europe, leading to something resembling the United States of Europe. France also believed German troops within a European army would be far easier to control than an independent German military force under an alliance.

The Americans felt strongly that placing army units from member countries in a unified NATO command, led by an American general, was the most efficient solution both to defending Europe and to containing a rearmed Germany. Under this plan, each NATO member country would be responsible for raising its own soldiers, with NATO providing planning, coordination, control, and the leadership structure.

There were protracted and sometimes heated discussions for and against each solution. Ultimately the idea of allowing Germany to re-create and rearm its military prevailed. There would not be a stand-alone European army, and American general Eisenhower was appointed as NATO's first supreme allied commander in Europe (SACEUR). By tradition and in recognition of America's position as NATO's most powerful country and de facto leader, every SACEUR since Eisenhower has been an American.

The idea of an independent European army has never gained currency. Even in 1999 when the European Union set up its own military establishment, called the European Security and Defense Policy (ESDP), it chose an alliance modeled after NATO's. Both NATO and the ESDP are in Brussels, a short taxi ride from each other. Scores of American and European officials spend hours debating how the two military organizations should function together without competition.[6]

Fueled by the Soviet threat and lubricated with American dollars, NATO continued to expand. Greece and Turkey joined NATO in 1952. Germany finally joined NATO in 1955. (The Soviet Union and its allies countered with the formation of the Warsaw Pact, which remained NATO's archenemy until the dissolution of the Soviet empire in 1989.) Spain became NATO's sixteenth member in 1982.

At this stage in its life cycle, NATO was still a Western European alliance with a laser-like focus on one objective, to stop a Soviet invasion of Europe at the Elbe River, the boundary of Churchill's so-called Iron Curtain. Then in 1991 the unexpected happened: the Soviet Union collapsed. The West went to sleep one night under the ever-present threat of nuclear annihilation by the Soviets and woke up the next morning to find the Soviet Union was no more. The Iron Curtain had not only been lifted, it had also ceased to exist. NATO's awesome deterrent power had kept Europe safe for forty-two years. The alliance's security umbrella had made it possible for the West to defeat the Soviet Empire without firing a shot.

During the Cold War years, while protected by NATO, which was largely underwritten by American power and dollars, Europe rebuilt itself. It emerged from the devastation of World War II in the shiny new form of the European Union, a breathtaking integration of Europe's many nations into an increasingly closer economic and political grouping that still continues.

The European Union was mainly the result of European ingenuity, hard work, political acumen, and strategic vision. But the powerful concept of an integrated Europe at peace and of a size that would enable it to play a leading role in the world was recognized and supported from its infancy by the United States.[7] By championing Europe's security and ensuring that NATO had the money and military resources it needed, the United States had freed the Europeans to focus their political and financial resources mainly on rebuilding Europe and then on creating the European Union. (At the height of the Cold War with the Soviet Union, the United States had 375,000 troops permanently stationed in Europe. Today there are around 80,000.[8])

Providing for Europe's security after the war is an investment of which Americans can be justly proud. The integration of Europe through the European Union has virtually eliminated military conflict in Europe. As important as it was for Europe, a stable union is an equally important development for the United States, considering the lives and dollars Americans invested in two horrendous European wars during the last century.

With the collapse of the Soviet Empire, NATO had met all the objectives of its founding treaty. It had kept "the Russians out, the Americans in, and the Germans down."

Let me hasten to add that keeping the Germans "down" was not intended to be demeaning. The Germans themselves recognized the enormous benefits to them of an integrated Europe with Germany permanently fixed at its center. The Germans kept that strategic vision firmly in mind as they anchored their future to a virtually subordinate partnership with France. Within a few years France and Germany would become the engine propelling the European Union's growth, a position they maintain today.

Should NATO have been disbanded when the Soviet Union collapsed given that the alliance had met all its founding objectives? I think not. It would have been, in my opinion, almost negligent to disband an alliance that had become essential to the security of the Euro-Atlantic countries and was at the center of the wider transatlantic relationship. Should NATO's future have been elevated to the top of the transatlantic alliance's discussion agenda? Of course. But hindsight is 20/20, and in the high-speed transition of European geopolitics that was then taking place, there was little energy left for the political leadership to do anything but watch the world change.

As General Scowcroft, then the U.S. national security adviser and an architect of the policies that had managed the fallout from the cataclysmic changes in Europe, put it, "I'm sorry that because we were fixed on near-term goals that we didn't think hard enough about how NATO had to change going forward. We focused on a 'Europe whole and free,' but what did that mean? What did it mean to NATO to have the reason for the alliance, the glue that held it together disappear? We never faced up to that."[9]

The disintegration of the Soviet Union left the Central and Eastern European members of the now defunct Warsaw Pact floating in a no-man's-land between Western Europe and Russia, the successor to the Soviet Union. These erstwhile satellite states, having just emerged from decades of dictatorial rule, had one overriding strategic objective—to institutionalize and defend their newfound freedoms.

To institutionalize their rebirth, these countries looked to membership in the European Union. For their defense, however, they wanted to join NATO. More than anything else, these countries wanted the ironclad guarantee that Article 5 of the NATO treaty—an attack on one NATO member would be treated as an attack on all—would provide them. Who knew what a future Russia might look like? It was better to acquire the insurance of a NATO membership as quickly as possible. Thus NATO was soon swamped with membership inquiries from states that had just months before been part of the Warsaw Pact, created to battle NATO!

An excellent analysis of what then occurred comes from Zbigniew Brzezinski, the former national security adviser under President Jimmy Carter. He said that

> NATO's role then changed. It became the framework for stabilizing a suddenly unstable geopolitical situation in central and eastern Europe. It is now easy to forget that even after the dissolution of the Soviet bloc in 1989–90—the emancipation of Eastern Europe, the reappearance of independent Baltic states, and the reunification of Germany—the resented Russian army remained deployed, as during the Cold War, on the banks of the Elbe and, until 1994, in the former Soviet satellite states. Although the army's eventual withdrawal was all

but inevitable, the uncertainties regarding regional security, border issues, and fundamental political identity in the former Soviet bloc were complex. With the emerging EU in no position to offer reassuring security, only NATO could stably fill the void.

What followed was less the product of strategic design than the result of history's spontaneity. The latter is often confusing and contradictory, and yet ultimately decisive. That was largely the case with NATO's expansion eastward. Initially, Russia's new leadership acceded reluctantly to it . . . only on second thought, shortly thereafter, did Russia begin to object. . . . In any case, there was no practical way of preventing the spontaneous surge of the central and eastern European states toward the only Western institution that could simultaneously assure their security and help define their political identity.

One has to remember that the central and eastern Europeans were in a mood of enthusiastic emancipation from the Soviet Union's almost five-decade and rather heavy-handed domination. They were determined to become an integral part of the free Europe and disinclined to become a geopolitical no man's land between NATO and Russia. If the central and eastern European states had been left out, the Europe divided in two by the Cold War, instead of becoming one, would have become a Europe divided into three: the NATO states in the west; a West-leaning but insecure central and eastern Europe, as well as the newly sovereign but unstable Belarus and Ukraine, in the middle; and Russia in the east. How such an arrangement could have peacefully endured is difficult to imagine. An enlarged NATO has proved itself to be by far preferable to the instability or even violence (à la Ukraine or Georgia recently) that almost certainly would have at some point ensued in a central and eastern Europe left to its own uncertain devices between a reunified Germany in NATO and a resentful Russia still tempted to view the region as part of its "near abroad."[10]

But in this rush to absorb the newly freed nations of Central and Eastern Europe, NATO and the West sowed the seeds of future tension with Russia. Scowcroft, who once taught Russian history at West Point, has never been entirely comfortable with NATO's expansion to Russia's doorsteps. He remembers being surprised at the Russians acquiescing to NATO's expansion. "They complained, but they acquiesced. And I think I underestimated what it was really doing to Russian attitudes. I think we all did. We were humiliating Russia, not intentionally, but nevertheless that was the net result." Likewise, Scowcroft questions whether NATO really benefited from the expanded membership. "We should have asked ourselves, what are we trying to do? . . . For example, what does Albania bring to NATO? You can say well, it helps us democratize Albania, but is that the job of NATO?"[11]

Since its inception in 1949, NATO had seen itself, and had been viewed by others, as a purely defensive organization. This singular mission expanded after the demise of the Soviet Union, as NATO began to absorb the newly freed nations on its eastern borders, and as the geopolitical threat profile changed. From facing the Cold War threat of an attack against the European mainland, NATO's mission now changed to anticipating and meeting threats from distant lands that could be thousands of miles from Europe. Defense Secretary Robert Gates described this change during a 2010 NATO conference held in Washington, D.C.

> At the strategic level, the greatest evolution in NATO over the last two decades is the transition from a static, defensive force to an expeditionary force—from a defensive alliance to a security alliance. This change is a result of a new security environment in which threats are more likely to emanate from failed, failing, or fractured states than from aggressor states; where dangerous, non-state actors often operate from within nations with which we are not at war, or from within our own borders; and where weapons proliferation and new technologies make possible the specter of chaos and mass destruction in any of our capitals.[12]

Between 1995 and 1999, as described in chapter 4, the alliance's mission had become more elastic and NATO's military power, for the first time, had been used proactively to stop a series of civil wars in Bosnia and later in Kosovo. So what was next? Indeed, what was this new NATO?

Gathering in Washington, D.C., in the spring of 1999 to celebrate the fiftieth anniversary of the alliance's founding, NATO leaders decided to tackle this question head on during an exercise they undertake every ten years to develop an updated strategic concept, or its mission statement for the next decade. (NATO's new strategic concept was adopted at the alliance's meeting in Lisbon in November 2010.)

NATO saw its future challenges as having been transformed from preventing Soviet tanks from rolling into Western Europe to addressing far more complex and global threats, including the proliferation of weapons of mass destruction (WMD) and non-state-sponsored terrorism. To meet these threats, NATO believed it had no choice but to go where the threats were, and it adopted an "out-of-area" strategy. Now, instead of hunkering behind the Elbe River and watching for Soviet tanks to come through the Fulda Gap, NATO would instead travel anywhere in the world to confront and stop the new threats to Euro-Atlantic security.

The out-of-area strategy was adopted on April 4, 1999, after a fair amount of dissent. Not everyone liked the idea of converting NATO into a world policeman. After all, the main reason the new entrants had joined the alliance was primarily to buy insurance against potential threats by Russia. It would soon become clear that, while the differences over NATO's transformation into a global crisis manager had been papered over by diplomatic phraseology, not every member had signed on to the new mission statement with equal exuberance.

It is also interesting to compare the dense sixty-five articles in the 1999 *The Alliance's Strategic Concept* (see appendix B) with the tightly written and clear fourteen articles of the 1949 founding treaty. As NATO's role has changed, its mission statements have transitioned from military precision to bureaucratic phraseology. As Article 52 of the strategic concept illustrates,

> The size, readiness, availability and deployment of the Alliance's military forces will reflect its commitment to collective defence and to conduct crisis response operations, sometimes at short notice, distant from their home stations, including beyond the Allies' territory. The characteristics of the Alliance's forces will also reflect the provisions of relevant arms control agreements. Alliance forces must be

adequate in strength and capabilities to deter and counter aggression against any Ally. They must be interoperable and have appropriate doctrines and technologies. They must be held at the required readiness and deployability, and be capable of military success in a wide range of complex joint and combined operations, which may also include Partners and other non-NATO nations.[13]

With the perspective of a decade it is now obvious that NATO members have been unable or simply have not been interested in living up to the commitments they agreed to at their 1999 meeting in Washington, D.C. For example, this clause was at the heart of the new strategic concept adopted there: "The size, readiness, availability and deployment of the Alliance's military forces will reflect its commitment to collective defence and to conduct crisis response operations, sometimes at short notice, distant from their home stations, including beyond the Allies' territory."

This mismatch between what NATO wishes to do and the resources that its members will actually commit to help it meet its commitments continues in the Strategic Concept adopted during November 2010 in Lisbon. (This is included as appendix E.) Facing significant cuts in its budget and staff, NATO still proposes to set up an anti-ballistic missile defense shield, a cyber-attack shield. It's committed to go anywhere in the world to defend Western interests, and insists against all evidence to the contrary that the alliance, "has a unique and robust set of political and military capabilities to address the full spectrum of crises—before, during and after conflicts."

Or as Gen. John Craddock, who until April 2009 was NATO's SACEUR, describes it, "All good words, the challenge today—as then—is not in the development of what NATO wants to do, should do, or feels compelled to do. The challenge for NATO is to match its level of ambition with its political will to resource the means to accomplish its ambitions—or more specifically—creating and sustaining military capability. . . . Absent that . . . the disconnect between the vision . . . and the political will to commit the resources will continue."[14]

Meanwhile, Stopford, the former Coca-Cola executive, still works at NATO, and his rebranding efforts for the alliance continue. "NATO lost its primary rationale on the day the Warsaw Pact closed up business. It has been casting around for a different identity and role so it remains relevant. The jury seems to be out on whether it has succeeded," the *New York Times* observed in 1988, when NATO hired the brand management executive.[15] Twenty-two years later, the alliance is still looking for the fizz for its brand.

NATO, INC.

The simple acronym "NATO" belies the size of the organization. In fact, the twelve foreign ministers who signed the North Atlantic Treaty in Washington, D.C., on that historic spring day in 1949 would be truly amazed if they could see their creation today. The alliance's organization is laid out in table 1.

Table 1. NATO Organizational Chart

CIVILIAN STRUCTURE
    NATO Headquarters
    Permanent Representatives and National Delegations
    International Staff (IS)
        Private Office (PO)
        Public Diplomacy Division
            Academic Affairs Unit
            Archives
            NATO Library
            Media Library
            TV-Radio Studios
            Fellowship and sponsorship programmes
            NATO Information and Documentation Centre, Kyiv, Ukraine
            NATO Information Office in Moscow
            Allied Contact Points in Partner Countries
            Science for Peace and Security
        NATO Office of Security (NOS)
        Executive Management
            Recruitment Service
            NATO Internship Programme
        Division of Political Affairs and Security Policy
            Partnership for Peace Documentation Center

Division of Operations
> Civil Emergency Planning
> Euro-Atlantic Disaster Response Coordination Centre (EADRCC)
> NATO Situation Centre

Division of Defence Policy and Planning

Division of Defence Investment
> Explosive Ordnance Disposal and Ammunition Storage Training Team
> The Group of National Directors on Codification (AC/135)
>> NATO Codification System
> The NATO Naval Armaments Group (NNAG) (AC/141)
> The NATO Air Force Armaments Group (NAFAG) (AC/224)
> The NATO Army Armaments Group (NAAG) (AC/225)
> The CNAD Ammunition Safety Group (AC/326)
> Life Cycle Management Group (AC/327)

NATO Office of Resources (NOR)

NATO Headquarters Consultation, Command and Control Staff (NHQC3S)

Office of the Financial Controller (FinCon)

Office of the Chairman of the Senior Resource Board (SRB)

Office of the Chairman of the Civil and Military Budget Committees (CBC/MBC))

International Board of Auditors for NATO (IBAN)

NATO Production and Logistics Organisations (NPLO)

MILITARY STRUCTURE

The Military Committee

International Military Staff
> Plans and Policy Division
> Operations Division
> Intelligence Division
> Cooperation and Regional Security Division
> Logistics, Armaments and Resources Division
> NATO Situation Centre
> Financial Controller
> NATO HQ Consultation, Control and Communications Staff (HQC3)
> Partner Country Representation
> NATO Training Group
> Committee on Women in the NATO Forces
> NATO Military Audiovisual Working Group

Allied Command Operations (ACO)
 Supreme Headquarters Allied Power Europe—SHAPE—Mons, BE
 Joint Force Command HQ Brunssum —Brunssum, NL
  Command Component Maritime HQ Northwood, UK
  Command Component Air HQ Ramstein, GE
  Joint Headquarters Northeast—JHQ NORTHEAST—Karup,
   DA (deactivated)
  Headquarters Allied Force Command Heidelberg, GE
 Joint Force Command HQ Naples—Naples, IT
  Command Component Maritime HQ Naples, IT
  Command Component Air HQ Izmir, TU
  Command Component Land HQ Madrid, SP
  Joint Headquarters South—JHQ SOUTH—Verona, IT (deactivated)
  Joint Headquarters Southcentre—JHQ SOUTHCENT—Larissa, GR
  Joint Headquarters Southeast—JHQ SOUTHEAST—Izmir,
   TU (deactivated)
  NATO Headquarters Sarajevo
  NATO Headquarters Skopje
  NATO Headquarters Tirana—NHQT
 Joint Headquarters Lisbon—Lisbon, PO
 Rapidly Deployable Corps Headquarters
  Allied Command Europe Rapid Reaction Corps (ARRC)
   HQ—Rheindalen (Germany)
  EUROCORPS HQ in Strasbourg (France)
  Multinational Corps Northeast—Szczecin (Poland)
  Rapid Deployable Italian Corps—Milan (Italy)
  Rapid Deployable Turkish Corps HQ—Istanbul (Turkey)
  Rapid Deployable German-Netherlands Corps HQ—Münster
   (Germany)
  Rapid Deployable Spanish Corps HQ in Valencia (Spain)
  NATO Deployable Corps—Greece
 Other Staffs and Commands Responsible to SACEUR
  The Reaction Forces (Air) Staff—RF(A)S—Kalkar—GE
  NATO Airborne Early Warning Force (NAEWF)
  Immediate Reaction Forces (Maritime)
  ACE Mobile Force—AMF—Heidelberg, GE
  Naval Striking and Support Forces—STRIKFORNATO—Naples (IT)
  Standing Naval Force Atlantic—STANAVFORLANT

Standing Naval Forces Mediterranean—STANAVFORMED

Standing Naval Forces Channel—STANAVFORCHAN

Allied Command Transformation (ACT)

Headquarters Supreme Allied Commander Transformation—HQ SACT—Norfolk, US

Joint Warfare Centre—JWC—Stavanger, NO

NATO Joint Force Training Centre—JFTC—Bydgoszcz, PL

NATO Maritime Interdiction Operational Training Center— NMIOTC—Souda Naval Base, Crete, GR

NATO Undersea Research Centre—NURC—La Spezia, IT

NATO School—Oberammergau, GE

Other NATO Command & Staff Organisations

Canada-US Regional Planning Group—CUSRPG

NATO Airborne Early Warning and Control Force Command— NAEW&CFC—Mons, BE

Combined Joint Planning Staff—CJPS—Mons, BE

ORGANISATIONS AND AGENCIES

Logistics

Senior NATO Logisticians' Conference (SNLC)

NATO Maintenance and Supply Organisation (NAMSO)

The NATO Maintenance and Supply Agency (NAMSA)

NATO Pipeline System (NPS)

Central Europe Pipeline System (CEPS)

NATO Pipeline Committee (NPC)

The Central Europe Pipeline Management Organisation (CEPMO)

Central Europe Pipeline Management Agency (CEPMA)

The Committee of Chiefs of Military Medical Services in NATO (COMEDS)

Production Logistics

Conference of National Armaments Directors (CNAD)

NATO Medium Extended Air Defence System Design and Development, Production and Logistics Management Agency (NAMEADSMA)

NATO EF 2000 and TORNADO Development Production and Logistics Management Agency (NETMA)

NATO Helicopter Design and Development Production and Logistics Management Agency (NAHEMA)

NATO HAWK Management Office (NHMO)

Standardisation

The NATO Standardisation Organisation (NSO)

NATO Committee for Standardisation (NCS)

Office for NATO Standardisation (ONS)

NATO Standardization Agency (NSA)

Civil Emergency Planning

Senior Civil Emergency Planning Committee (SCEPC)

Civil Emergency Planning Boards and Committees

Euro-Atlantic Disaster Response Coordination Centre (EADRCC)

Air Traffic Management, Air Defence

The NATO Air Traffic Management Committee (NATMC)

The NATO Air Defence Committee (NADC)

Military Committee Air Defence Study Working Group (MC-ADSWG)

NATO Air Command and Control System (ACCS) Management
Organisation (NACMA)

NATO Programming Centre (NPC)

Airborne Early Warning

The NATO Airborne Early Warning and Control Programme
Management Organisation (NAPMO)

Communication and Information Systems

NATO C3 Organisation

NATO CIS Services Agency (NCSA)

NATO Consultation, Command and Control Agency (NC3A)

NATO Headquarters Consultation, Command and Control
Staff (NHQC3S)

The NATO Frequency Management SubCommittee (FMSC)

Frequency Management Cooperation in NATO

NATO Headquarters Information Systems Service (ISS)

NATO CIS Operating and Support Agency (NACOSA)

Electronic Warfare

NATO Electronic Warfare Advisory Committee (NEWAC)

Meteorology

Military Committee Meteorological Group (MCMG)

Military Oceanography

The Military Oceanography (MILOC) Group

Research and Technology

Research and Technology Organisation (RTO)

Education and Training
>   NATO Defense College (NDC)
>   The NATO School—Oberammergau, Germany
>   NATO Communications and Information Systems (NCISS) School
>   The NATO Training Group (NTG)
>   *Project Steering Committees/Project Offices*
>   Alliance Ground Surveillance Capability Provisional Project Office
>   (AGS/PPO)
>   Battlefield Information Collection and Exploitation System (BICES)
>   NATO Continuous Acquisition and Life Cycle Support Office (CALS)
>   NATO FORACS Office
>   Munitions Safety Information Analysis Center (MSIAC)

Source: NATO, accessed August 22, 2010, http://www.nato.int/cps/en/SID-B2657127-FB99B5EB/natolive/structure.htm.

NATO is run from its political headquarters on Boulevard Leopold III in Brussels, Belgium. Here NATO's senior, political decision-making body, or its "board of directors," which is called the North Atlantic Council, oversees the military alliance through its appointed "CEO," or NATO's secretary-general. The alliance's sizable bureaucracy of around fourteen thousand personnel reports to the NAC through the secretary-general. All twenty-eight member countries are represented on the NAC by a full-time, ambassador-led delegation, resembling a mini embassy at NATO.[16]

In 2002 NATO established the NATO-Russia Council (NRC) to promote relations between the alliance and Russia. As part of the NRC structure, Russia was invited to send an ambassador-level permanent representative to Brussels. This allows NATO and Russia to discuss common issues at the top political level. The NRC has taken on added significance after the November 2010 NATO Summit in Lisbon where the Alliance invited Russia to join in discussing a common anti-ballistic missile shield.

Here is how NATO describes the function of the headquarters staff:

> The NATO Headquarters provides a site where representatives from
> both the civilian and military side of all the member states can come
> together in order to make political decisions on a consensus basis.
> It also offers a venue for dialogue and cooperation between partner

countries and NATO member states, so that they can work together in their effort to bring about peace and stability. . . .

There are approximately 4,000 people working at NATO Headquarters on a full-time basis. Of these, some 2,000 are members of national delegations and staffs of national military representatives to NATO. There are also about 300 members of missions of NATO's partners' countries. There are approximately 1,200 civilian members of the International Staff or agencies located within the Headquarters and about 500 members of the International Military Staff, including 100 civilians. . . .

Meetings at NATO Headquarters take place throughout the year, creating a setting for dialogue amongst member nations. There are more than 5,000 meetings every year amongst NATO bodies.

The key advantage to having permanent delegations at NATO Headquarters is the opportunity for informal and formal consultation on a continuous basis. Consultation between member states is a key part of the decision-making process at NATO, allowing Allies to exchange views and information prior to reaching agreement and taking action.[17] (emphasis added)

I have stressed the last two paragraphs because they are central to NATO's cardinal operating principle of reaching decisions by consensus. The key to understanding NATO is to remember that it functions under one inviolable rule: every decision must be unanimously agreed to by every member country. In fact, no votes are cast during its deliberations. Unanimity ensures that every member's voice carries equal weight. Ultimately, all twenty-eight member countries as diverse as the United States, Turkey, Germany, Bulgaria, Croatia, Latvia, and the remaining twenty-two others must agree on every issue unanimously for the alliance to take any action (see table 2).

Commendably democratic in principle, making decisions by consensus has regularly interfered in NATO's operations. During the Kosovo campaign, for instance, the alliance's air force "endured strong interference by NATO's political leadership, which revealed tension between NATO's . . . political objective (preserve the alliance) and the . . . military objective (destroy or compel Serbian forces to depart Kosovo and halt ethnic cleans-

Table 2. NATO Member States with Dates of Accession

Date	Country	Enlargement	Notes
April 4, 1949	Belgium	Founders	
	Canada		
	Denmark		
	France		France withdrew from the integrated military command in 1966 to pursue an independent defense system but returned to full membership on April 4, 2009.
	Iceland		Iceland, the sole member that does not have its own standing army, joined on the condition that it would not be expected to establish one. However, its strategic geographic position in the Atlantic made it an invaluable member. It has a Coast Guard and has recently contributed a voluntary peacekeeping force, trained in Norway for NATO.
	Italy		
	Luxembourg		
	Netherlands		
	Norway		
	Portugal		
	United Kingdom		
	United States		
February 18, 1952	Greece	First	Greece withdrew its forces from NATO's military command structure from 1974 to 1980 as a result of Greco-Turkish tensions following the 1974 Turkish invasion of Cyprus.
	Turkey		
May 9, 1955	Germany	Second	Joined as West Germany; Saarland reunited with it in 1957 and the territories of Berlin and the former German Democratic Republic reunited with it on October 3, 1990. The latter was a member of the rival Warsaw Pact from 1956 to 1990.
May 30, 1982	Spain	Third	
March 12, 1999	Czech Republic	Fourth	Member of the rival Warsaw Pact (1955–91) as part of Czechoslovakia.
	Hungary		Member of the rival Warsaw Pact (1955–91).
	Poland		Member of the rival Warsaw Pact (1955–91).
March 29, 2004	Bulgaria	Fifth	Member of the rival Warsaw Pact (1955–91).
	Estonia		Member of the rival Warsaw Pact (1955–91) as part of the Soviet Union.
	Latvia		Member of the rival Warsaw Pact (1955–91) as part of the Soviet Union.
	Lithuania		Member of the rival Warsaw Pact (1955–91) as part of the Soviet Union.
	Romania		Member of the rival Warsaw Pact (1955–91).
	Slovakia		Member of the rival Warsaw Pact (1955–91) as part of Czechoslovakia.
	Slovenia		Previously part of Yugoslavia (1945–91, nonaligned).
April 1, 2009	Albania	Sixth	Member of the rival Warsaw Pact (1955–68).
	Croatia		Previously part of Yugoslavia (1945–91, nonaligned).

Source: "Member states of NATO," *Wikipedia*, last modified December 28, 2010, http://en.wikipedia.org/wiki/Members_of_NATO.

ing). This chasm between . . . objectives fostered friction and frustration among senior officers, which worked against a rapid conclusion of the air campaign."[18]

And during the prelude to the American-led invasion of Iraq, France and Germany vetoed Turkey's request for air defense missiles to protect it against a retaliatory attack by Iraq, which shares a border with Turkey. "This is a most unfortunate decision," Nicholas Burns, at that time the U.S. ambassador to NATO, said angrily. "Because of their [France's and Germany's] actions, NATO is now facing a crisis of credibility." In Washington, Secretary of State Colin Powell said the treaty bound all allies to defend Turkey: "I hope that NATO will now realize that they have an obligation to assist a NATO member."[19]

As noted, the NAC, the alliance's top decision-making body, meets under the chairmanship of the secretary-general, who is appointed by the member countries to a four-year term. Anders Fogh Rasmussen, a former Danish prime minister, became the secretary-general in 2009.

In another demonstration of the consequences of NATO's consensus rule, as chapter 6 will illuminate in more detail, Rasmussen almost did not become secretary-general. Turkey refused to approve the appointment, and with this one holdout Rasmussen's candidacy could not move ahead. It took the power and prestige of the American president to overcome Turkey's objections.

The rest of the alliance's ten thousand staff work in three broad groups: a civilian structure, a military structure, and organizations and agencies. The scope and complexity of NATO's framework are evident in table 1.[20] The civilian structure is NATO's executive division and includes the secretary-general's private staff, a public diplomacy division, and the financial controller. The organizations and agencies section is a support group whose functions include logistics, maintenance, meteorology, and standardization.

The military structure is the heart of NATO. Under this branch are the two most important NATO strategic commands: the Allied Command Operations (ACO) and the Allied Command Transformation (ACT). The ACO is responsible for planning and executing all the operations that the North Atlantic Council has agreed to undertake. The ACO operates from the Supreme Headquarters Allied Power Europe (SHAPE), located in Casteau, near Mons, Belgium, and reports to the SACEUR.

By continuously transforming NATO's capabilities, the ACT helps NATO remain relevant. For NATO's military forces, the ACT is responsible for proactively developing and integrating innovative concepts, doctrines, and capabilities, and for improving their armaments and tactics. In spite of the important role that ACT plays in keeping NATO relevant, the command has an almost invisible profile and is relatively unknown even in military circles. During my remarks in November 2009 to a group of seniors at the United States Military Academy, none of the cadets I encountered had heard of the ACT. On another occasion, a senior American military officer, now serving in Afghanistan, mistook the ACT for the Atlantic Council, the well-known think tank in Washington, D.C.

I mentioned this lack of awareness to the new ACT commander, Gen. Stéphane Abrial, a former head of the French air force. It did not surprise him at all. "I was posted to the United States Air Force University in Alabama some years ago. Most officers there didn't even know what *NATO* was," he told me with a smile.

The ACT's leadership, like the SACEUR, had also been an American preserve until 2009, when General Abrial took over as Supreme Allied Commander Transformation (SACT). The reason for the change from American to French command of ACT makes for an interesting sidelight. France decided to leave NATO's integrated military structure during the 1960s because then president Charles de Gaulle of France believed that embedding France's nuclear deterrent, the force de frappe (strike force), in NATO's unified military command would mean enmeshing the powerful French air arm in NATO's American-led bureaucracy. De Gaulle also maintained that as an American-led organization, NATO was aimed ultimately at preventing Europe from ever having its own military force. He was also concerned about the scarcity of French officers in important NATO positions.

The decision to leave NATO's military structure caused friction between France and its NATO allies. The Americans were particularly miffed because even though France left NATO's integrated military command, it did not give up its seat on the North Atlantic Council, NATO's de facto board of directors. This position meant France could commit NATO to a war without worrying about dispatching its military in the campaign. "We ought to tell the French to rejoin the military structure or get out of NATO," an exasperated senior former U.S. administration official told me. "That dog won't hunt any more."

After his election in 2008, French president Nicolas Sarkozy decided to bring France back into NATO's military structure as long as the allies addressed the lack of French officers in key NATO commands. As a result, a French general became SACT and headed to Norfolk, Virginia. A change in command brings in an entirely new group of officers who accompany the new commander, and the ACT now has a distinctly French feel to it, including, as I found out on a recent visit, all that wonderful French hospitality and strong coffee.

At regular intervals, when matters of great import are to be discussed, the North American Council's meetings are organized at the defense or foreign ministerial level. Even more important decisions call for a meeting at the level of heads of state or governments. At these high-powered meetings, the ambassadors take a backseat to their defense or foreign ministers and their countries' presidents or prime ministers.

In the humdrum of daily work this decision-making process seems to work fairly well. But, as Gen. Wesley Clark found out in the NATO military action against Kosovo (the only war that NATO had ever fought until its deployment in Afghanistan), in a fast-moving battle scenario the process can become badly skewed when every target that needs to be bombed requires preapproval from twenty-eight foreign ministries.

Even though NATO does not have a standing army, it does boast a few common defense capabilities. Most significantly it owns and operates a fleet of five airborne warning and control systems aircraft and three Boeing C-17 long-range transport aircraft.

The AWACS airplanes provide air surveillance, early warning, and command and control, and the C-17's heavy lift capabilities, but only for those member countries *that subscribe to the programs.* Sixteen NATO nations subscribe to the AWACS program, and ten use the C-17s. Interestingly, both programs fall under the control of the NAC, which means any of the twenty-eight NATO countries can prevent the subscribing states from using their paid-for capabilities.

Following the terrorist attacks on the United States in 2001, NATO sent the AWACS aircraft to patrol U.S. territory. At the request of Turkey in 2003, they were sent to guard Turkish territory against the possibility of an attack arising from the Iraqi conflict. And they infrequently contribute to the security of major events, such as the 2004 Olympic Games in Athens.

FINANCING NATO

With a budget of around $7 billion,[21] NATO employs over fourteen thousand military and civilian staff scattered in dozens of European and two North American locations. The actual budget is much greater because most of its employees are paid by their home nations even though their positions are a permanent part of the NATO bureaucracy. It is virtually impossible to find out what these additional costs are.

In addition to the fourteen thousand permanent employees, NATO deploys forces in a number of missions, including some thirty-four thousand troops in Afghanistan and fifteen thousand in Kosovo. The countries that contribute the troops also pay their expenses. "Contribute" is the operative word in NATO deployments because, contrary to popular belief and as noted earlier, the alliance does not maintain standing forces.[22] Thus member states must contribute troops and pay for their expeditions as needed.

These national expenditures have assumed serious consequences for NATO in Afghanistan. For instance, it was reported that "Poland spends $1 billion annually—10 percent of its defense budget—to maintain its 2,600-member contingent in Afghanistan."[23] This expenditure was hampering Poland's plans to modernize its armed forces and the president wanted NATO to set an exit strategy from the war. When I asked a senior NATO military official what was the biggest lesson he would draw from the alliance's experience in Afghanistan, he did not hesitate to say, "Never again." NATO's operating budget pays for running its permanent bureaucracy shown in table 3. These common funds, as NATO call them, pay for the alliance's ongoing costs, and NATO refers to the funds' allocation among all the member countries as burden sharing.

How are the common charges allocated to each NATO member? History, the country's defense budgets, their gross domestic product (GDP) and ability to pay, the countries' visible contribution to the West's defense, politics, and a bit of black magic—all play a part. Table 3 shows how the common funds budget for 2008–9 was divided among the twenty-six member countries. The addition of two more members does not materially affect either the ratios or the following explanation.

Members pay their share of the common funds through separate allocations under three categories that broadly follow the three sections of table 1. The United States made a common funds payment for fiscal year 2009 of $721 million that was assigned as follows.

Toward NATO's civilian budget, the United States allocated $71 million, which was paid through State Department funds.

> The NATO civil budget supports the alliance's Brussels headquarters and its international civilian staff, which is responsible for policy planning of operations and capabilities. . . . The civil budget covers standard administrative tasks, such as personnel, travel, communications, utilities, supplies and furniture, security, and the NATO headquarters project, for which construction began in 2010. In addition, this budget is used for several program activities, including public information, civil emergency planning, and the work of the science committee.[24]

To NATO's military budget, the United States paid $409 million through the Department of the Army.

> [The] military budget is, in most years, the largest of the three accounts. More than half of this fund is used to pay for operational and maintenance costs of the international military staff, its headquarters in Mons, Belgium and subordinate commands in different NATO geographical areas. . . . This budget also covers the cost of administering the alliance's military-related activities and organizations, including international military headquarters, the Airborne Early Warning and Control System (AWACS) fleet operations, which accounts for a significant portion of the U.S. share.[25]

Table 3. NATO Common Budgets Contributions and
Cost Shares, 2008/2009

(expressed in percent, with all 26 members contributing)

MEMBER STATE	CIVIL BUDGET	MILITARY BUDGET	NSIP
Belgium	2.3550	2.6702	2.6702
Bulgaria	0.3188	0.3188	0.3318
Canada	5.7671	5.0000	5.0000
Czech Republic	0.8829	0.8829	0.8829
Denmark	1.3246	1.8184	1.8184
Estonia	0.1021	0.1021	0.1021
France	13.0265	12.4547	12.4547
Germany	15.2809	16.6856	16.6856
Greece	0.6500	0.6500	1.1029
Hungary	0.6700	0.6700	0.6700
Iceland	0.0657	0.0550	0.0250
Italy	7.5000	7.8609	8.2550
Latvia	0.1341	0.1341	0.1341
Lithuania	0.2046	0.2046	0.2046
Luxembourg	0.1250	0.1587	0.1587
Netherlands	3.1965	3.3833	3.3833
Norway	1.2821	1.6190	1.6190
Poland	2.3782	2.3782	2.3782
Portugal	0.8000	0.6500	0.6500
Romania	1.0090	1.0090	1.0090
Slovakia	0.4219	0.4219	0.4219
Slovenia	0.2459	0.2459	0.2459
Spain	4.3097	4.2297	4.2297
Turkey	2.0000	1.8000	1.8000
United Kingdom	14.1394	12.0542	12.0542
United States	21.8100	22.5428	21.7258
Total	100.0000	100.0000	100.0000

Source: U.S. Department of Defense. In Carl Ek, "NATO Common Funds Burdensharing:
Background and Current Issues," Congressional Research Service Report RL 30150,
January 27, 2009.

The U.S. funds for the National Security Investment Program (NSIP) budget, or $241 million, is paid through the U.S. military's construction appropriations. This category "involves the collective financing of a wide variety of NATO support functions, including, for example, command, control, communications, and information hardware and software; logistics activities; harbors and airfields; training installations; transportation; and storage facilities for equipment, fuel, and munitions."[26]

It is worth noting that "[w]hen burden-sharing contributions are negotiated, the alliance reportedly has taken into consideration the United States' worldwide security responsibilities" and expenditures, and adjusts its share of common funds accordingly.[27] For instance, in table 3, note that the percent of the common budget allocated to the United States is around 7 percent larger than Germany's. But in 2003, U.S. GDP was $10.3 trillion while the combined GDP of the other (at that time) eighteen NATO allies was $8.9 trillion. If NATO common funds assessed were based solely on GDP, the U.S. share would have been 53.6 percent and Germany's would have been 9.8 percent.[28] So the oft-heard criticism in the United States that America's NATO allies are not spending enough to carry their own weight does not refer to the common funds. The member countries, including by the United States, universally recognize them as being reasonably fairly allocated.

As I have mentioned earlier, the costs for maintaining NATO forces in action are, by far, the more significant of the two categories of expenditures borne by each member, and are funded through the member countries' national defense budgets. The difference between the two expenditures can be dramatic. For instance, NATO common funds for 2009 totaled approximately $3.6 billion.[29] Meanwhile, America's share for NATO operations in Afghanistan (America had around sixty-eight thousand troops in Afghanistan during 2009), for which the United States alone must bear the costs under NATO practice, were $3.6 billion per month.[30]

In the end, though, NATO is a military alliance dedicated to defending the security of its members against aggression. Members' payments into the common funds are their insurance premium against attack by an aggressor country. And nothing reflects the members' belief that NATO would ride to their rescue if they were attacked than Article 5 of the North Atlantic Treaty. Attack one of us, and you attack us all, so this famous saying goes. A simple enough statement, it would seem, and as true now as it was sixty years ago when NATO was founded.

Would that it were so.

CHAPTER THREE

One for All, All for One

The Parties agree that an armed attack against one or more of
them in Europe or North America shall be considered an attack
against them all.

—Excerpt from Article 5 of the North Atlantic Treaty

An early spring sunshine bathed Estonia in April 2007. It had been
an unusually gray and cloudy winter, and as the sun warmed the
still chilly air over the countless parks and squares of this pretty
Baltic country, the Estonians were out in force to enjoy nature's bounty.
Almost sixteen years after the collapse of the Soviet Union, Estonians had
just about forgotten their years of enslavement under the Soviets. Not only
was Estonia a free country again, it was also part of the European Union,
the exclusive club of twenty-seven European countries that had become
the largest economic and most successful political union in the world.

To ensure its freedom and security Estonia had also joined NATO, the
world's most powerful military alliance. As a member of NATO, Estonia
was protected by the alliance's fabled Article 5 that guaranteed that any
attack on Estonia would be considered an attack on every NATO member.
Should danger ever threaten Estonia again, Germany, France, Britain, and
even the mighty United States would come with their armies to end the
danger. So even though an increasingly dynamic Russia sat just around the

corner, the Estonians could rest easy knowing that their growing prosperity and security were guaranteed by the might of the entire Western world. Estonians basked in the warm sun and counted their blessings.

To top it all, on April 27 the Tallinn City Council had begun to dismantle and relocate *Pronkssõdur* (the Bronze Soldier) from the center of the city to the Tallinn Military Cemetery. Erected by the Soviets to memorialize the Red Army's reconquest of Estonia, the six-foot-tall bronze statue had been controversial from the day it had been installed. A source of pride to the ethnic Russians of Estonia, it was widely disparaged by everyone else as nothing but another symbol of the hated Soviet occupation. Now, against Russia's wishes, the Estonians had banished it to the outskirts of Tallinn. With NATO's ring of steel around it, Estonia did not have to worry about Russian anger any more. The Estonian spring seemed complete.

At around 2 p.m. the Estonians found they could not access their bank accounts over the Internet. An hour later the heavily trafficked government computer servers, used for everything from paying taxes to obtaining licenses, were inaccessible. Then e-mail delivery ceased. Shortly thereafter international banks found they could no longer conduct transactions with Estonian banks. The postal system's computers stopped working. Within hours Estonia, which prided itself on being one of the world's most Internet savvy countries, had ceased to function.[1]

Over the course of the next three weeks, the country was electronically dismembered as the Web servers of Estonia's parliament, ministries, corporations, newspapers, and banks were knocked off line. Pro-Russian graffiti began to appear on the Estonian president's Web page, and pro-Russian messages began to appear on the government's servers. It did not take long for the Estonians to realize that in return for humiliating the Russians by removing their *Pronkssõdur*, they had struck back with a massive cyberattack and brought Estonia to its knees. Although it was an electronic blitzkreig, or cyber aggression, against a NATO member, it was an act of aggression nonetheless.

"A three-week wave of massive cyber-attacks on the small Baltic country of Estonia, the first known incidence of such an assault on a state, is causing alarm across the western alliance, with Nato urgently examining the offensive and its implications," wrote Ian Trainor of the *Guardian*.[2]

Alarm bells rang across NATO for more than one reason. "Estonia's president, foreign minister, and defence minister have all raised the emergency with their counterparts in Europe and with Nato," Trainor reported.[3] The Estonians pulled NATO's emergency chain. A NATO member was attacked, and under Article 5 of the North Atlantic Treaty, it was an attack on every member of the alliance. The entire Western world was now bound by treaty to come to Estonia's aid.

Or was it?

NATO's reply quickly revealed that Article 5, the heart of the alliance's security guarantee to its members since 1949, was no longer the invincible shield every NATO member believed it to be. A sobered Estonian defence minister was forced to concede, "At present, Nato does not define cyberattacks as a clear military action. This means that the provisions of Article V of the North Atlantic Treaty, or, in other words collective self-defence, will not automatically be extended to the attacked country."[4]

Two main obstacles prevented the alliance from invoking an Article 5 emergency in Estonia. As Estonia's defense minister noted, NATO did not (and does not, as of December 2010) define cyber attacks as a clear military action. An equally large problem for NATO was the inability of cyber warfare experts to definitively trace the origin of the attacks to Russia.

One of the essential ingredients of an Estonian-style cyberattack is that the aggressor commandeers hundreds and even thousands of computers located outside the country under attack and then uses these "robot attackers" to bombard the target with electronic hits. After launching its robot attackers, the aggressor country can just sit back and watch its malevolent creations electronically slice the enemy to pieces without revealing the source of the attack.

James A. Lewis, director of the technology and public policy programs at the Center for Strategic and International Studies, described the complexities of this new form of warfare in his postmortem of the attack on Estonia:

> The attacks caused grave concern among NATO officials, in large part because, at first, Russia was blamed. This attribution was wrong, in the sense that the attacks were not launched from Russian govern-

ment computers. Like many things in cyberspace, it was difficult to tell who was at the other end of the Internet. Attribution in the Estonia case was made even harder by the use of "botnets." Botnets—short for robot networks—are the big new thing in cyber crime. A cyber criminal takes remote control of a computer by surreptitiously loading software on it. Most consumers don't know that their computers have been compromised. Some botnets are huge, using tens of thousands of computers around the world. Having these gigantic criminal networks simultaneously send thousands of messages every minute overburdened Estonian servers and caused them to crash.[5]

The long-term military implications of the cyberattack on Estonia were stunning, especially for NATO's ironclad guarantee of mutual self-defense offered by Article 5. Technology had transformed NATO's ring of steel around its members to a fence of tissue paper. Article 5, designed to respond to Soviet tanks and armor coming through the Fulda Gap in Germany, had been outflanked by tens of thousands of robot networks attacking from around the world. These attackers were silent, invisible, and virtually impossible to identify.

The cyberattack against Estonia demonstrated that, today, aggression against a country need not involve territorial invasion. A crippling first strike can as easily be launched by attacking a country's cyber infrastructure and, for that matter, its electrical or energy infrastructure (both of which are increasingly computer controlled).

The Estonian cyberattack was the beginning of a wave of similar intrusions. Since then, dozens of cyber intrusions into corporate, defense, and government installations have been reported by the media. The targets of these attacks include some of the world's most heavily guarded installations.

In November 2008 the *Daily Telegraph* reported that Russian computer hackers had penetrated one of the world's most protected organizations, the Pentagon, which is America's military headquarters and the center of its worldwide command and control network. "The electronic attack was so serious that Adm Michael Mullen, the chairman of the Joint Chiefs of Staff, briefed President George W. Bush and Robert Gates, the defence secretary. . . . The attack struck computers within the US Central Command, which oversees Iraq and Afghanistan."[6]

In July 2009 a complex cyberattack was launched simultaneously against a number of American targets including "the White House, Department of Homeland Security, Department of Transportation, Federal Aviation Administration, National Security Agency, State Department, US Postal Service, US Treasury Department and Voice of America. A Pentagon site, defenselink.mil, was also targeted . . . as was a site for US forces in South Korea."[7]

To its credit, immediately after the Estonian cyberattacks, NATO went into high gear to plan cyber defenses for itself and its members against this growing threat. NATO's policy on cyber defense was approved in January 2008, and heads of state and governments endorsed it at the Bucharest Summit in April. The Cooperative Cyber Defense Centre of Excellence (CCDCOE) was set up in Estonia, and NATO's Military Committee adopted a cyber defense concept.[8] Located in Tallinn, NATO's CCDCOE is still an embryonic operation with a staff of thirty supported by a handful of alliance members: Estonia, Latvia, Lithuania, Germany, Italy, the Slovak Republic, and Spain. These sponsoring nations share the costs for financing the facility and in turn benefit from its research.

Given the speed with which cyberattacks are being mounted, their increasing sophistication, and NATO's perennial budget woes, it is doubtful whether NATO will ever have the financial resources to combat cyber warfare. "It is hardly two months into the new year, but we [NATO] already face shortfalls of hundreds of millions of euros . . . the alliance faces very serious, long-term, systemic problems," U.S. Defense Secretary Robert Gates told NATO leaders in February 2010.[9]

That same month Vice Adm. Michael McConnell, USN (Ret.), who had served as President Bush's director of national intelligence, compared the danger of cyber war to the nuclear threat that the Soviet Union had posed during the Cold War. He said that "if America went into a cyber war today, we would lose."[10]

If the United States, with its trillion-dollar defense and security budget, finds itself in this vulnerable position, what chance would NATO ever have to defend its own computer systems, much less those of its members against cyberattack? This form of warfare could force an adversary to capitulate before a single soldier set foot on enemy soil.

It is pointless to start thinking of cyberattacks as an Article 5 trigger until NATO believes it is capable of thwarting such an attack, which it is not. A year after Estonia was crippled by the Russian cyberattack, NATO announced it would be unable to invoke the mutual defense clause in future cyberattacks. The alliance backpedaled on cyber warfare in true bureaucratic fashion by setting up another NATO department, the Cyber Defence Management Authority (CDMA), in 2008.

However, NATO indicated that the new authority's launch was postponed because of "'technical and bureaucratic problems' despite there already being 'a substantial agreement on the concept.' . . . Despite strong pressure from some Eastern European members, and in particular Estonia, the competencies of the new authority will fall exclusively on Article 4 of the North Atlantic Treaty 'for the foreseeable future,'" the NATO official said. So member countries will be able to consult one another "in case of cyber attacks but will not be bound to 'assist' each other as foreseen in Article 5 of the Treaty." Invoking Article 5 is "'completely excluded' in case of cyber attack at this stage, according [to] a NATO official involved with cyber defence dossiers. Instead, NATO is exploring ways to coordinate a 'political and technical response. . . .'"[11]

Cyberattacks are but one element of a whole series of new technology-driven threats confronting NATO members today. Each of these threats contains the seeds of multiple Article 5 triggers. Let's take another example—namely, the protection of earth-orbiting satellites, which are as necessary for warfare today as are guns and bullets.

Without the ubiquitous global positioning system (GPS), the ability of the United States to wage high-technology war would come to a screeching halt. Without GPS satellites that guide bombs, drones, artillery shells, helicopters, special force attack teams, missiles, and dozens of today's military systems, much of America's fearsome arsenal would be useless. The European Union's Galileo system, an enhanced version of GPS, has come online and will, by 2014, provide European defense establishments with a choice of tracking systems. NATO's arsenal of precision weapons uses the U.S. GPS system and undoubtedly will also begin using Galileo as it becomes available.

GPS technology relies on a constellation of twenty-four satellites to function. With NATO's almost total reliance today on this GPS technology, would an enemy's destruction of some of its satellites constitute an Article 5 attack? This scenario is not just around the corner; it is already a reality.

On January 19, 2007, the *Washington Post* reported that in the previous week the Chinese military had used a ground-based missile to hit and destroy one of its aging satellites orbiting more than five hundred miles in space. It was a high-stakes test, demonstrating China's ability to target regions of space that are home to U.S. spy satellites and space-based missile defense systems. China shrugged off the ensuing worldwide protests, stating, "Beijing considers [space] a key part of the push to modernize its military and increase its ability to compete in high-tech warfare."[12]

Given its inability to invoke Article 5 in the case of cyber security, I do not believe NATO will consider satellite destruction an event that would trigger invoking Article 5. Without including cyber and space warfare in its definition of "attack," however, does NATO's Article 5 have any relevance in the twenty-first century?

Cyber and space warfare are but two new threats that confront NATO military strategists today, according to Dr. Rob de Wijk, director of The Hague Centre for Strategic Studies and a professor of international relations at Leiden University in the Netherlands. He has this wake-up call for NATO:

> As NATO considers its future strategic posture, it must take into account three dramatic new security challenges that will impact the interests of its members. First, it must account for the impact of rising poles [China, India, and Russia, for instance] in the international system. Second, it must prepare for the security impact of the competition among world powers for scarce resources. Third, NATO must consider how climate change will impact international security and Alliance interests. These three principal challenges in this emerging strategic environment require that NATO reconsider its role and mission.[13]

During the Cold War NATO's only adversary, the Soviet Union, was sufficiently deterred by the retaliatory power of Article 5 to never launch an attack against the West. The article is still at the heart of everything NATO does and remains NATO's cutting-edge deterrent. But the Soviet Union was a well-defined state. Today's adversaries are elusive and stateless. Operationally, they function in the same manner as today's international corporations, which harness the Internet and other readily available technology tools to manufacture the components for its products in one country, put them together in another, and deliver the finished products around the world.

Today's technically sophisticated enemy can trigger powerful bombs with cell phones and use inexpensive, off-the-shelf software to break into the video feeds of American pilotless drones in Afghanistan. The enemy's knowledge is easily transferable over the Internet. It is this enemy and this new form of warfare that NATO will need to confront in the future. And this enemy will not be as easily deterred by the threat of Article 5 as was the Soviet Union. This enemy is more likely to look at the mutual self-defense clause and just shrug.

This largely defanged threat of an Article 5 response was behind the decision of two Eastern European NATO members—Poland and the Czech Republic—in 2008 to agree to the installation of American antimissile systems on their territories. The United States explained the missiles' installation on Russia's doorstep by saying that the missiles were meant to defend Europe and the United States against an attack from Iran. The missiles, the Americans insisted, could also defend Russia if the Russians supported the missile deployment.

The North American Council, NATO's policymaking board, was not consulted about the deployment of the Russia-facing missiles. It is not hard to see why the Bush administration decided not to consult its NATO partners before making this important military move. It would not have passed muster. The Eastern and Central European members of NATO would have heartily agreed with the American move, but the Western Europeans would not have wanted to provoke Russia. Without the latter's support, the initiative would have never received NATO's endorsement.

So why did Poland and the Czech Republic break with their European NATO partners? Here is how Senator Richard Lugar, a strong supporter of NATO and one of the Senate's shrewdest foreign policy experts, explained it at his September 2009 appearance before the Atlantic Council in Washington, D.C.: "Iranian missiles never constituted the primary rationale for Polish and Czech decisions to buy into the Bush Administration's plan. Rather, it was the waning confidence in NATO, and Article Five in particular, that lent the missile defense a political credibility that exceeded the military merits of the plan."[14] The quote is even highlighted in the transcript of the senator's prepared speech.

NATO's Central and Eastern European members are far more phobic about Russia than are the original Western European founding members, which see Russia as sometimes prickly but in the end a valuable business partner. Senator Lugar placed into the public record a fact that is discussed within security and defense circles but has not seen much illumination in the media; that is, confidence in NATO and its Article 5 is a rapidly diminishing commodity.

These Central and Eastern European countries recognize that an Article 5 defense of their territories is increasingly unlikely. They no longer believe NATO is willing to defend them against the most probable forms of attack today. To ensure their security, these NATO members would much rather have American missiles and American troops on their soil. A potential aggressor would think twice about taking actions against them that might also impair the capabilities of American missiles or injure American troops.

NATO—A FORCE FOR INSTABILITY

Americans, Canadians, and Western Europeans believe the origins of today's threats lie far from Europe's borders, and that premise in turn leads them to view NATO's mission in global terms. For the Central and Eastern European members of NATO, however, barely two decades removed from their Soviet enslavement, all threats emanate from Russia. It is as though NATO has morphed in two, with a new NATO that looks primarily over the horizon and with the old NATO still fixated on Russia. The Central and Eastern Europeans seem to have joined the old NATO.

Even though most of the recently freed states of the former Soviet Empire are also members of the European Union, it is to American-led NATO that they look for their security. These countries give the United

States the main credit for the disintegration of the Soviet Empire. When it comes to pulling the trigger, as Senator Lugar testified, these new NATO members would much rather put their fate in American hands than, in their opinion, the more negotiation-prone EU states.

As a result, the Central and Eastern Europeans often favor America's interests ahead of those of the European Union. These newer members of NATO were ardent supporters of the American-led invasion of Iraq, even though NATO had refused to be a part of it. And, as noted, both Poland and the Czech Republic quickly acceded to America's request to base missile defense systems on their soil even in the face of Russia's strong opposition to American weapons being stationed near its border.

If Estonia showed that Article 5 no longer provides the bullet-proof mutual security umbrella for NATO members, the short-lived 2008 war between Georgia and Russia illuminated another, equally dangerous aspect of the mutual defense clause: Article 5, when coupled with the diverging notion of what constitutes a threat within the alliance, actually has the potential to increase the threat of geopolitical instability in Europe.

On August 7, 2008, throwing caution and common sense to the wind, President Mikheil Saakashvili of the Baltic country of Georgia decided to take his country to war with Russia. Why the Columbia University–trained lawyer who had worked briefly for one of New York's prestigious and best-connected law firms would take Georgia (population 5.4 million, GDP $12 billion[15]) to war with Russia (population 146 million, GDP $1.12 trillion[16]) speaks volumes about the nature of today's NATO; its hazy promise, via Article 5, of security for European states; and its potential for abuse as a foreign policy tool against Russia.

As discussed in chapter 2, after the Soviet Union collapsed, NATO expanded eastward until it was positioned less than four hundred miles from the borders of Russia. Two states lay between Russia and the new NATO borders—the Ukraine and Georgia.

While it had never been comfortable with NATO's steady eastward expansion, Russia had been unable to do anything because of its weakened economic condition after the collapse of the Soviet Union. In 2006, however, when NATO began to court the Ukraine and Georgia, Russia's condition had materially changed. Then, a newly enriched Russia, flush with petrodollars, put up a red flag. There you shall not go, Russia essentially told NATO, and drew a line in the Caucasian sands.

Russia insisted that it considered both Georgia and the Ukraine to lie within its "near-abroad," or its sphere of influence, and that it would consider NATO's expansion into these two countries as a direct threat to its security and national interests. One does not have to be a Russophile to agree with Russia's position. Think about how the United States would react if Mexico and Canada announced they were about to join a military alliance headed by Russia. It would be enough to make the U.S. government invoke the Monroe Doctrine, which for more than a century, has warned foreign powers not to set up in America's backyard.[17]

"Unlike the Baltic States, Ukraine and Georgia were part of the Soviet Union. They were not [Russian] satellites," said Brent Scowcroft, the former U.S. national security adviser who also taught Russian history at the United States Military Academy. "And with respect to Ukraine and Russia, there is a deep historic tie. Kiev was the heartland of Russia until the Mongol invasion in the thirteenth century, when the Russians fled north into the forests where the Mongols wouldn't follow them."[18] In other words, beyond the fact that by including Georgia and the Ukraine, NATO's border would abut Russia's, NATO was now planning to absorb two states that had been an integral part of the Soviet Union for centuries and that had sizable Russian populations.

Russian sensitivities, however, did not carry much weight during the Bush administration. Both President Bush and Vice President Dick Cheney were determined to make NATO membership for Georgia and the Ukraine a primary plank of American security policy. Accordingly, the United States let it be known that it would strongly push for providing membership action plans (MAPs), or checklists to ensure a country is qualified to join NATO and the preliminary steps before membership is granted, at the alliance's next summit scheduled for April 2008. This "ministerial," in NATO parlance, would bring together the heads of state of all NATO countries.

The stage was now set for the tragedy that would soon descend on Georgia and the Western alliance. It would be a play in three acts. When the curtain fell, Georgia would be left severely wounded—economically and militarily—and its chances for joining NATO would be demolished for the immediate future; Russia would forcibly establish a No Trespassing sign over its backyard, show NATO to be a paper tiger, and score a strategic blow against the United States; and the growing divide between the United States and its Eastern European and Western European allies would be further increased.

In mid-March, recognizing Russia's rising hostility to NATO extending membership to the Ukraine and Georgia, Germany, France, Greece, Italy, Norway, and Spain decided to oppose the MAP provision to the two countries. But the Americans' push for moving Georgia and the Ukraine through the final goal post quickly received support from the East European countries of Lithuania, Latvia, Estonia, Slovakia, Slovenia, Bulgaria, Romania, Poland, and the Czech Republic, as well as from Canada. It was not the first time that Eastern European NATO members had chosen to support the United States over their Western European NATO neighbors. A bifurcated NATO seemed to be emerging from the rock-solid alliance of the past.

Lacking unanimous consent—NATO's sine qua non for making decisions—NATO denied military action plans to Georgia and the Ukraine, but in an attempt to please everybody, NATO let it be known that it had in principle decided to welcome the two countries. It was not a question of whether the military action plans would be provided but when.

"Today, we make clear that we support these countries' applications for MAP," Secretary-General of NATO Jaap de Hoop Scheffer said after the alliance's March 2008 meeting in Bucharest. "Therefore, we will now begin a period of intensive engagement with both at a high political level to address the questions still outstanding pertaining to their MAP applications. We have asked [NATO] foreign ministers to make a first assessment of progress at their December 2008 meeting."[19]

The Ukrainians, it turned out, weren't quite sure they wanted to join NATO, but Georgia was ecstatic with the communiqué. It seemed to the Georgians that they had virtually bypassed the MAP step. Without taking the final examination, Georgia believed it had received a passing grade.

Georgian president Saakashvili said, "I think we should be very happy," and added that it appeared as though Georgia had "suddenly jumped over the technical stage" of an action plan with the promise of full membership. "MAP is not as important when you have a commitment to accept us as members," he said. "Here we got a 100-percent guarantee, at least formally, for membership."[20]

Add to this the outspoken support of the United States, the world's sole superpower and NATO's leader, the Georgians must have begun to believe they were now NATO members in all but name. It would have been hard for them not to believe that Georgia had been welcomed into the exclusive club whose members had all sworn to consider an attack against one to be an attack against all. Buttressing Georgia's almost-realized NATO credentials were two thousand of its soldiers fighting in Afghanistan under the NATO banner.

No matter that the formalities were not yet complete, the Georgians must have concluded that should their country ever be invaded, it would be covered by NATO's Article 5 clause. Indeed, their American friends would see to that. Georgia's president had no way of knowing that this hypothesis was about to be tested on the battlefield.

Friction had simmered for years between Georgia and its breakaway province of South Ossetia, ever since the latter declared independence in 1990. As the war of words escalated in 2008, Russia increased its support for Abhkazia and South Ossetia (which has a large Russian population), including handing out Russian passports to its ethnic brethren there. It did not help that "Mr. Saakashvili, a close American ally who has sought NATO membership for Georgia, is loathed at the Kremlin in part because he had positioned himself as a spokesman for democracy movements and alignment with the West," reported the *New York Times*.[21]

As tensions grew between Georgia and Russia, America's support for Georgia seemed to move from mere words to action. Just days before hostilities broke out between the two countries, Joseph R. Wood, Vice President Cheney's deputy assistant for national security affairs, led a team of security officials to Georgia, a signal that would have been impossible for both Georgia and Russia to miss.

On August 7, 2008, Georgia decided it had had enough and launched a mortar attack into South Ossetia, killing numerous civilians and Russian peacekeepers.[22] It was a miscalculation of enormous proportions.

To the Georgians' considerable surprise, Russia counterattacked, using all the nonnuclear might of the Russian armed forces. Not only did Russia send its forces into South Ossetia, but Russian armored columns also poured into Georgia itself. Together with airborne elements of the Russian military, they occupied Georgia's main port and naval installation.

An alarmed NATO was soon contemplating the destruction of an almost-NATO member. Russia had called both Georgia's and NATO's bluff. And by extension it had laid down the gauntlet for the United States. Make my day, Russia's president Vladimir Putin seemed to be saying.

Now into this witch's brew was tossed a measure of a deadly potion—namely, the American presidential election cycle. U.S. senator John McCain, then the Republican candidate for president, was determined to use the Russian counterattack against Georgia as a lever to force NATO or the United States to take military action against Russia. "We should immediately call a meeting of the North Atlantic Council to assess Georgia's security and review measures NATO can take to contribute to stabilizing this very dangerous situation," McCain said.[23]

Moreover, in the face of certain defeat against overwhelming odds, McCain urged Saakashvili to keep fighting. Saakashvili said McCain called him during the war and told him "not to surrender and not to say no to freedom" when "some well-known world figures were telling us to stop resistance." The Georgian president maintained that McCain was quite clear and said that the United States will stand by Georgia and "we will all be Georgians."[24]

Senator McCain was using the war between Georgia and Russia to burnish his security credentials, but in the process he was creating a geopolitical flash point in a volatile region. Had he succeeded in his attempts at injecting NATO or the United States into this conflict, the results would have catastrophic. Thankfully, NATO did not rise to the bait. After first making bellicose remarks—"We will not allow Russia to wield a veto over the future of our Euro-Atlantic community," warned Secretary of State Rice[25]—even the hawkish Bush administration let the incident drop off the radar screen.

President Sarkozy of France personally intervened and ultimately worked out a cease-fire between Russia and Georgia. As things stand, the province of South Ossetia is permanently lost to Georgia. The Russian parliament, the Duma, passed legislation in 2009 to recognize its independence, which is under the protection of the Russian military.

The negotiated cease-fire was another example of the European Union's rapidly developing Common Security and Defense Policy. It was an entirely European effort. President Sarkozy, then serving in the rotating six-month tenure of the EU presidency, worked out its details, and an EU military mission immediately followed to ensure that the terms of the cease-fire were observed.

Meanwhile, the American people were not impressed by Senator McCain's bellicosity on behalf of Georgia. He lost the presidency to Senator Barack Obama. McCain did, however, win Georgia's highest state honor, the Order of the National Hero of Georgia, at a lavish public ceremony in Tbilisi on January 11, 2010.[26]

Another point is worth pondering: would matters have been different were Georgia already a NATO member when it went to war with Russia? In the conflict's early stages, it was not clear that Georgia had fired the first shot. Would the twenty-six European members of NATO, Canada, and the United States have been prepared to defend Georgia against the Russian counterattack by agreeing to send NATO troops to forcibly take back the two provinces absorbed by Russia? It is impossible to know, but I tend to doubt it.

The Central European and Eastern European NATO members may have supported NATO's military aid to Georgia, if offered, and they would probably have had strong backing from then U.S. president George Bush. But Canada and most, if not all, of the Western European NATO members, I believe, would likely have voted no. And it takes only one dissenting vote to stop any NATO action in its tracks.

There is little unanimity among NATO members on the threats confronting the alliance, especially when it comes to Russia, as I discovered during the question and answer session following my remarks at one of the top military institutions in the United States in November 2009. One of the questioners asked me why NATO had not responded more strongly against Russia's invasion of Georgia. Before I could answer, one of the German officers at the institution interjected, "My country has a large and growing relationship with Russia. Why does NATO provoke Russia by expanding to its borders? I can tell you if NATO had gone to war at that moment, my country would not have joined you."

Assuming the U.S. Congress had supported using military force in Georgia, the American administration may well have gone ahead with military action, using the same coalition-of-the-willing strategy that it had employed to fashion the invasion of Iraq. And Europe would have woken up one morning staring at Cold War 2.0.

One final perspective on the conflict between Georgia and Russia comes from Dr. Edgar Buckley, a former assistant secretary-general of NATO, and Dr. Ioan Mircea Pascu, a member of the European Parliament and former minister of defense of Romania. They have recently argued that although Georgia is not a member of NATO, many believe that Russia's use of force against it was a challenge to the alliance "and revealed weaknesses in its practical ability, and perhaps even its resolve, to stand up to Russia and defend allies in comparable circumstances."

Dr. Buckley continued, "That Article 5 did not apply to Georgia, but would apply in the event of an armed attack against any NATO member—misses the point. The allies concerned want more explicit reassurance that Article 5 will be invoked in the case of an attack against their territories and that they will be rapidly and adequately defended."[27]

This observation brings us back full circle to a key dilemma that NATO faces: it is rapidly becoming an alliance with a split perception of what constitutes a threat. This fact dilutes the alliance's central commitment to its members of mutual defense. Western European countries are far less threatened by Russia, the only real potential threat to NATO, than are the alliance's Central European and East European members.

It is not in the interest of the Western Europeans to disrupt their growing ties with Russia, an already significant trading partner and their largest source of energy. Having to launch a territorial defense against Russia—albeit a resurgent, self-confident Russia—is simply not in their cards, at least for now. And that means NATO will not be able to convince its Eastern European and Central European members, from whose perspective Russia is the real threat, that Article 5 wields much power anymore.

In fact, it is worth recalling that none of the wars that NATO has been involved in since the end of the Cold War—Bosnia, Kosovo, and Afghanistan—were triggered by an Article 5 situation. They have instead been under the remit of Article 4: "The Parties will consult together whenever, in the opinion of any of them, the territorial integrity, political independence or security of any of the Parties is threatened."

In the case of Bosnia and Kosovo, NATO used force to prevent civil wars in its backyard from spreading out into the rest of Europe (see chapter 4). In the case of Afghanistan, as discussed in chapter 2, NATO did invoke Article 5 after 9/11, but the United States did not want NATO's help and fought the Taliban by itself. It was only two years later that NATO chose to get involved in Afghanistan under a UN mandate. The same could be said for NATO's antipiracy naval deployment in Somali waters.

So Article 4 appears to be a far more workable mutual defense clause and much more applicable to today's realities. Unlike Article 5, which is invoked only after an attack on a member nation, Article 4 can be used during the lead-up to any situation that might *potentially, in the future* harm alliance interests. Because it focuses on consultation and cooperation for the purpose of responding to potential threats against member states, Article 4 would seem to be much more useful, on a day-to-day basis, to a NATO that no longer has a single, well-defined enemy.

There is no question that Article 5 will continue to be at NATO's heart. Its "one for all and all for one" declaration is the bond that holds NATO members to their alliance. So, the central challenge that the Alliance faced at the November 2010 NATO Summit in Lisbon was to answer two questions: What does Article 5 mean in the twenty-first century, and can all twenty-eight NATO members agree to its meaning? What follows is how NATO's Strategic Concept adopted in Lisbon addresses the challenge (full text of the Strategic Concept in appendix E):

4A. *Collective defence.* NATO members will always assist each other against attack, in accordance with Article 5 of the Washington Treaty. That commitment remains firm and binding. NATO will deter and defend against any threat of aggression, and against emerging security challenges where they threaten the fundamental security of individual Allies or the Alliance as a whole.

I wonder if the Estonians and Georgians are reassured.

But how has NATO fared as a combatant? Has it lived up to its expectations as the world's most powerful military alliance? And has it done so especially in its first war outside the European continent, the jurisdiction that the alliance was created to defend?

CHAPTER FOUR

NATO at War

Why are we spending all these billions of dollars to have an army
if you won't ever let me use it?
—*Secretary of State Madeleine Albright to Gen. Colin Powell,*
chairman of the Joint Chiefs of Staff[1]

"I was the first Secretary of State that took NATO to war," former secretary Madeleine Albright proudly told a gathering of NATO officials and experts at the Palais d'Egmont in Brussels on July 7, 2009.[2]
Anders Fogh Rasmussen, the NATO secretary-general designate, had just
appointed Albright to chair a group of Euro-Atlantic experts that Rasmussen had put together to help draft recommendations to guide the creation
of NATO's new strategic concept, or the operating guidelines that would
govern the alliance's operations for the next decade. Albright's keynote
address at the meeting was her official debut in her new position. Always
blunt and direct, she was in top form. "NATO has always been part of my
life," she said, recounting the alliance's history from her uniquely personal
perspective.

Its birth was hastened by the Communist takeover, in 1948, of my
native country. From then until the fall of the Berlin Wall, NATO had
the dual role of shielding freedom in the West while preserving hope

in Europe's east; as a daughter of Prague living in America, I had one foot on each side of that divide.

A decade ago, I had the privilege of welcoming Hungary, Poland and the Czech Republic into our alliance and of working with many of you to end terror and ethnic cleansing in Kosovo. . . . As these events reflect, NATO has been the most successful alliance in history; as current events dictate, it remains a pre-eminent actor on the world stage.

But she also had words of caution for her audience. "Each year, across the globe, there are fewer people who recall NATO's creation, fewer who remember its Cold War resolve, and fewer who have a clear sense of why NATO's survival and success should matter to them."

The phrase "the most successful alliance in history" is commonplace when referring to NATO, and the phrase is more than merited, as chapter 2 clearly demonstrated. The alliance's deterrence power, similar to a massive coiled spring ever-ready for action, kept Europe safe for forty years until, in 1989, the Cold War ended and the Soviet Union collapsed from within, without NATO's intervention.

But after the Cold War, when NATO's military machine did have to be used, the results have been less than inspiring. Without the threat of nuclear incineration to focus NATO members' minds on a common foe, the political bands that held the allies together to make NATO a fearsome war machine weakened. Thus, among the many kudos in Albright's speech, she also injected words of warning: "We have a firm foundation upon which to build. This does not mean that our job will be easy or that NATO's future is assured."

In 1999 Albright was determined to goad NATO into a war against Serbia, a part of the rapidly disintegrating Federation of Yugoslavia. Serbia's leader, Slobodan Milosevic, had begun to use brutal methods to stop the Serbian province of Kosovo from gaining independence from Serbia. Human rights violations, refugees, and ethnic cleansing, seemingly eradicated from Europe, had again begun to rear their ugly heads. Statesmen in Europe and America were coming to the reluctant conclusion that force was the only way the world was going to halt the unfolding catastrophe.

This area was Europe's backyard, but Europe still had no institutions that could be used to build a wartime consensus and organize armies in a campaign to force Milosevic's hand. The European Union had decided it would focus on integrating Europe's civil, commercial, and economic differences. The security pillar for the European Union would be tackled later. Consequently, there was no equivalent of the North Atlantic Council to make political decisions to deploy a European security force, no military council to advise the politicians on deployments, and no European military staff to execute the orders. When it came to organizing and projecting European power, NATO was the only game in town.

Set up as a defensive alliance to ensure the security of its members' territory, NATO had already crossed the Rubicon of being used for offensive purposes during the Bosnian campaign in 1992. As we shall soon see, NATO members agreed then, for the first time in the alliance's history, to use NATO assets in an offensive action to enforce UN resolutions.

In the case of Kosovo, however, there was little prospect of gaining a UN resolution to legitimize a NATO attack because of Russian opposition on the Security Council. The NATO nations themselves would have to approve and legitimize any use of force, and if they did decide to go to war, then it would have to be without the imprimatur of the United Nations.

Kosovo would be a large and complicated campaign that would require a strong American presence to achieve success. U.S. military resources were what made NATO a fighting force. Most NATO members, with a handful of exceptions, had not maintained military forces that could hold their own in a modern war.

The presence of American forces was also necessary to stiffen the Europeans' spine so they would undertake an offensive mission without backing from the United Nations. A senior American military officer who saw active service during the campaign told me that even Britain, a potent military power, made it clear to him that the country would not go to war against Kosovo unless the Americans did.

The U.S. military wasn't sure it wanted to lead NATO to war in Europe. Milosevic might be a nasty person, but he had not attacked a NATO member country. There was also strong public sentiment on both sides of the Atlantic that NATO, Bosnia notwithstanding, was still a defensive alliance.

Then the military had to contend with the Powell doctrine, which was named after Gen. Colin Powell, the popular chairman of the Joint Chiefs of Staff, who turned out to be Albright's main opponent in the Pentagon. The Powell doctrine, then the mantra of the America's armed forces, was a direct outcome of the Vietnam War. It stipulated America would never again go to war unless it did so with overwhelming force and a clearly defined exit strategy. Those terms meant the U.S. military would have to use overwhelming land forces in Kosovo, and that option was not feasible in Washington, D.C., where the Republicans, then in the majority, loudly opposed an American commitment in Kosovo.

House Majority Whip Tom DeLay typified the Republican opposition to the Kosovo mission during a speech on April 28, 1999: "President Clinton has never explained to the American people why he was involving the U.S. military in a civil war in a sovereign nation, other than to say it is for humanitarian reasons, a new military/foreign policy precedent."[3]

Presidential candidate Pat Buchanan, speaking to the NBC television program *Meet the Press* on April 25, 1999, voiced the other undercurrent of opposition to the war. "What are we doing bombing and attacking this tiny country that has never attacked the United States?" Buchanan asked. "I believe . . . it is now becoming basically no longer a war for Kosovo but a war to save NATO's credibility and NATO's face."[4]

In President Bill Clinton's administration, Secretary Albright had emerged as the champion of using NATO in Kosovo. She maintained Milosevic was akin to the proverbial school bully, ferocious until someone stood up to him, faced him down, and landed a few punches. That is what it took to make the bully turn tail and run.

Start bombing Serbia, show the bully Milosevic we mean business, and it will be over in three days, Albright assured President Clinton. NATO, after all, was the world's greatest military alliance while Serbia, a state of marginal geopolitical importance, had a population of 7.5 million and few modern military capabilities. It would not even be a fair matchup.

Albright won the day. She convinced President Clinton that the United States had to intervene militarily in Kosovo to stop a potential human rights catastrophe. Gen. Wesley Clark, then the SACEUR, ordered the air strikes. NATO, created to defend the West against the Soviet Union, began the first war under its own authority and waged it against the ministate of Serbia.

In the end, however, Albright guessed wrong. It turned out that NATO was not ready for war, but Milosevic was. Anticipating trouble, he had dispersed and hidden his military assets. Using the NATO attack as a pretext he began a systematic elimination of thousands of Muslims and forced hundreds of thousands of Albanian Kosovars to flee Serbia.[5] Instead of preventing atrocities, NATO's involvement had done the opposite. Now the Western powers had no alternative but to keep escalating the air war.

Wars are rarely won with air strikes alone, but an invasion of Serbia would mean committing troops against a well-entrenched enemy. There was no question that ultimately NATO would prevail, but the leaders of NATO's member countries would have to convince their citizens, citizens of a peaceful and increasingly prosperous Europe, that they had to sacrifice their citizens' lives to get the job done. In America, the administration would have to explain why America's national interests were tied up in a country that most Americans had never heard of. Neither Europe nor America was ready for a bloody land conflict with casualties.

There might be awkward questions, for example, about why NATO, the world's most powerful alliance, had failed to stop Milosevic with threats alone when its threats had made the Soviet Union blink. Besides, citizens might want to know why a defense alliance believed it could invade a country without first getting the imprimatur of the United Nations.

So NATO kept escalating the air war. America's precision-guided weaponry was still a work in progress while the Europeans' investment in high-tech weaponry was practically nonexistent. To keep their pilots safe, the air strikes were generally kept to fifteen thousand feet or higher. The high-altitude bombing resulted in a growing number of bombing errors, including a direct missile hit on the Chinese Embassy in Belgrade that killed three and injured another twenty people. It turned out that American intelligence had used an out-of-date map to guide the missile to its target, which was two hundred yards away from where the bomb landed.

In a bizarre explanation for the growing number of deaths caused by bombing errors, Jamie Shea, then NATO's spokesman, said, "When we started this operation, we were conducting around 30 [sorties] a day. Now we are conducting up to 350 attacks every night. There has not been a ten-fold increase where bombs have gone astray."[6]

It would take NATO eleven weeks to force Milosevic to agree to a truce. In those eleven weeks the Serbs would murder thousands of ethnic Albanian Kosovars in Europe's first acts of ethnic cleansing since World War II. NATO was powerless to stop the atrocities because no NATO country wanted to send its troops into Serbia during hostilities. At the end of eleven weeks, with its inventory of precision-guided weaponry almost depleted, an alarmed Washington encouraged Russia to work out a truce, and it did.

Once it was safe, fifty thousand NATO troops, under the UN flag (one of Milosevic's requirements before he would agree to a truce), moved into Kosovo to maintain the peace and to oversee the nation-building operation. Ten years later ten thousand NATO troops still remained in Kosovo. NATO secretary-general Rasmussen expects that most of the troops will leave Kosovo by the end of his four-year term, or in 2012.[7] This withdrawal date is fourteen years and three American presidents from the time NATO attacked Serbia with the expectation that the war would be over in three days.

Besides the sorry state of NATO's readiness to wage war in 1999, the eleven-week Kosovo war showed that even in a time of conflict, NATO still made decisions using its cumbersome committee structure. The SACEUR, ostensibly in command of all NATO forces in Europe, did not have the authority to make any important battlefield decisions without permission from the alliance's two powerful committees—the North Atlantic Committee and NATO's Military Committee (NATO MC)—which had been set up within NATO to balance military action with the political interests of each member state. Because every battlefield decision required unanimity, one dissenting country could overrule General Clark, NATO's battlefield commander.

Although NATO decided to rely on airpower to force Milosevic to his knees, General Clark could not select those bombing targets he considered vital to conduct the war he had been asked to fight. Instead, the nineteen member countries had to approve targets in the Kosovo campaign before air strikes could be launched. The NAC and NATO MC had to reach consensus separately to bomb each target, with every member of each committee making a decision based on the potential political fallout in its country over the proposed target. It drove General Clark mad with frustration.

"The foreign ministries, or in the American case, the State Department, ran the day-to-day process at NATO headquarters through nations' ambassadors, who met in the North Atlantic Council or NAC," Clark explained. The defense ministries were represented within the ambassadors' teams and also by a military representative of the Chief of Defense who sat on the NATO Military Committee, a body subordinate to the NAC. Thus, "the foreign ministries had the upper hand and the last word in working the issues."[8]

The results of this obtuse form of decision making on the battlefield were predictable. At one point Clark had secured French and American approval to attack the Serb television transmitter, "only to have NATO balk when some of the ambassadors questioned whether the target was truly military," he explained.[9]

Back in Washington, America's military leaders watching NATO at war in Kosovo became increasingly disillusioned. But the first indication that NATO had lost its allure for the Pentagon would come two years later, after the 9/11 terrorist strikes in New York; Washington, D.C.; and Pennsylvania. As noted earlier, in spite of NATO's first invocation of Article 5 and the Europeans' offer to fight shoulder to shoulder with the United States, America would essentially say to NATO, "Thanks but no thanks. We'll call you when we need you."

"We will never let anyone tell us who we can and can't bomb again," Secretary of Defense Rumsfeld told General Clark after 9/11.[10] Clearly, the secretary was referencing his disdain for NATO's predilection for making war by committee.

The military engagement in Kosovo and the earlier breakup of Yugoslavia were hugely complicated issues. Volumes have been written to describe the cultural, historical, political, and economic ramifications of the breakup of Yugoslavia, which was the confederation of six republics—Serbia, Croatia, Bosnia and Herzegovina, Macedonia, Slovenia, and Montenegro—as well as two provinces, Kosovo and Vojvodina. My objective in this book is not to describe these complexities or to provide a history of that bloody breakup or to ascribe blame or responsibility for what happened in Kosovo. My focus here is to point out that the war in Kosovo demonstrated NATO was considerably different from the image most people had of the alliance. Instead of a well-oiled and powerful military alliance that was ready for action, NATO was shown to be a slow-moving, bureaucratic organization that had difficulty defeating a petty dictator of a tiny country.

Although the Kosovo campaign is recognized as NATO's first war, it was the second time NATO resorted to force in Europe. Between 1992 and 1994 NATO played an important role in supporting the UN peacekeeping effort in the Bosnian-Serbian conflict.

More than a hundred thousand people died and almost two million became refugees before the war ended with the December 1995 Dayton Agreement, the cease-fire accord signed in Dayton, Ohio. NATO's resolve to aggressively implement the UN sanctions through using a sustained and powerful air bombardment of militarily important targets was the key factor in ending this bloody conflict.[11]

In the Bosnian campaign NATO acted with the approval of the United Nations. This endorsement made it far easier to reach a consensus at meetings of the North Atlantic Council, NATO's highest political decision-making body. Moreover, under the umbrella of the United Nations, the authority NATO had to use force as it saw fit was broad and flexible.

For instance, the NAC planned and approved a series of massive air strikes in July 1995. Thus, in August 1995 NATO could respond quickly to a series of brutal massacres carried out by the Serbs. Within a few days, NATO aircraft operating out of Italy and from two American aircraft carriers hit 338 targets. The sustained lethality of the attacks forced an end to the Bosnian war.

It is worth recalling that NATO owes its legitimacy to the United Nations. A review of the North American Treaty that established NATO in 1949 makes that quite clear (see appendix A). The designers of the treaty went out of their way to ensure the auspices of the United Nations covered their newly minted Western alliance. They did so in the opening sentence of the treaty's preamble: "The Parties to this Treaty reaffirm their faith in the purposes and principles of the Charter of the United Nations and their desire to live in peace with all peoples and all governments."

The drafters and signatory countries of the North American Treaty were careful to thread the United Nations, especially its Security Council, into the fabric of their treaty. As Article 7 demonstrates: "This treaty does not affect, and shall not be interpreted as affecting in any way . . . the primary responsibility of the Security Council for the maintenance of international peace and security."

The imprimatur of the United Nations made all the difference for the Europeans during the Bosnian campaign. "Public opinion in Europe sees the United Nations as the main source of legitimacy, and NATO is more legitimized if it is linked to the United Nations, rather than an independent body making its own decision," Fernando Valenzuela, the former ambassador from the European Union to the United Nations, told me.

NATO's involvement in Kosovo, meanwhile, was an action that was largely driven by the United States and was halfheartedly supported by some NATO members. Italy and Greece, for instance, worried about the influx of refugees into their countries as a result of the NATO campaign. It would, however, have been virtually impossible to convince the UN Security Council to authorize a NATO campaign in Kosovo. Russia, a permanent, veto-bearing member of the Security Council, had long-standing national interests in the region, resented NATO's presence there, and would have opposed such a resolution.

In the end the Kosovo campaign proved controversial. As the the *Leiden Journal of International Law* pointed out, "There is no unanimity in the international community about the legality of NATO's use of force in Kosovo in order to avert a humanitarian catastrophe. NATO has acted without Security Council authorization and its arguments for a humanitarian intervention are legally inconsistent."[12]

So under what authority did NATO go to war over Kosovo? Jamie Shea, the NATO spokesman during the Kosovo campaign, responded to just such a query on the British Broadcasting Corporation call-in program *Talking Point on Air* on April 20, 1999:

Vladimir, New Zealand: This action violates NATO's own charter which commits it to force only if one of its own member states is attacked.

Jamie Shea: That is not correct. Article 5 of the NATO treaty says that the obligation to use force applies to self-defense. It does not say that NATO cannot use force for other purposes. That then has to be done on a voluntary basis, as the countries are participating. *There are other articles in the treaty that commit the allies to working for a peaceful international order based on the principle of the UN.*[13] (emphasis added)

Shea is of course correct. Article 4, as seen in chapter 3, specifically grants the opportunity for NATO members to consult each other whenever any of them believes the "territorial integrity, political independence or security of any of the Parties is threatened." Certainly the NATO members had consultations, and the alliance's top political decision-making body, the North Atlantic Council, had judged the civil wars resulting from the breakup of Yugoslovia posed a danger to the NATO members that were adjacent to Kosovo. But the conflicts in both Bosnia and Kosovo changed NATO forever.

What Bosnia and Kosovo did was open a window through which NATO could peer at life after the Cold War. The alliance had gone into action beyond the territorial borders of its member states, albeit still within Europe. But now a precedent had been set. NATO had decided that instability in its backyard was too risky for peace in Europe and had to be stopped. And the allies had realized that when it came time to find a vehicle for coordinating military action in Europe, NATO was still the only choice available.

What was not apparent then, however, was the Europeans' feeling of weakness and embarrassment that fifty years after World War II, a prosperous European Union still had to rely on the United States to handle the crisis in Europe's backyard (see chapter 5).

Critics may point out that NATO's actions in Kosovo left something to be desired; for instance, the number of atrocities increased even as NATO's attacks against Serbia began. The air campaign could also have been far better executed. But what cannot be discounted is NATO's success in ultimately controlling the spread of instability from Bosnia and Kosovo.

As Javier Solana, NATO's secretary-general from 1995 to 1999, put it, "NATO's Kosovo operation was a major challenge in the history of the Atlantic alliance. For the first time, a defensive alliance launched a military campaign to avoid a humanitarian tragedy outside its own borders. For the first time, an alliance of sovereign nations fought not to conquer or preserve territory but to protect the values on which the alliance was founded. And despite many challenges, NATO prevailed."[14]

With the Kosovo intervention NATO had moved into new territory. The alliance had demonstrated that there was still a reason for NATO's existence even after the Cold War had ended.

With this second wind filling their sails, NATO leaders gathered in 1999 for their annual summit in Washington, D.C. It was also a time to celebrate the fiftieth anniversary of alliance and, as happens every ten years, to update NATO's strategic concept for the following decade. As these excerpts from the strategic concept demonstrate, NATO's military campaigns in Bosnia and Kosovo permanently changed how NATO thought of itself.

Military Capabilities: The Concept reaffirms Allies [*sic*] determination to strengthen Alliance defense capabilities by ensuring forces that are more mobile, sustainable, survivable and able to engage effectively on the full spectrum of NATO missions.

New Missions: The Concept calls for improvements in NATO's capability to undertake new missions to respond to a broad spectrum of possible threats to Alliance common interests, including: regional conflicts, such as in Kosovo and Bosnia; the proliferation of weapons of mass destruction and their means of delivery; and transnational threats like terrorism.[15]

The 1999 Strategic Concept, which NATO unanimously adopted on April 24 (see appendix B), committed NATO to go anywhere in the world to preserve and protect the safety and security of its members. Now, the whole world was its playing field.[16]

NATO's adoption of the out-of-area mission would turn out to be a momentous decision. Two years later, on 9/11, the world would change forever. And NATO would get its wish to prove that it was still very much in business, in the mountains of Afghanistan.

In December 1979 I was skiing in Gulmarg, the capital of Indian Kashmir. I will never forget the breathtaking sight of the entire horizon filled with mountains that towered over sixteen thousand feet around us. Another memory from this trip will forever stay with me. It must have been around three or four o'clock in the morning when my bearer prodded me awake and in a hushed voice said, "Sir, the Russians are crossing into Afghanistan." He pointed in the direction where about two hundred miles away Russian armor was pouring into the country.

Ultimately although over a hundred thousand Soviet troops fought in Afghanistan, they would fail to conquer this hardy land of fierce warriors who detest foreign occupation more than anything. Over the centuries, countless invaders have met this same fate, as one after another they gave up their dreams of forcing their will on the Afghans and left.

What the Afghans lacked in modern armor and weaponry they made up in bravery, fighting skill, and intimate familiarity, acquired over generations, with their trackless, inhospitable terrain. Once the United States decided to become a silent partner of the Afghan resistance and began to funnel money, intelligence, antiaircraft missiles, and other deadly weaponry to the Afghans, the Soviet force was doomed.

After ten long years and an estimated forty thousand to fifty thousand casualties, a humbled and mauled Russian army hobbled back across the Friendship Bridge to Soviet Uzbekistan. Their Afghan misadventure marked the beginning of the end of the Soviet Empire.

Not in my wildest dreams did I imagine that twenty years after the Russians were thrown out of Afghanistan with American help, America itself would be bogged down in an Afghan campaign. As of this writing, over a hundred thousand American soldiers and tens of thousands of allied troops are encamped in Afghanistan. It is their turn now to try their luck against the Afghans. Just as the Russians were in their time, the newcomers are equipped with fearsome new weapons: unmanned aircraft, or drones; laser-guided munitions; and night vision goggles. And just as the Russians before them, after nine years of war, the might of the Western powers appears no closer to prevailing by force against the Afghans.

To this war NATO has hitched its new incarnation as an alliance that will go anywhere in the world to fight against the forces of evil to defend

Euro-American peace and stability. As of December 14, 2010, there were 131,730 NATO troops deployed in Afghanistan under ISAF command. Of these, 90,000 are from the U.S. military, 33,458 belong to the other twenty-seven NATO countries, and there were 8,272 troops from twenty non-NATO nations.[17] (The troop numbers are approximate because they change daily.)

It is the first real test of NATO's out-of-area mission statement adopted in its 1999 Strategic Concept. Further, it has become NATO's existential battle, not only because a continuous stream of European soldiers are being killed for the first time in almost three generations, but also because the war in Afghanistan, just as those in Bosnia and Kosovo, has put the alliance under a microscope. The picture of NATO that has emerged is quite different from the expectations of both its friends and enemies.

NATO entered Afghanistan in its role as the leader of the UN-sanctioned ISAF. The United Nations set up the force in December 2001 to use the opportunity that the Americans' victory over the Taliban and al Qaeda opened to stabilize and reconstruct Afghanistan after twenty years of devastating internecine war. The UN resolution calls upon the ISAF to "provide security and law and order, promote governance and development, help reform the justice system, train a national police force and army, provide security for elections, and provide assistance to the local effort to address the narcotics industry."[18]

Initially led by the United States, the ISAF's mission was limited to Afghanistan's capital, Kabul. Afghan president Hamid Karzai then requested that the United Nations invite NATO to join the ISAF. Karzai's request was the opportunity NATO had been waiting for. It was the alliance's out-of-area moment.

NATO took over the leadership of the ISAF in August 2003. The NATO contingent is the largest component of the ISAF, but non-NATO countries, such as Australia, Saudi Arabia, the Ukraine, and Jordan, are also represented. Table 4 provides a breakdown of troops from every country participating in the ISAF's mission.

The immediate problem NATO faced was a mismatch in what the alliance's military leaders expected from NATO member nations and what

Table 4. International Security Assistance Force: Troop Contributing Nations

Albania	250	Germany	4665	Poland	2515
Armenia	40	Greece	70	Portugal	105
Australia	1550	Hungary	335	Romania	1010
Austria	3	Iceland	4	Singapore	40
Azerbaijan	90	Ireland	7	Slovakia	230
Belgium	590	Italy	3300	Slovenia	75
Bosnia & Herzegovina	10	Jordan	6	Spain	1270
Bulgaria	525	Republic of Korea	0	Sweden	485
Canada	2830	Latvia	115	The Former Yugoslav Republic of Macedonia*	215
Croatia	280	Lithuania	145	Turkey	1795
Czech Republic	460	Luxembourg	9	Ukraine	10
Denmark	750	Mongolia	40	United Arab Emirates	25
Estonia	155	Montenegro	30	United Kingdom	9500
Finland	100	Netherlands	1885	United States	62415
France	3750	New Zealand	225		
Georgia	175	Norway	470	Total	102554

Source: NATO, "Troop Contributing Nations," accessed July 1, 2010, http://jsaf-live.web drivenhq.com/troop-contributing-nations .html.

Note on Numbers: Totals are approximations and actual numbers change daily. Number of troops should be taken as indicatives.

*Turkey recognizes the Republic of Macedonia with its constitutional name

these nations were prepared to deliver. Many NATO countries (and especially their populations) assumed the alliance was headed to a largely peaceful environment where their troops would help stabilize and rebuild Afghanistan. When they arrived, they found themselves in the middle of a war that they had assumed had ended. NATO forces had to fight as they tried to build.

This breakdown in communications mystifies former U.S. ambassador to NATO Nick Burns. "I feel this very personally, because I was present at the creation of this policy in 2003 when NATO made the collective decision to go in. We decided to go into a combat mission—it wasn't for a peacekeeping mission—and some of the allies are acting as if this was a humanitarian mission."

The reality of waging a war in Afghanistan has proved to be a highly contentious issue for the Europeans. A German Marshall Fund poll conducted during 2009 showed that the preponderance of the NATO countries surveyed, with the exception of the United States, wanted their forces totally withdrawn. More than half of the Western Europeans and two-thirds of the Eastern Europeans wanted to reduce their commitments or remove their soldiers from Afghanistan.[19]

In a report prepared in February 2009 for members and committees of the U.S. Congress, the Congressional Research Service pointed out that

> NATO's effort in Afghanistan is the alliance's first "out-of-area" mission beyond Europe. The purpose of the mission is the stabilization and reconstruction of Afghanistan. . . . Taliban and al-Qaeda insurgents are providing stiff resistance to the operation, Afghanistan has never had a well-functioning central government, the distance from Europe, and the country's terrain present daunting obstacles to both NATO manpower and equipment. Stabilization and reconstruction must take place while combat operations continue. And, although the allies agree upon the general political objective of the ISAF mission, some have had differing interpretations of how to achieve it.
>
> *Politically, the mission in Afghanistan is likely to remain important for NATO's future. Several key NATO members, above all the United States, view*

the Afghanistan mission as a test case for the allies' ability to generate the political will to counter significant threats to their security. These countries believe Afghanistan provides a test of will against the concrete danger of international terrorism although some allies may disagree with this assessment. . . .

Over the past several years, NATO governments have also repeatedly pledged to develop capabilities making their forces more expeditionary, flexible, and "deployable." This mission in Afghanistan provides a hard test of these capabilities and commitments.[20] (emphasis added)

Once it became obvious that the ISAF's mission was in a sense premature—UN peacekeeping and stabilization forces go into a region *after* the fighting has stopped—it encountered an immediate problem: many NATO members did not wish to involve their military in a fighting war and had opted out of the fighting in writing. This situation meant NATO did not have an integrated fighting force on the ground. Having volunteered to go to Afghanistan and to stake its reputation on the war, NATO was faced with a conundrum of its own making as part of the forces the alliance sent to Afghanistan could not be used on the battlefield.

"What's going on in Afghanistan right now is critically important for the future of NATO because we [the United States] and NATO have made it into a NATO project," Senator Chuck Hagel told me. "There is a significant difference of opinion among the twenty-eight NATO members on that war. If that wasn't the case then why do we have a situation where each nation has conditions on its troops being there?" he asked rhetorically. "Some of them there are there just because they wanted to put a few people in there. They won't fight or take casualties, but they are there. I'm not second-guessing their decision, I'm not saying that is right or wrong, but those are the facts. So, for us to skip around that, and act like this is a unified NATO command, is totally untrue. If it was a NATO effort all those NATO troops in there would be fighting side by side, as the United Nations did in Korea. So this is really an untruthful fabrication; we have invented it."

This hugely important statement comes from one of America's most knowledgeable foreign policy experts, who has always been and continues to be one of NATO's strongest supporters. Connect the dots in Hagel's statement, and it is obvious that NATO is increasingly more of a liability than an asset to the American effort in Afghanistan. It is not carrying its own weight. Yes, a few NATO members are fighting the Taliban and suffering most of the casualties, but the rest of the membership is simply there to show the flag. NATO's commitment to fight out of area is already ringing hollow.

The most abrasive issue in Afghanistan, particularly for the U.S. military, is its NATO allies' use of national caveats. Here's how the Congressional Research Service Report describes them and their impact on military effectiveness:

> At the outset, NATO leaders faced considerable difficulty persuading some member states to contribute forces to ISAF. . . . Many allies committed forces to the NATO operation, then imposed restrictions—"national caveats"—on tasks these forces could undertake . . . almost half the forces in ISAF have some form of caveats . . . restrictions that allied governments, or their parliaments, place on the use of their forces . . . caveats do pose difficult problems for commanders who seek maximum flexibility in utilizing troops under their command. . . . Some nations will not permit their troops to deploy to other parts of Afghanistan. . . others prohibit their troops from participating in combat operations unless in self-defense. NATO commanders . . . have had to shape the conduct of the mission to fit the capabilities of and caveats on those troops.[21]

National caveats come in different forms. Under the previous German government of Chancellor Gerhard Schroeder, German troops were not permitted to engage in combat operations, which meant German soldiers could not take part in integrated patrols. Under the present government of Chancellor Merkel, German troops can engage in combat to defend German positions, but they still cannot engage in counterinsurgency operations.[22]

The inability to give orders to all of the forces under his command is a serious handicap for any commander. In a war it can easily become a matter of life and death. John Brophy, a civilian employee of the U.S. Army serving in the Space and Defense Lab, and Dr. Miloslav Fisera, of the University of Defense in Brno, Czech Republic, looked at the deadly impact of national caveats in the Afghan war.[23]

In September of 2006, a combined British-Afghan National Army patrol encountered a numerically superior enemy force and for 14 days the ISAF patrol held out without reinforcement. Some reports allege that reinforcement was available, but could not immediately deploy because of national caveats. . . .

Other reports suggest that Canadian forces assigned to ISAF . . . suffered numerous casualties because other contingents could not support them.

"The largest offensive operation by NATO in recent years was Operation Medusa . . . it nearly failed on Day Four . . . because the national caveats meant that the Canadians simply did not have the support that they needed from other countries."

There have also been some public "accusations" that during Operation Medusa, at least 12 Canadian soldiers died because they could not get support from other national contingents because of these combat-restrictions. There have been no further public details on this alleged incident, and these rumors have not been confirmed. . . .

These incidents suggest that caveats affect not only senior multinational commanders, but even small-unit commanders who must depend on reinforcements from neighboring national contingents in emergency circumstances.

Finally, it is . . . already clear that caveats are an increasingly contentious issue which is threatening not only the combat capability of NATO, but is actually threatening to "drive a wedge" between NATO nations. Some observers contend that caveats are preventing military success in Afghanistan, and, by extension, are endangering the alliance itself.[24]

Former U.S. secretary of defense Donald Rumsfeld once likened NATO's way of making war with national caveats to a basketball team that practices together for months, only to have some players refuse to participate when the game starts. My own feeling is the Europeans are simply not as threatened with the geopolitics of Afghanistan as are the Americans. The Europeans are not convinced that if the Taliban are not stopped on the streets of Kabul or Kandahar, they will need to be fought in Amsterdam or Berlin. Most of them are there simply out of loyalty to the United States.

"I have interpreted the involvement of Europeans and Canadians in Afghanistan as being motivated, in large part, by a desire to make a show of solidarity, without actually believing that the mission is of critical importance," Andrew Bacevich told me. He recalled the rupture between the United States and its allies over the Iraq War and suspects "that people on both sides of that divide saw it as regrettable and wish to find ways to repair relations by making a show of supporting the U.S.-led mission in Afghanistan. I don't think German troops are in Afghanistan because the German government views the future of Afghanistan as a vital interest of Germany or of Europe. So there is this less than full-hearted commitment."

As serious as national caveats are, they may soon take a secondary role to the fact that a number of NATO countries are just plain tired of the unending war in Afghanistan and are getting ready to leave. The Dutch forces, which numbered 1,770 at the end of 2009, were down to 190 as of December 14, 2010, and will be gone by the end of 2010 (the Dutch government collapsed when the prime minister tried to extend the Dutch troop deployment beyond 2010).[25] The Canadian Parliament has decreed its troops must withdraw by the end of 2011. There are strong signals that the Italians and Germans will also begin packing their kit bags before too long. Britain, always the stalwart American ally has made it clear there will be no British combat forces in Afghanistan after by 2014. Soon, the war in Afghanistan will revert to becoming an all American project.

The United States keeps asking its NATO allies to pull their weight in Afghanistan but to no avail. There was a time when NATO members marched in lockstep with the United States. But that is not the case anymore.

The German Marshall Fund discovered in 2009 that only 55 percent of the Central and Eastern Europeans and 65 percent of Western Europeans believed NATO was essential. The split between the Western European NATO members and the rest of the alliance came into sharp focus when the German Marshall Fund asked European countries whether they would be willing to trade NATO expansion for Russian oil and gas. While 41 percent of Western Europeans said they would, only 28 percent of the Central and Eastern Europeans agreed. Finally, in perhaps the most important finding, all across Europe people preferred global leadership by the European Union rather than by America.[26]

The last two chapters will not make for pleasant reading for those who believe NATO is still destined to continue being the most successful military alliance in history. Whether its future will be as storied as its past is an open question, however. Much depends on removing the rose-tinted glasses through which the transatlantic allies have always viewed NATO and to recognize reality. NATO is simply not the alliance it used to be. But that does not mean it is not important or useful. NATO still has a key role to play in Euro-Atlantic security, but it must share its role in the future with Europe's own security establishment, the European Union's Common Security and Defense Policy.

To an American audience accustomed to reading about the never-never land the Europeans have created for themselves by letting the United States bear all of the costs of keeping them safe, the fact that Europe even has a security establishment will come as a surprise. The average American has been convinced for a long time that the Europeans will never invest their euros in defense matters. They are portrayed as too busy expanding the European Union and building a comfortable life to worry about keeping themselves safe.

But how then does one explain the following forecast by the European Institute for Strategic Studies?

The good news is that in the coming years, based on their current procurement plans, EU countries should have a number of new strategic capabilities such as: A400M and more C-17 transport planes; A330 air tankers; Euro-fighter, Rafale and Joint-Strike-Fighter jets;

and Franco-British aircraft carriers. EU defense ministries will also be able to use Galileo—a satellite navigation system—to guide their equipment and define their positions. All this equipment will greatly add to the military prowess of Europe's armies in the future.[27]

It turns out that since 2001, as the European commitment to NATO was waning at best, its commitment to a European security establishment has been gaining strength. The idea of a European security establishment has always been greeted with gales of laughter in America. While the Europeans are not there yet, the course is set. As the Europeans have proven over the last sixty years, when it comes to strengthening the European Union, they may take two steps forward and one step back, but they eventually achieve their goals. As we are about to see, the Europeans have already created a potent military organization that simultaneously recognizes that the EU is a grouping of sovereign states while being able to deploy military and civilian missions under an integrated EU command.

CHAPTER FIVE

At the Crossroads of NATO and the European Union

In the past, the United States has been ambivalent about whether NATO should engage in security cooperation with the EU. Well, that time is over.

—*Secretary of State Hillary Rodham Clinton*

Bright sunlight glanced off the Egyptian freighter on March 3, 2009, as it sailed into the Gulf of Aden, fifty-seven miles off the coast of Yemen and headed for the United Arab Emirates. The early morning sun lit up the choppy waves of the gulf as the deck watch scanned the horizon of these troubled waters, infested with Somali pirates that use small groups of fast-moving boats to hijack commercial vessels and kidnap their crews, holding them from ransom. Another day of uneventful sailing would take the Egyptians into safer waters, but they were not to experience that luxury.

A well-armed skiff had evaded detection and appeared off the Egyptian ship's starboard bow, spraying it with gunfire and wounding one of the sailors. Frantically, the Egyptian captain radioed for help and ordered full steam ahead. This kind of event happens with breathtaking regularity these days as Somali pirates get ever more sophisticated in their well-paying business. Hundreds of millions of dollars are handed over by the owners of hijacked vessels to the ragtag but well-armed and organized band of modern-day pirates.

But on this morning events would unfold differently. Before the pirates could board the ship, the German warship *Rheinland-Pfalz* and its helicopter responded to the Egyptians' call for help. A brief fire-fight ensued after which the pirates were captured. The commercial carrier continued its voyage. The pirates would ultimately find themselves in a Kenyan courtroom, facing prosecution for piracy.

The German frigate flew a flag that exhibited a blue field with a circle of gold stars—the universally recognized symbol of the European Union. The German navy ship is part of a flotilla that includes warships from Spain, Germany, France, Greece, Italy, Sweden, Belgium, and the Netherlands. As part of the European Union Naval Force (EU NAVFOR), the flotilla now patrols the pirate-infested waters off Somalia under the European Union flag in an operation called Atalanta.

Over twenty warships and aircraft, as well as eighteen hundred soldiers, sailors, and airmen from EU countries are part of Atalanta, the first ever naval operation launched by the European Union. Operation Atalanta is Europe's response to a UN mandate that authorizes the world community to protect commercial sea-lanes against piracy. It is entirely funded by EU states and was organized and deployed under the framework of the EU's Common Security and Defense Policy (CSDP), making it possible for the states to plan and execute crisis management missions thousands of miles from Europe's borders.

Launched in December 2008 for one year, Operation Atalanta is the largest antipiracy effort off Somalia. Its naval flotilla contains more than twice the number warships deployed by either NATO or the United States. The naval force proved to be so effective in the first few months of its deployment that its tenure was extended through the end of 2010.

The naval flotilla has a broad mission: "to provide protection for vessels chartered by the World Food Programme for Somalia; provide protection for merchant vessels; employ the necessary measures, including the use of force, to deter, prevent and intervene in order to bring to an end acts of piracy and armed robbery; . . . to arrest, detain and transfer suspected pirates."[1] This duty must come as a surprise to Euro-skeptics who believe the Europeans can never put together a military force of any consequence.

If the internecine political issues NATO faces in Afghanistan leave an impression of the Europeans being in disarray and having a halfhearted commitment to hard power, Operation Atalanta provides a dramatically different perspective. It is a reminder of what the European Union is now capable of accomplishing militarily when its member nations perceive a clear threat to their national interests. Atalanta also demonstrates that with the CSDP, the Europeans finally have a platform to build consensus around a security issue, organize and fund a multinational operation to deal with the threat, and execute it with precision.

Rear Adm. Peter Hudson, from Britain's Royal Navy, is commander of Atalanta from the operational headquarters in Northwood, on the outskirts of London. Rear Adm. Giovanni Gumiero of Italy commands the naval force from his force headquarters based on the Italian frigate ITS *Etna*, which sails in the seas off Somalia. Operation Atalanta, however, is under the overall control of the European Union, which is a governmental unit set up by European nations. Just as any other political entity, the European Union has the authority to sign agreements and treaties with other countries. This ability gives the EU a significant advantage over NATO, which is in the end a military alliance whose operations are under the political control of a committee—namely, the North Atlantic Council—that reports to twenty-eight governments.

The difference is evident in the way the European Union designed and launched Atalanta. It has mandated,

> The military personnel involved in the [Atalanta] operation can arrest, detain and transfer persons who are suspected of having committed or who have committed acts of piracy or armed robbery. . . . They can seize the vessels of the pirates or the vessels captured following an act of piracy or an armed robbery and which are in the hands of the pirates, as well as the goods on board. The suspects can be prosecuted . . . by an EU member state or by Kenya under the agreement signed with the EU on 6 March 2009 giving the Kenyan authorities the right to prosecute. *An exchange of letters concluded on 30 October 2009 between the European Union and the Republic of Seychelles allows the transfer of suspected pirates and armed robbers apprehended by ATALANTA.*

> . . . This [Seychelles] arrangement constitutes an important new con-
> tribution to the counter-piracy efforts. This new agreement is based
> on the same conditions and framework as the Kenyan agreement.[2]
> (emphasis added)

This 8.3 million-euro budget for running Atalanta's two headquarters is shared by the EU member states, with each country's payment being established on the basis of its GDP. The ships, helicopters, military person-nel, and operating costs are borne by the contributing countries and estab-lished according to their involvement in the operation, with each country continuing to bear the cost of the resources it provides.

The operation's successful record is testimony to the seamless co-operation and interoperability of military forces from a number of differ-ent European Union countries. Unlike the NATO forces in Afghanistan that are chronically short of troops and equipment promised by some of the alliance's member nations but never delivered, Rear Admiral Hud-son's naval flotilla has received what was promised. Compared to the seem-ingly endless efforts to have all NATO countries function as one integrated military force in Afghanistan, Atalanta appears to work like a well-oiled machine.

The countries participating in Atalanta work so well together that its operations have already broken new ground. Their innovative use of so-phisticated technology and procedures make Atalanta the trendsetter for multicountry naval operations.

Its ships patrol an area that stretches from the south of the Red Sea, through the Gulf of Aden, and into part of the Indian Ocean, including the Seychelles. The territory is comparable to that of the Mediterranean. So, communications and the melding of naval command and control pro-cedures from a host of countries into a unified operating network are the keys to operational success. Here Atalanta has excelled, according to the magazine *Naval Technology*:

> A Maritime Security Centre acts as a control room for the EU Navy.
> Officers from European forces monitor computer screens showing
> the position of EU naval and merchant ships spread over a 4,800km

radius. A website has been set up through which the merchant shipping community can log planned routes and naval forces can put out alerts and provide advice to people travelling through dangerous waters.

EU NAVFOR spokesperson Ryan Wallace says this capability has allowed the naval forces to help vulnerable ships travel through the area using intelligence at a level never enjoyed before. . . . The Royal Navy, as part of EU NAVFOR, has made its satellite communications compatible with other naval forces, including Nato, the US Satcom control in the Indian Ocean and other forces patrolling the region. . . .

"It is the first time a lot of these countries outside the coalition have ever talked to each other in a military command so we had to draw on a lot of the experience of other forces [to be able to integrate the EU NAVFOR technology] as well to be able to get the system running at their end," Wallace says.[3]

The results of these innovations were clearly manifested in early March 2009 when Bloomberg reporter Gregory Viscusi happened to be on board an Atalanta warship as it went into action. As Viscusi watched, "three naval vessels and two helicopters from an international force responded to internet chat room alerts using GPS navigation to locate a German-operated cargo freighter in the Gulf of Aden that had come under attack by nine pirates. Both US and European naval forces, previously communicating on completely different military radio frequencies, responded and the attackers were arrested."[4]

The naval mission's success has already influenced the views of senior military leaders in Europe about the European Union's ability to successfully organize and deploy multinational missions. It is an important benefit in a global recession as defense budgets shrink.

Atalanta's British commander must have raised quite a few eyebrows in London when, in the midst of reviewing Britain's strategic defense expenditures, he told the *Financial Times* that from a UK perspective, "we've been pleasantly surprised at the success we have had. It [has] exposed to us that across the EU's goals, we can deliver effectively through *missions of this nature. We need to reflect upon this and see how it changes our relations for the future. My personal view is it is for the positive.*"[5] (emphasis added)

While NATO has had to struggle in performing every mission it has launched since 1999—Bosnia, Kosovo, and Afghanistan—the CSDP appears to have moved out much more smoothly to fill the European Union's security, stability, and defense needs. Since its founding in 1999, the CSDP has launched twenty-seven missions in Europe, Africa, the Middle East, Central Asia, and the Baltic region. Table 5 shows the scope of these deployments as of May 2009.

Most of the missions have been far smaller in scale than the ones NATO has undertaken, and most of them have been nonmilitary missions, such as deploying to Guinea-Bissau to reform its security sector and to the Democratic Republic of the Congo to assist the Kinshasa police. But it is interesting to note that in its ten years of existence the CSDP has undertaken far many more missions than has NATO in its sixty years. And, I might add, the same European countries that have been tying NATO up in knots since the end of the Cold War are the ones that have made a success of the CSDP.

While the forces in most CSDP missions number in the hundreds, the European Union's mission to the landlocked African country of Chad mobilized a force of over ten thousand troops, to ensure that a force of thirty-seven hundred would be in theater continuously over the duration of the mission. With a price tag of over a billion dollars, this mission represented an important milestone, for it demonstrated that the European Union could integrate, deploy, maintain, and operate a sizable, multicountry military force at a great distance from Europe, a specialty that is generally not attributed to the European Union.

The EU Force to Chad and the Central African Republic (EUFOR TChad/RCA) consisted of troops from twenty-three of the twenty-seven EU states and, significantly, from three non-European Union countries—Albania, Croatia, and Russia—whose forces operated under the integrated EU command.[6] Albania and Croatia provided force protection platoons. Russia provided four heavy lift helicopters and their crews.

Under Irish and French command, the mission ran under the CSDP framework from March 2008 to April 2009.[7] Authorized by a UN Security Council resolution, the mission's objective was to protect more than 200,000 refugees from Darfur and some 225,000 people displaced by internal fighting in Chad and the Central African Republic. It was the most

Table 5. CSDP Missions Through Mid-May 2009*

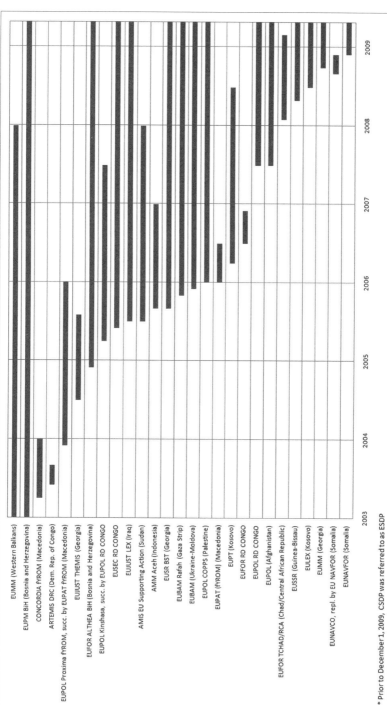

* Prior to December 1, 2009, CSDP was referred to as ESDP

Adapted from ISIS Europe, "Chart and Table of CSDP and EU missions," European Security Review no. 44, May 2009, http://isis-europe.org/pdf/2009_artrel_276_isis-esdpchart-may09.pdf.

demanding military mission that the European Union had launched thus far. Besides the logistics involved, the theater of operations encompassed over 280,000 square kilometers, or more than half the size of France.[8]

After the European Union approved the mission and Chad and the Central African Republic cleared it, elite Irish rangers supported by Special Operations Forces from Austria, Belgium, France, and Sweden prepared four operating zones in January 2008. The entire force was deployed and in operation by the summer. Lt. Gen. Patrick Nash of Ireland was the operations commander of the mission and ran his command from the operational headquarters (made available to the mission by the French military) in Mont-Valérien, near Paris. Brig. Gen. Jean-Philippe Ganascia of France was the "in theater" force commander in charge of the military forces on the ground.

The deployment was not an insignificant military feat. Thousands of tons of military equipment, fuel, and water had to first be shipped to Douala, Cameroon, on the East African coast—a two-week journey from Europe. Then it had to be transported another seventeen hundred kilometers to Chad, a distance equivalent to traveling from Rome to Stockholm, using containers, trucks, and other vehicles on rough roads. Camps had to be built from scratch in the middle of the desert to house the thirty-seven hundred troops.

To reach the operations zone in the center of Africa, an air bridge was established from Europe to N'Djamena, Chad, and a sea-land bridge was set up from the port city of Douala in the Cameroon to Chad. Ultimately, over 2,400 units (containers and vehicles) of equipment would be transported through Cameroon, and 540 air transport flights would fly troops and equipment directly from Europe to Chad.

Italian troops installed a field hospital of fifteen air-conditioned, interlinked tents that contained operating rooms, X-ray equipment, a pharmacy, and dentistry unit. To ensure that the insurgents understood early on that the Europeans meant business, the multinational special force units carried out reconnaissance missions deep into hostile territory.

To minimize the loss of life, once the force was fully established, extensive operations using air and ground assets were undertaken to target specific areas of concern and to display the force's military capabilities. Long-range patrols were sent throughout the area of operations to project EUFOR Tchad/RCA as a credible force with a significant deterrent effect. A coordinated information campaign underpinned the military deployment. UN personnel, who would ultimately take over from the EUFOR, were colocated in EUFOR's camps, and the military provided a security umbrella that enabled the deployment of the UN force after EUFOR Tchad/RCA completed its mission.

One of the questions I was most interested in asking the force commander, General Nash, was whether he had the authority to take military action as necessary or whether his force was constrained with national caveats of the kind that prevented most of the European members of NATO from participating in the Afghan war.

"I asked for and got extremely robust rules of engagement," Nash told me. He wanted the highest level of rules possible to ensure the mission was successful in completing its mandate and for the security of the soldiers. "I have no quibbles with the European Council in this respect because they approved what I wanted to do in Chad," he said.

Nash's military preparations proved prescient. The EU force found itself militarily engaged in the first month of the deployment. "There was a major altercation near the Sudanese border, I mean a major firefight," Nash told me. "We had to bring in helicopters to support the troops and to extricate them. Our troops found themselves engaged against regular military units and lost one soldier in the engagement. But we dealt with it strongly and taught them a good lesson."

Within weeks after the first engagement, an Irish contingent was attacked by a well-organized rebel force outside the town of Goz Beida in Chad. It was another serious firefight, and the rebel militia sustained a number of casualties. During a number of subsequent occasions, Belgian and Austrian troops fought off attacks in northern Chad and killed many of the enemy. Nash also went out of his way to speak about the French and Polish troops attached to his force. They never hesitated to engage the enemy to defend the mission's mandate.

And what about the national caveats? Neither the EU countries nor the Russians had any caveats that impacted their troops ability to use force to achieve their mission. Nash went out of his way to praise the Russian military force: "The Russians put their helicopters and crews under the European Union command and executed their missions brilliantly." The general could not help taking this American to task for asking about European caveats. "You know, the Americans talk a lot about caveats, but the United States is the biggest offender with caveats. You rarely allow your troops to operate under international command."

During March 2009, ceremonies were held both in Chad and in the Central African Republic to transfer mission responsibility to UN forces. A significant number of countries that contributed troops to EUFOR Tchad/ RCA agreed to "re-hat" their troops with the UN forces' blue berets and stayed in the region. The remainder of the force returned to Europe by the end of May 2009.

The seventeen-month Chad/Central African Republic mission demonstrated the European Union's objective of using military deployments to further geopolitical goals that Europeans consider to be in their national interest. "Stabilization of the Darfur region is an important objective for Europe," General Nash said to me. "Security is a precondition for development, and the military operation will reinforce and complement other European Union initiatives, political, economic and diplomatic."[9]

It is instructive to also compare the execution of the European Union's mission in Chad to the difficulties the NATO-led International Security and Assistance Force faced in Afghanistan. The mission to Chad encountered numerous political problems as it was being organized, but it overcame them and completed its objectives on time. In contrast to the CSDP-organized mission to Chad, the NATO-led ISAF continues to be plagued with innumerable political and operational problems years after it landed in Afghanistan.

For instance, on January 21, 2010, seven years after the NATO deployment to Afghanistan, Gen. Stanley McChrystal, then the commander of all NATO and U.S. forces in Afghanistan, publicly criticized German NATO troops for not doing an adequate job. The four-star general said, "Like all the troops in Afghanistan, German forces needed to live with the greater risk." He thought that the Germans had "to change the way they have dealt with the situation so far" and that he planned "to deploy American troops in the German sector in the near future."[10] (I must point out that the German reluctance to engage in war has nothing to do with bravery or skill. Germany is still burdened with its World War II Nazi history that makes warfare a hugely sensitive issue for the country.) Worse, at least two countries, the Netherlands and Canada, have decided to call it quits and go home before the Afghanistan mission has achieved its objectives. Other European NATO members could follow this precedent given the level of unease in Europe for the decade-old war in Afghanistan.

In fairness, I must again point out that the ISAF mission in Afghanistan is far larger and more complex than was the EUFOR Tchad/RCA mission. But the fact remains that military forces from the *same* European countries populate both NATO's ISAF and the European Union's CSDP missions. Both organizations draw from the same pool of Europeans. So it is legitimate, it seems to me, to ask why this difference in commitment, attitude, and performance exists between the two operations.

I believe that ultimately the reason for the disparities is that NATO is led by the United States and the CSDP is a European enterprise. Increasingly over the last decade America and Europe have largely ceased to "find a strategic consensus," as Nicholas Burns, former senior American official and ambassador to NATO, put it. The two sides simply do not share a similar vision about global threats and how to respond to them. Unless this divide is repaired, NATO will, in Burns's words, "splutter" and continue on its path of "being hollowed out." [11] To rebuild the consensus between Europe and the United States, and to avoid the fate Burns sees for NATO, I believe that NATO and the CSDP must be bridged. Chapter 7 deals with my recommendation in more detail.

One does not read much about the CSDP in the American media. But then it did not cover much about the European Union either as it was realizing its landmark achievements such as replacing the currencies of eleven EU countries with a common European currency (the euro) and consolidating the increasing amounts of national sovereignty that member nations handed over to EU organizations.

The Americans' inattention to developments in the European Union has often led to unpleasant surprises because they do not understand the powerful entity that the Europeans have been creating these sixty years. General Electric, for instance, was shocked in 2001 to discover that the European Union could block its attempted merger with Honeywell, even though American antitrust authorities had approved the transaction and both were American companies. I recall attending a Foreign Policy Association lunch for Mario Monti, then the European competition commissioner, whose office made the decision to reject the deal. Although the European Union's deliberations were at a key stage then, no one from General Electric or Honeywell showed up.

In February 2010, the European Parliament voted to reject a data-sharing deal with the United States that would have allowed American authorities to monitor the financial transactions of Europeans. Even though some countries in the European Union were in favor of the deal, that power now rests with the European Parliament, not with individual nations. I wonder how many Americans are even aware a European Parliament, with an ever-increasing amount of clout, exists.

For over half a century, the Europeans have gone about the task of creating, if not a United States of Europe, certainly a Europe of united states. The Common Security and Defense Policy is part of this progression to build European institutions to, as the Europeans say, "an ever closer Union."[12] It is not a European army but an army of Europeans that, increasingly, is a far better fit for the majority of European crisis management objectives than is NATO.

The European Union originated in "communities" that were set up to handle specific cross-border European functions. The first community, which kick-started the union, was the European Coal and Steel Community established in 1951. Germany, France, and four other countries gave the organization the responsibility of managing their steel production. It was a revolutionary step considering that coal and steel were then the raw materials for manufacturing the tools of war.

The idea came from France and Germany, the two nations that have been historically most associated with triggering European conflicts and that were the largest producers of coal and steel. By agreeing to the Coal and Steel Community, the two most powerful industrial countries of Europe were ceding control of their coal and steel production. Not only did the community go a long way in rebuilding trust between Germany and its closest neighbors, but it also proved a resounding success. Between 1952 and 1960, the European Economic Community's (the EEC became the

EU in 1993) coal and steel production went up by 75 percent and industrial production by 58 percent.[13]

It is worth recalling that as soon as he learned of the French-German negotiations to set up the Coal and Steel Community, then U.S. secretary of state Dean Acheson immediately recognized the strategic vision that the community concept represented. With Germany and France locked in a tight embrace, there was the first real chance in centuries to eliminate war on the European continent. Acheson urged President Harry S. Truman to support this French-German initiative. The president did. And the rest, as they say, is history.

Based on the success of the Coal and Steel Community, the Europeans set up a number of other groups, each designed to bring Europe's countries closer together: the European Atomic Energy Community (EURATOM), the European Economic Community (the EEC), and so on. For a while in the 1950s the Europeans thought they could develop a European Defense Community to leverage the success of the other groups and set up a European military force. The financial and political problems proved daunting, especially in light of the emergence of NATO in 1949 to connect North America's might to a common European defense.

The Europeans decided instead to focus their energies and limited budgets in building the EEC (the European Union's predecessor). It left the defense of Europe to NATO and, more specifically to its leader, the United States—the only power in the world that had the financial and military clout to blunt the threat of an increasingly belligerent, nuclear-armed Soviet Union.

This division of labor—a European-led project to build a peaceful Europe that is ever more integrated and and an American-led project, NATO, to ensure Europe's security—proved eminently successful (as chapter 2 has shown). In spite of the emergence of the CSDP, it continues to this day. This arrangement is the genesis of the often heard American criticism that the European states can lavish social benefits on its citizens because they do not have to pay for their defense. While true to some extent even today, this critique no longer reflects the true state of affairs in Europe, given that the total defense budget of the European Union states is around $350 billion.

The European Union's growth is reflected in a series of treaties that represent binding commitments by the member states. Each treaty requires the signatures of the heads of state of government of *all* member states. The European Union dates its founding to the Treaty of Rome, signed in 1957. The important Treaty of Maastricht, signed in 1993, coined the phrase "European Union" and defined the so-called three pillars on which it is based.[14] The first pillar consolidated the communities and set up the groundwork for the euro, and the third pillar dealt with justice and home affairs policy. The second pillar established the union's Common Foreign and Security Policy (CFSP), which makes it possible for the union's members to take joint action in foreign and security affairs. The Common Security and Defense Policy is the operational part of the CFSP.

The CSDP, though codified in European Union law under the Treaty of Maastricht, remained unused for a number of years. Nothing could really take the place of NATO as long as Europe was minutes away from being incinerated by the Soviet Union's missiles. The end of the Cold War in 1991 removed this threat. As the Soviet Union collapsed, NATO and the United States led the Europeans in the conflicts in Bosnia and Kosovo. As explained in chapter 4, no other institution but NATO could undertake these campaigns in Europe's backyard. America's and NATO's leadership in European security fifty years after World War II ended was a frustrating and sobering reminder to the Europeans that they needed to put their security house in order and develop their own security plans.[15]

Britain and France decided to change Europe's security deficit. At a meeting in Saint-Malo, France, in December 1998, the two countries proposed aggressive steps to fire up the European Union's dormant CSDP. (This landmark agreement and call to action, known as the Saint-Malo Declaration, is reproduced in appendix C.)

The two powers proclaimed, "The European Union needs to be in a position to play its full role on the international stage. . . . To this end the Union must have the capacity for autonomous action, backed up by credible military forces, the means to decide when to use them and a readiness to do so, in order to respond to international crises."

In a great leap forward, the two nations envisioned military actions in which NATO might not be involved. In such instances, they said, "the

Union must be given appropriate structures and a capacity for analysis of situations, sources of intelligence and a capability for relevant strategic planning, without unnecessary duplication." The joint declaration goes on to say that "Europe needs strengthened armed forces that can react rapidly to the new risks, and which are supported by a strong and competitive European defence industry and technology."[16]

The United States was caught completely off guard by the Saint-Malo Declaration, especially the British role in triggering the agreement, according to David Armitage of the U.S. State Department. "The Saint-Malo declaration injected life into the European security debate and opened the door . . . to American reservations. It occurred . . . four months before NATO's 50th anniversary, and just one month before the introduction of the euro, the single European currency.

"According to one Pentagon official, Washington felt 'betrayed' by the British . . . [because] there was no advanced warning by the British, and that the surprise reflected not only the substance of the Saint Malo proposal but also the process of notification."[17]

The Saint-Malo Declaration was then enshrined in 1999 as the European Security and Defense Policy, which encompassed both a specific policy and a set of dedicated institutions that the European Union could use to plan, approve, and execute joint crisis management actions.[18] (In December 2009, with the Treaty of Lisbon, the ESDP formally assumed its original name, Common Security and Defense Policy. For consistency I used CSDP throughout this book and disregard its formal introduction only in 2009.)

These "institutions" that the European Union set up to execute its security and military missions took the form of two committees: the policy-making group, or the Political and Security Committee (PSC), and the Military Committee (MC). It is important to note that the PSC is a body of the Council of the European Union, which is the main decision-making body and represents the member states. The European Union also set up its own Military Staff and a Situation Centre to provide intelligence and monitoring functions. These institutions were embedded into its policy-making bureaucracy and are located in Brussels.

These CSDP structures provide the European Union with a firm foundation to build an even more robust security and defense structure in the future. The European Union describes the organization this way[19]:

"*The Political and Security Committee* (PSC) meets at the ambassadorial level as a preparatory body for the Council of the European Union. Its main functions are keeping track of the international situation, and helping to define policies within the Common Foreign and Security Policy (CFSP) including the CSDP. It prepares a coherent EU response to a crisis and exercises its political control and strategic direction.

"*The European Union Military Committee* (EUMC) is the highest military body set up within the Council. It is composed of the Chiefs of Defense of the Member States, who are regularly represented by their permanent military representatives. The EUMC provides the PSC with advice and recommendations on all military matters within the EU." It is chaired by a four-star general from an EU state.

"*The European Union Military Staff* (EUMS) composed of military and civilian experts seconded to the Council Secretariat by the Member States and officials of the Council General Secretariat." It is chaired by a lieutenant general, seconded from one of the EU states. The EUMS is the engine of the CSDP. The staff totals two hundred military and civilian personnel, which is an indication of the stage of development of the European Union's security and defense establishment. It is dwarfed by the military organizations of many of the union's larger members and is overshadowed by NATO's fourteen thousand officials.

For good measure the union's Satellite Centre based in Madrid, Spain, and the Institute for Security Studies based in Paris were attached to the CSDP machinery to provide the CSDP with mapping and analytical support.[20] By 2003 the European Union's CSDP was operational with a military staff of around two hundred personnel, remaining the same size in 2010.

To provide a strategic framework for the security and defense policy, the European Union adopted the European Security Strategy in 2003 (see appendix D). In 2004 the European Union's Defense Agency (EDA) was set up to support the member states in their efforts to improve those military capabilities needed for the ESDP. It does so by promoting research and development and armaments cooperation, and by strengthening the European Union's defense technological and industrial base.

Recognizing that crisis management operations in the future would require small, mobile units, in 2007 the European Union also set a target of organizing nine battle groups. Each battle group consists of fifteen hundred troops and can be deployed within two weeks.

The entire security and defense structure is under the responsibility of the "High Representative (HR) of the Union for Foreign Affairs and Security Policy." This position and its responsibilities are what make the CSDP unique because the HR is responsible for the European Union's security and defense activities, diplomatic service, and the distribution of foreign aid. Consolidating these functions gives the European Union a powerful crisis management tool (see chapter 7). If winning hearts and minds is the future of crisis management, the European Union now appears light years ahead of other organizations.

It was inevitable that the project to develop an all-European security organization with the clear objective of deploying European security forces would collide with the organization that felt it had all the security needs of Europe covered: NATO. What did the Europeans' sudden burst of activity in the security and defense policy realm mean for NATO? That the development came on the eve of the launch of Europe's single currency just added to the Americans' sinister forebodings. The euro was already being touted as a competitor to the U.S. dollar. Now, the Americans wondered, were the Europeans also launching a competitor to NATO?

Planning, command, and control are essential ingredients of successful military missions. Soon, the European Union started to talk about adding an independent operational planning staff to the CSDP. This component was the last straw, and the United States, with the strong support of Britain, insisted that there be no conflict or duplication between NATO and the CSDP. Madeleine Albright, then the U.S. secretary of state, laid down the law. "We enthusiastically support any . . . measures that enhance European [security] capabilities," Albright said. But, she maintained, the CSDP had to fit in with the existing security framework in Europe, namely, NATO. Albright then set out three standards for measuring whether the Europeans were meeting American requirements for the CSDP—standards that have since become known as the three Ds.

The key to a successful European security and defense initiative was to focus on practical military capabilities, Albright explained. "Any initiative must avoid preempting Alliance decision-making by *de-linking* [CSDP] from NATO, avoid *duplicating* existing efforts, and avoid *discriminating* against non-EU members."[21] (emphasis added) The pressure was on the European Union to work out an agreement with NATO that would let them divide the security pie. One wonders what the Europeans really felt at being told there were limits to their developing a European defense and security strategy.

The nondiscrimination clause was particularly important for the United States. At that time there were four countries that were NATO members but not EU members. Turkey was one of them (and it still is not an EU member). And the European Union, for internal political reasons, was not very clear about including Turkey in the CSDP-NATO consultations to determine which organization should respond to a crisis. Turkey, for its part, used its veto powers and refused to let NATO discuss any working arrangement with the European Union.

At the same time it was clear that the Europeans were determined to implement the CSDP and create a security force that was staffed by Europeans and controlled by the European Union. To make its point the European Union announced the formation of the European Rapid Reaction Force by 2003. The force would comprise sixty thousand troops that could be sent to distances of four thousand kilometers within sixty days of a crisis and be able to sustain itself for up to a year.

The CSDP initiative was getting serious, and ways had to be found to let the CSDP coexist with NATO for maintaining transatlantic harmony. Under American pressure, the European Union agreed that Turkey would be treated in the same way as any other nonmember. A live-and-let-live compromise was soon reached between it and NATO.

Known as the Berlin Plus agreement, the compromise hammered out in 2003 declared that the European Union would check with NATO before launching a CSDP mission. NATO would have rights of first refusal. If NATO did not want to perform the mission, only then could it be run by the CSDP. To avoid duplication (and, I suspect, to keep CSDP under control), NATO agreed to allow the CSDP use of NATO's planning, command, and control staffs, and the Europeans agreed to not add this capability within the CSDP. NATO also agreed to let the CSDP use NATO's physical assets as long as NATO was not using them. Finally, NATO's Deputy SACEUR (DSACEUR) would take charge of the CSDP missions deployed under Berlin Plus.

Upon conclusion of the Berlin Plus agreement followed the European Union's first peacekeeping mission, which headed to the Former Yugoslav Republic of Macedonia. This would be the first and only time the CSDP would use the Berlin Plus arrangements. Though the agreement has only been used once, this attempt to control the growth of CSDP is still around. Although NATO-philes insists Berlin Plus represents the limits of cooperation between the EU and NATO, it is in reality increasingly irrelevant as the Europeans have continued to deploy mission after mission without any regard to it.

Alarm bells sounded in Washington during June 2003 as the European Union launched Operation Artemis, a military mission to the Congo, without consulting NATO. The Bush administration, as had the Clinton administration before it, assumed the Europeans would not launch missions without discussing them first with NATO. Operation Artemis made history as the first European military operation outside Europe and the first CSDP mission undertaken without any NATO support.

By May 2009 a total of twenty-seven CSDP missions had been deployed. Fourteen were still under way, and thirteen had been successfully completed. Of the fourteen ongoing missions, six were in the Balkans, Caucasus, and Eastern Europe; three in the Middle East; one in Central Asia; and four in Africa. These missions have cost the European Union more than $1 billion, with individual nations directly paying another $2 billion. The CSDP funding follows the same formula that NATO uses: once a nation decides to contribute forces to a mission, it pays the costs for those forces. The CSDP, just as NATO does, pays for the common expenses, such as headquarters and communications. These common charges amount to around 10 percent of a mission's budget.

The lesson from a decade of CSDP missions is that the Europeans will ultimately do what they perceive is in their national interest. The CSDP has proven itself successful in building consensus and in resolving political issues surrounding military missions. It is instructive that the EU mission in Chad/CAR almost stalled in November 2007 for lack of critical logistical support, but European leaders stepped in and made sure the mission remained on track. European diplomats held a series of emergency meetings in Brussels until "a shortfall of helicopters and fixed-wing aircraft had been solved by further contributions from France, Belgium and Poland . . . a French government spokesman said . . . that President Nicolas Sarkozy had authorised additional resources to help 'unblock' the situation."[22]

As efficient as the rollout of the CSDP has been, the Europeans do not think of it in terms of a mechanism for the defense of Europe; instead, they view it more as projecting European security interests by supporting the United Nations and other peacekeeping missions. "The [CSDP] has a completely different purpose from European territorial defense. *For the time being*, the [CSDP] is more for soft wars—intended to keep the peace by helping the United Nations cope with conflict management—but not real defense," Fernando Valenzuela, the European Union's ambassador to Russia, told me. "In fact when we talk of [the CSDP] it is a bit misleading, because it is not really defense in the traditional way as we talk about. In fact the ESDP has nothing to do with the defense of European Union territory. It is a defense which is projected towards the outside, and not really intended to defend the territory of the European Union." (emphasis added)

Valenzuela's observation that the CSDP is not meant to defend Europe is what one hears throughout the European security and diplomatic establishment and in European think tanks. Even with a growing defense and security identity, the Europeans looks to NATO when they think about defending Europe. I will discuss this point in the last chapter because it does not make complete sense. Further, an examination of the Treaty of Lisbon, which the Europeans adopted in December 2009, shows it is not necessarily true.

But there is one more NATO fault line that needs to be explored beforehand, that is, the future impact of Islam and Europe's growing Muslim population on NATO.

CHAPTER SIX

Islam, Turkey, and NATO

If they do not accept us, we will not lose anything, and they [the European Union] will choose to be a Christian club.

—*Prime Minister of Turkey Recep Tayyip Erdogan*

On September 30, 2005, the conservative, mass-circulation daily newspaper in Denmark *Jyllands-Posten* printed twelve cartoons, many of which depicted Islam's Prophet Muhammad in unflattering poses. One, which could be easily interpreted as comparing the Prophet to a terrorist, depicted him with a rocket in his turban; another showed him as a knife-wielding Bedouin.

Islam's founder, Prophet Muhammad, prohibited the creation of portraits or other forms of iconography to portray his likeness because he did not want followers of Islam to worship him as Christians did Jesus Christ. He also forbade Muslims from using him as an object of prayers. As a result, Muslims consider it a sin to depict the Prophet's likeness in any form. To wake up one morning and see the Prophet portrayed in a cartoon would be bad enough, but to see him portrayed as a terrorist outraged Muslims in Denmark. Over thirty-five hundred Danish Muslims staged peaceful protests to condemn what in their opinion was the worst kind of blasphemy.

After other European newspapers reprinted the cartoons, they triggered outrage among Muslims across the Middle East, sparking protests, economic boycotts, and warnings of possible retaliation against the people, companies, and countries involved.[1] Muslims around the world felt transgressed against and showed it.

Muslim clerics in Denmark and France brought lawsuits against the *Jyllands-Posten* and the satirical magazine *Charlie Hebdo,* which had reprinted the cartoons, for publishing these images. They viewed them as offensive, insulting, degrading, and as likely to stir up hatred or to promote discrimination.

The Organisation of the Islamic Conference, an association of fifty-seven Islamic states promoting Muslim solidarity in economic, social, and political affairs, condemned the cartoons. Eleven of its ambassadors traveled to Denmark to meet with Danish prime minister Anders Fogh Rasmussen to lodge a protest and to ask for actions that would soothe Muslim feelings.

The Danish prime minister refused to meet with the ambassadors. To Rasmussen it was a simple case of European secular values colliding with the religious bonds that hold Muslims back from living an enlightened secular life. "This is a matter of principle. I won't meet with them because it is so crystal clear what principles Danish democracy is built upon that there is no reason to do so," said Rasmussen. "The press needs to be critical—I need to bear that as prime minister and religions must do so as well," he added.[2]

Rasmussen could have chosen to hold the meeting to assuage the feelings of the Muslim minority in Denmark and the rapidly growing Muslim community in Europe, but he did not. The reactions over the ensuing months ranged from protests and lawsuits within Denmark and Europe to boycotts, burned flags, and sacked embassies abroad. The political manipulation of these depictions by Muslim extremists also generated violent unrest that led to over two hundred deaths across the Muslim world.[3]

Three years later, seemingly oblivious to the fact that Rasmussen still generated hostility in Muslims around the world, the North Atlantic Council—NATO's governing board—recommended that he be the next secretary-general of NATO. Turkey, NATO's only Muslim majority country, immediately said it was opposed to Rasmussen's candidacy and blocked the appointment. The links between Europe's growing Muslim population, Turkey, and NATO had suddenly taken center stage. What amazed many observers was that Rasmussen, an elected official, disregarded not only the sensitivities of one of his country's fastest-growing minorities but also the position that European courts have increasingly taken against hate speech and the incitement of religious tensions.

"In European jurisdictions, free speech is an important value, but it is balanced against other values," Erik Bleich of Middlebury College pointed out.[4] Bleich has been studying the Danish cartoon controversy from the perspective of modern jurisprudence in the European Union and is writing a book on it. Limiting racist speech is an important goal in most European countries, according to Bleich, and it sometimes outweighs the right to free speech.

"In the 1980s and 1990s, countries like Germany, France, Austria, and Belgium began passing laws against Holocaust denial. . . . You cannot go to these countries and say the Holocaust never happened," Bleich said, "or that it happened, but it was not that bad; or that it happened and it was a good thing it happened. You can be arrested, tried, and convicted. Brigitte Bardot—fabulous French actress of yesteryear and ardent animal rights activist today—has five convictions for hate speech [for incendiary remarks against European Muslims for their ritual sacrifice of sheep on Eid, a major Muslim holiday].

"Whatever one thinks of these cartoons—that they are offensive or anodyne, that they should be punished or heralded—in the prevailing European legal context of the time, it was not radical to argue that some of these images constituted illegal hate speech," Bleich concluded.

Rasmussen almost did not make the transition from his old job as prime minister of Denmark to the position of NATO's secretary-general. In fact, there was a fair amount of astonishment, even among NATO members, when his name was announced. That NATO would elect a leader who was still universally reviled in Muslim lands struck many observers as a short-sighted decision by an alliance that had bet its all on the outcome of the Afghan war, a war in which winning the hearts and minds of Afghanistan's and Pakistan's Muslims, is NATO's first priority.

"NATO Disses the Muslim World" was the headline of Stephen Kinzer's article in the *Guardian* newspaper when it first became known that Rasmussen was the leading candidate to fill the role of secretary-general.

". . . it seems utterly unbelievable that Nato is about to name as its new secretary general a figure whom millions of Muslims detest more than almost any other European, Prime Minister Anders Fogh Rasmussen of Denmark. Rasmussen, as Nato seems to have forgotten, was Denmark's leader when a Copenhagen newspaper published cartoons depicting the prophet Mohammed in ways that outraged Muslims around the world. When ambassadors from 11 Muslim countries asked to meet him to discuss ways of calming the anger that was building in their homelands, he refused to receive them.

"If Nato decides that the figure most directly associated with this scandal should be its new secretary general, how can it expect to win the public support in Afghanistan and Pakistan that is crucial to the success of its vital mission?" Kinzer asked rhetorically. "This choice would not be simply tone-deaf. It would do more to alienate Muslims from Nato than almost any other step the alliance could take. What can Nato be thinking? Proceeding with this appointment would suggest that it has lost all contact with reality. *Rasmussen's qualifications are not the issue – what matters is the way his appointment would be perceived in the world's most explosive region.*"[5] (emphasis added)

The announcement that the former Danish prime minister was being considered for NATO's leadership position caused blood pressure to rise higher in Turkey than anywhere else. A NATO member for over fifty years, Turkey fields the alliance's second largest military force after the United States and is a staunch Western ally. It must have seemed to Turkey, where Islam is the predominant religion, that with its announcement NATO had gone out of its way to insult Muslims in general and Turkey in particular.

In an interview with France 24 on April 3, 2009, immediately after Prime Minister Rasmussen announced his candidacy as secretary-general of NATO, Turkish prime minister Recep Tayyip Erdogan told the radio station he "was opposed to his Danish counterpart Anders Fogh Rasmussen's bid for NATO's top job because he doubted he [Rasmussen] could contribute to global peace."

Besides criticizing Rasmussen's stance during the crisis over the cartoons of Prophet Muhammad, Erdogan reminded his TV audience that Rasmussen had also failed to act on Turkey's requests to ban a Denmark-based TV station linked to the Kurdistan Workers' Party (PKK), which the United States and the United Nations consider to be a terrorist organization. "How can those who have failed to contribute to peace, contribute to peace in the future? We have doubts . . . and my personal opinion is negative," he said at a conference in London.

As noted earlier, NATO makes decisions by consensus. Without Turkey's approval, Rasmussen could not be approved as the alliance's next leader. And Turkey's approval began to look increasingly doubtful as Muslim countries around the world rallied in opposition and looked to Turkey, as NATO's only Muslim majority country, to block it. Overnight, Turkey had become the conduit for transmitting global Muslim concerns into NATO's hallways.

"Muslim countries have asked Turkey to veto Danish Prime Minister Anders Fogh Rasmussen as the next NATO chief," Turkish prime minister Tayyip Erdogan told German newspaper *Welt-Online* on March 28, 2009. According to the newspaper, "Erdogan said he talked to Rasmussen by telephone on Friday and told him the Turkish people were upset . . . A very serious reaction emerged in countries with Muslim populations during the cartoon crisis. . . . Now these countries have started to call us and tell us not to allow it."[6]

As the leader of the Islamist-rooted Adalet ve Kalinma (AK, or Justice and Development) Party, Erdogan said that he could not contradict his party's principles. He told Rasmussen that "he can appreciate what that means." And, echoing the opinions expressed in the *Guardian*, Erdogan went on to say, "Turkey is concerned that at a time when NATO faces rising demands in Afghanistan, a secretary general with such an approach could affect the alliance's relationship with the Muslim world."

The stage was now set for a major confrontation between the twenty-seven NATO members that supported Rasmussen's candidacy and the one, Turkey, that did not. It was a face-off that had all the hallmarks of an impending political disaster for the alliance. In short, the confrontation over the selection of NATO's next secretary-general had been transformed into a geopolitical storm.

Fortunately for all concerned, the crisis reached a boiling point at the annual meeting of NATO's heads of state that was held on April 4, 2009, in Strasbourg-Kehl.[7] There, four months into his presidency of the United States, Barack Obama engaged in immediate and forceful personal diplomacy to forestall disaster. In a series of meetings, first one-on-one with Rasmussen and then Erdogan, and then with both of them together, the men reached a compromise that allowed Turkey to support Rasmussen's candidacy for secretary-general of NATO. It had been a close call, but disaster was averted. Or had it only been forestalled?

Had Turkey's threat to veto Rasmussen materialized, the collateral damage would have been felt far beyond NATO. For one thing, it would have moved NATO into uncharted territory because religious sensitivities for the first time would have derailed a decision within the Western alliance. And the argument made by the Taliban and al Qaeda that the West was on a crusade against Islam would have gained further currency. The end result would have been a major setback to NATO's already shaky position in Afghanistan. Just as important for Europe's future, the fallout from such a NATO debacle would, in all probability, have ended Turkey's quest for membership in the European Union. America would have been caught in the cross fire of trying to decide whether it should continue supporting its European allies against Turkey, thereby damaging a partnership that American presidents of both parties had spent a half century cultivating.

Ironically, one of Rasmussen's first acts as NATO's secretary-general was to call on the very Islamic nations he had spurned five years earlier to exhort them to send Muslim soldiers to fight in Afghanistan, where the mostly Christian Western forces were increasingly bogged down by the Muslim Taliban.[8] The irony of asking these Middle East leaders, who often use their troops to keep democracy out of their own countries, to send their troops to Afghanistan to spread democracy seems to have escaped Rasmussen!

This election of NATO's secretary-general revealed a whole new set of fault lines that were previously just under the surface of the alliance's veneer. These interlinked fault lines reflect the pressures of Europe changing to a more diverse continent with a growing Muslim population and the struggle within Europe about living up to the European Union's pledge to allow Turkey into the European Union. Both of these issues are playing out against a Turkey that has transformed its previously one-dimensional, Western-oriented foreign policy into one that has 360-degree optics that include not just Europe to its west but also the entire Middle East, Central Asia, and Russia as part of its national interest. While Turkey still considers itself to be a Western-oriented country, the wider lens will inevitably mean its national interests will sometimes diverge from those of the West and NATO will have to adjust its objectives to Turkey's sensitivities to maintain NATO's cardinal rule of unanimous decisions.

NATO's decision to select Rasmussen as its secretary-general without receiving prior endorsement from Turkey was perplexing to say the least. Turkey is NATO's pivotal member today. Not only does it have the largest military force in NATO after the United States but it is also the only Muslim majority country within NATO. (Albania is also a Muslim majority country, but its impact on NATO is far smaller by comparison.) Turkey's membership keeps NATO from being viewed as a Western, Christian alliance and gives it some legitimacy in Afghanistan.

But another issue that makes Turkey a pivotal NATO member is its ongoing political conflict with the island of Cyprus. This dispute is a permanent obstacle to any formal collaboration between the European Union and NATO, making it impossible for the two to officially work together, in Afghanistan (where both sides have an important role to play) or anywhere else. As I argue in chapter 7, without this collaboration, NATO's future success as an alliance is far from assured.

As an example of what this lack of collaboration means in practice, consider the European Union's mission to help train the Afghan National Police (EUPOL Afghanistan). This allied task is critical in Afghanistan. Without a well-trained Afghan National Police force, NATO will not be able to turn over responsibility for law and order to the Afghans, one of the conditions for ending the alliance's military involvement in Afghanistan.

NATO cannot provide mission-critical intelligence information to EUPOL or security for EUPOL's trainers because Turkey has vetoed both actions. It has the right to do so as a NATO member. Turkey will not permit NATO to collaborate with this EU mission because Turkey is not yet a member of the European Union. One of the biggest obstacles to its membership is the objection from Cyprus, which is an EU member.[9]

Turkey and Cyprus have been embroiled in a dispute since 1994. Just as any other EU member, Cyprus has veto rights on other countries' future membership in the European Union, rights that it uses to block Turkey's application for membership.

After a Greek-backed coup and a Turkish invasion in response, the island of Cyprus was divided in 1974 into the Greek-Cypriot Republic in the south and the Turkish-Cypriot zone in the north. In 2004, the European Union approved the membership of Cyprus (technically, the Greek-Cypriot Republic) even though the Greek-Cypriots had rejected a UN plan for unifying the island, a plan the Turkish-Cypriots had accepted. Turkey began formal negotiations for its membership in 2005, after informal discussions that began as far back as 1999, but its application for membership has barely progressed.

Both Turkey and Cyprus have used this dispute to block official collaboration between the European Union and NATO, to the detriment of both organizations. In Kosovo, for instance, EU and NATO missions are on the ground at the same time. Although their staffs regularly interact in an ad hoc manner, there is no official contact between the two organizations and no formal recognition that the two are collaborating. The standoff between Cyprus and Turkey has become the biggest impediment to better relations between the European Union and NATO. "We have to get this problem out the way so that the European Union and NATO can start working together militarily," Amb. Marc Grossman told me. "It is a real barrier." Grossman served both as the U.S. ambassador to Turkey and as the undersecretary of state for European affairs.

Elements in the feud could be the inspiration for a Broadway comedy, were it not for its serious implications for the future of Euro-Atlantic security. A recent example illustrates how far the Turkish-Cypriot conflict has reached.

In a gesture of goodwill, NATO secretary-general Rasmussen was invited to address an informal meeting of EU defense ministers on the Spanish island of Majorca in February 2010. A European diplomat who was at the meeting told me that Rasmussen gave a fine speech, using a slide presentation, and promised the audience members he would send them a printed copy of the slides he had used. Rasmussen subsequently realized he couldn't do that because it would be considered an official communication between the European Union and NATO, which is blocked by the Turkish and Cyprus dispute. A neutral third party had to be found to take the printout and forward it to the defense ministers.

Thanks to these Byzantine politics, an island of minimal geopolitical consequence, with 800,000 people and with a GDP of $22 billion, has managed to block the entry of a critically important country, with a population of seventy-four million and a GDP of $794 billion, or about 1.3 percent of the entire world's GDP, into the European Union.[10]

"The European Union promised Turkey it would become a member of the Union, and we have to keep this promise," Ana de Palacio, Spain's foreign minister, told me during a conversation we had for my last book. That assertion may theoretically be true, but try telling it to Turkey as it stumbles over obstacles to get to first base with its membership. Not surprising, Turkish support for EU membership has fallen from 70 percent in 2004 to 42 percent in 2008.[11]

The fallout from the Turkish-Cypriot dispute is the single biggest obstacle to collaboration between the European Union's CSDP and NATO. As noted earlier, the CSDP is prohibited (mainly by Britain) from having its own planning or command resources. It is forced to use NATO's by means of the Berlin Plus agreement (see chapter 5). Under NATO's operating rules, any NATO member can review and block the use of the alliance's assets by the European Union. Turkey uses its rights in this regard to insist that Cyprus not be part of any CSDP mission that wishes to use NATO assets.

"I cannot imagine a more absurd situation," a senior NATO military official told me, "than these two key security organizations, both based in Brussels, within a few miles of each other, with twenty-one members in common, but are not on speaking terms." A senior EU official told me that continuation of the Turkey-Cyprus dispute also serves the purpose of those EU countries that do not wish to let Turkey into the EU. These countries don't have to dirty their hands by blackballing Turkey's membership, Cyprus does it for them.

It is easy to forget that both the CSDP and NATO draw from one pool of European defense assets. Thus the soldiers who are deployed as part of a CSDP mission one day and may be part of a NATO mission on another. The same inventory of tanks and airplanes serve the CSDP and NATO. Since both NATO and the CSDP require countries to make their soldiers and equipment available to either defense organization's missions and also to underwrite their expenses, the same pool of money from member countries pays for the missions.

If this standoff is not resolved soon, it will be impossible for both NATO and CSDP nations to achieve economies of scale in their defense expenditures. As the American secretary of state put it at a recent NATO meeting in Washington, D.C.:

> I know that in the past, the United States has been ambivalent about whether NATO should engage in security cooperation with the EU. Well, that time is over. We do not see the EU as a competitor of NATO, but we see a strong Europe as an essential partner with NATO and with the United States. . . . And we look forward to working together with the EU as it applies its Common Security and Defense Policy to determine how we can best support one another and the United Nations in addressing security challenges.[12]

None of this progress is going to be possible without a resolution of the rift between Turkey and Cyprus.

Cyprus is not the only reason that Turkey's EU membership is in danger of failing. In fact, were the Europeans so inclined, Turkey's membership would move smoothly into its final stretch. The real hurdle is a dramatic shift in European opinion with the majority no longer favoring Turkish membership. This turn is a result of demographic and cultural changes: a greatly visible and sometimes assertive Muslim population and the cultural adjustments Europeans feel they are being forced to accommodate people from a non-Christian religion and culture; a global financial crisis that, coupled with the forces of globalization, has shredded millions of European jobs; and an increasingly shrill but well-organized minority that has constructed a narrative around these trends to exploit European fears. In this charged environment, admitting Turkey and its seventy-five million

NATO headquarters, Brussels, Belgium. *The Council of the European Union*

German frigate and helicopter during EU Operation Atalanta on patrol off Somalia.
EU NAVFOR Atalanta

Somali pirates captured by the German navy as part of Operation Atalanta.
German Navy

Somali pirates being transferred to German frigate in Operation Atalanta.
German Navy

EU naval force patrols off the Horn of Africa. *The Council of the European Union*

Dutch frigate of EU Operation Atalanta intercepts Somali pirate skiffs.
The Council of the European Union

EUFOR Tchad/RCA patrolling the village of Birao, Central African Republic.
The Council of the European Union

Escorting a delivery convoy in Chad. *The Council of the European Union*

Mixed French-Slovenian patrol in Chad. *The Council of the European Union*

Polish helicopters arriving in theater, Chad. *The Council of the European Union*

French observation drone launch, Chad. *The Council of the European Union*

EU High Representative Javier Solana with Swedish armored column, Goz Beida, Chad. *The Council of the European Union*

Greek C-130 transport aircraft arriving in darkness at N'djamena, capital of Chad. *The Council of the European Union*

French tank in action, Chad. Note EUFOR insignia. *The Council of the European Union*

Lt. Gen. Patrick Nash, operation commander, EUFOR Tchad/RCA, visiting Abeche, Chad. *The Council of the European Union*

Brigadier General Ganascia, force commander EUFOR Tchad/RCA, transfers command from the European Union to the United Nations. *The Council of the European Union*

Muslims, who would become EU citizens if Turkey was granted EU membership, appears now to have become an uphill battle.

Turkey's transformation from a country that could be counted on to read from a standard Western script into a financially robust, self-confident nation with a far broader geopolitical outlook and an Islamic patina has also forced a number of European and American strategists to try and come to grips with Turkey's evolving place in Europe and in NATO.

"Turkey has emerged as a regional power," according to Shada Islam of the European Policy Centre in Brussels, one of Europe's leading think tanks. "It is building links with Iran and Syria and is moving beyond its backyard into Central Asia. A new self-assured, self-confident Turkey now looks at Europe and says, 'We are still waiting in line to join the European Union, but we have our own identity and our own ambitions, and oh yes, our own foreign policy.'" Having studied and written about Turkey, Muslims, and Europe for many years, Shada Islam says Europeans seem taken aback by Turkey's new identity, which emphasizes a desire to join the European Union but on its own terms.

If Europeans seem unsure about how to deal with the newly assertive and independent Turkey, America is also going through a process of soul-searching. The current entry for Turkey on the U.S. State Department's website introduces Turkey's foreign policy by offering this idyllic description: "Turkey's primary political, economic, and security ties are with the West, although some voices call for a more 'Eurasian' orientation. Turkey entered NATO in 1952 and serves as the organization's vital eastern anchor, controlling the straits leading from the Black Sea to the Mediterranean and sharing a border with Syria, Iraq, and Iran. A NATO headquarters is located in Izmir."[13]

Contrast this serene description with a November 2009 column in the *Wall Street Journal* titled "A NATO without Turkey?" In the piece, David Schenker describes quite a different Turkey from the State Department's vision:

> Nearly a decade after Islamists took the reins of power in Ankara, the central question is no longer whether Turkey should be integrated into Europe's economic and political structure, but rather whether Turkey should remain a part of the Western defense structure.

Recent developments suggest that while Turkey's military leadership remains committed to the state's secular, Western orientation and the defining principles of the North Atlantic Treaty Organization, the civilian Islamist government led by the Justice and Development Party (AKP) seems to have different ideas. Ankara is . . . aligning itself with militant, anti-western Middle East regimes abroad. . . .

It's time for NATO to start thinking about a worst case scenario in Turkey. For even if the increasingly Islamist state remains a NATO partner, at best, it seems Turkey will be an unreliable partner. . . . Absent a remarkable turnaround, it would appear that the West is losing Turkey. Should this occur, it would constitute the most dramatic development in the region since the 1979 Islamic Revolution in Iran.[14]

Writing in the *Philadelphia Bulletin* on April 6, 2009, Daniel Pipes put it even more bluntly. "Does Turkey Still Belong in NATO?" was the provocative headline of his column. He began his argument with this paragraph: "Smack on its 60th anniversary, the North Atlantic Treaty Organization finds itself facing a completely novel problem—that of *radical Islam, as represented by the Republic of Turkey*, within its own ranks."[15] (emphasis added)

While it is true that Turkey's foreign policy no longer operates under a banner that reads, "The West's foreign policy is Turkey's foreign policy," I am not convinced that the result is necessarily bad for NATO—not yet anyway. And whether it will be bad depends on the maturity with which the rest of NATO's members react to the new geopolitical reality that Turkey has carved out for itself as a country with the world's first democratically elected Islamist government with a foreign policy that is more balanced than it used to be and is more finely tuned to Turkey's national interests, as well as to those of NATO and the West in general and to those of the United States in particular.

In fact, the reverse is equally true. A prominent and Islamic NATO member benefits NATO. It keeps NATO from being thought of as an organization that excludes Muslims and is an enforcer of the West's policies. The image of NATO would be very different in Afghanistan without Turkey.

In this context, it is enlightening to read the description of Turkey's ruling party from one of its ministers of state. Contrary to the label more widely used by Western media, Mehmet Aydin, who is also a professor of philosophy and religion, says that the AK Party does not consider itself to be "moderate Islamist"; rather, it sees itself as a party comprising "moderate Muslims" whose religious ethics inspire their public service as individuals but *cannot be construed as part of their identities as political actors.*

Aydin's depiction is hardly the "radical Islam within NATO" image conjured by Pipes. According to Aydin, Turkey is still a staunch NATO ally that continues to think of itself as a European nation. "We carry our two identities as Muslim and European very easily without feeling any complex," the Turkish foreign minister said recently.[16]

Turkey's gradual but steady move to a more balanced foreign policy is the result mainly of two relatively recent developments: the collapse of the Soviet Union and the country's repeated observation that the West's geopolitical decisions, even if they involve Turkey, have not always been in Turkey's best interests. Turkey joined NATO for protection against the superpower to its north, the Soviet Union. As soon as it joined NATO, it could count on the protection of the United States through Article 5—its "one for all and all for one" clause—of the North Atlantic Treaty. Membership also meant Turkey was now regarded as an official part of the West and, more important for Turkey, a part of Europe.

The collapse of the Soviet Union removed its most dangerous threat and left Turkey as the most powerful state in the region after Israel, with which it developed a close relationship. At the same time, enlightened investment and industrial policies also made Turkey a regional economic force. Within a few short years Turkey capitalized on its newfound geopolitical flexibility and economic strengths by forging close links with all its neighbors: Syria, Iran, Iraq, and Russia, as well as Egypt, Saudi Arabia, the Gulf states, and Afghanistan. It has made wide inroads into the Caucasus and Central Asia. India and Pakistan have always been traditional allies.

From a NATO perspective, the thread that runs through all of these relationships is that—with the exception of Russia and India—they are all Muslim majority countries. Further, both India and Russia have sizable Muslim minority populations, with India's being the second largest in the world.

But unlike the viewpoint taken by commentators such as Pipes and Schenker, I view Turkey's expanding geopolitical bandwidth to be of significant potential benefit to the Western alliance. Given the wide gulf of credibility that now separates Muslims from Western powers, would it not be to the West's benefit to have as a NATO member and a potential EU member a country in which Islam and democracy coexist?

It is worth reiterating that a majority of Turkey's 99 percent Muslim population has twice given its government a vote of confidence. This bond of trust between the government and the governed is a scarce commodity in Turkey's neighborhood, the Middle East, where most nations have an authoritarian cast and an elastic concept of the balance between security and democracy.

The Turkish military, as a consequence of the ballot box, is increasingly less able to dictate the course of Turkish affairs. Commentators such as Schenker do not like this trend because the West has always assumed the Turkish military was all that prevented a secular Turkey from becoming a militant Islamic state.

I am not convinced that a country where the military comes rushing in to enforce secularism—a kind of on-again, off-again military dictatorship—makes for a stronger NATO member in today's world, with a far more dispersed balance of power than the two-superpower model that dominated geopolitics until the end of the Cold War.

Nor do I agree with the prevalent neoconservative opinion in the United States, as reflected by Pipes and Schenker, that working with a transformed Turkey America is "aligning itself with militant Islam." Rather, I believe that Turkey is a Muslim country in the same way that France is a Catholic country and Greece is Orthodox Christian country. And America's global interests are far better served by maintaining close relations with Turkey.

I do not mean to gloss over Turkey's shortcomings in areas such as freedom of the press and civil rights. Turkey is not, and may never be, a Jeffersonian democracy, and I realize there are many internal changes that Turks will have to make to their body politic, including their constitution, before Turkey finally qualifies to join the European Union. "But when you look at what Turkey has meant to the United States," Senator Hagel said, "and to NATO—a NATO member since 1952; the only NATO country on the Soviet border; did everything we asked it to do, whether it was the United Nations or with NATO; hugely important to our geopolitical security, our relationships, for the West's Muslim-Christian connections, the whole East–West linkage—any way you come at this, Turkey was and still is right in the middle of an enormously important part of the world. I don't know what ally would be able to lay claim to doing more for America's future and security, and we have a lot of good allies, than Turkey."

To understand the importance of Turkey today to the future of NATO, place yourself in the position of a Muslim living in the arc that spans Islamic lands from North Africa through the Middle East and into China. Chances are you have no formal education; you are poor, making do with pennies per day. You are living very much as your father and his father lived for centuries. Your condition is not much better than theirs was.

But in one respect you are different. Technology has connected you to the wider world. And when you look at the village's television set these days, or listen to the village's only shortwave radio, chances are more often than not you find the news dominated by American military presence in the Muslim countries Iraq, Afghanistan, Pakistan, Somalia, and Yemen. Are Iran and Syria next?

You might even hear that Western armies intend to remain in Iraq and Afghanistan for decades to ensure the countries are safe for their own cizens. You have already heard of the humiliations occurring in the prisons America set up there, the hundreds of thousands of Iraqis killed, and the scores that are killed daily by those buzzing unmanned airplanes that fly day and night over Pakistan and Afghanistan.

Before long you will come to believe that America makes war only on Muslim lands, and that presumption will lead you to think that America is at war with Islam. You will also associate Europe and NATO with this war because NATO is very much in the headlines these days and is equated with the United States. You will no doubt have heard that the United States intends to stay in Afghanistan for years to come, and that NATO intends to be there for as long as it takes—as the alliance's secretary-general has often promised.

"What is wrong with this picture?" I asked the EU ambassador to the United Nations, Fernando Valenzuela, when I spoke with him in the summer of 2009. With a wry smile, Valenzuela told me, "But we have Turkey!"

Valenzuela was not smiling, however, as he continued, "The risk of this whole thing [NATO war in Afghanistan] being perceived as a Western-led project is real." Talking about the seemingly perpetual war being waged by America, he observed that it tends to reinforce the central theme of al Qaeda's public relations machine: the West is waging a war against Islam. "*So how we win that war is very important,*" Valenzuela said. "And here Turkey is a very helpful element because it its involvement clearly means there is not a religious divide." (emphasis added)

"Turkey gives NATO a sense of legitimacy, in the sense that because NATO includes a Muslim country, it is therefore not against Muslims," said Soner Cagaptay, director of the Turkish Research Program at the Washington Institute for Near East Policy and an expert on U.S.-Turkish relations. "This is what Turkey provides NATO. It's huge."

Because most of NATO's future operations will probably be in Muslim countries, for NATO to sustain a façade that it is not an organization against Muslims, it must have a large Muslim country like Turkey as a member. NATO cannot afford to lose Turkey.

That Islam and Europe's Muslim community have the potential to influence the future direction of NATO is not yet a formal topic of discussion in the alliance. There is no mention of it, for instance, in NATO's new strategic concept adopted at the Lisbon Summit. As politically difficult as it may be, Europe's changing demographics mean that NATO's new strategic concept ought to have dealt with it.

During the 1950s there were few if any Muslims immigrants in Europe. Today there are twenty million, out of a total EU population of three hundred million. (By contrast, the Pew Research Center estimates the number of Muslims in the United States as less than two million.[17] The difficulty researchers in the United States face in this regard is that the U.S. census does not ask for a citizen's religious affiliation.) The largest percentages of Muslims are in France, at an estimated 8 percent of the population (five million); the Netherlands estimated at 6 percent (almost a million); Germany, 4 percent (four million); and the United Kingdom, 3 percent (two million). And Muslims exceed 20 percent of the population in some major EU cities.[18]

What makes the Muslim population in Europe different from that of the United States or Canada is the type of immigrant that travelled to Europe. While immigration to North America reflected mainly a professional class, Europe brought in manual laborers, or those who could fill construction and factory jobs and help rebuild Europe after the devastation of World War II. Many came from countries that had once been European colonies.

They were recruited to work in mines and factories and to drive buses. In some cases, entire Turkish villages in Anatolia moved to Germany. Most Europeans believed these workers would head home when their job was done. They never did.

Unlike their North American counterparts, who came in as doctors, engineers, and other highly skilled professionals, the Muslim immigrants in Europe, with the exception of those in Britain, neither had the skills nor had been given the opportunity to be integrated into their new home countries. The results two generations later were predictable.

According to Toni Johnson of the Council on Foreign Relations, "High crime rates and dependency on the social welfare system" and a "lack of economic opportunity among poor Muslim populations . . . contributed to tensions in recent years." In her paper, Johnson also cites Tom Winter of the University of Cambridge, who wrote, "As Muslims in Europe are overwhelmingly non-white, ongoing racial disharmony naturally impedes integration." Acknowledging that Muslims contend with problems stemming from their ethnic differences as well as their religious differences with their neighbors, Johnson discusses a finding from the EU Monitoring Center on Racism and Xenophobia: "Muslims face discrimination in all aspects of life, from housing to employment opportunities to education to cultural practices."[19]

The huge divide between the Muslim newcomers and native Europeans was clearly visible during the 2009 Swiss referendum against adding traditional minarets to mosques in Switzerland. Johnson points out,

So inflammatory were the campaign posters against the minaret in Switzerland, they were banned as racist in some Swiss cities. The attention and vehemence the media and some politicians place on symbolic issues like the minaret and the head scarf foster more alienation in Muslim communities, some analysts say. Muslims have also pointed out the media's double standard, which made much of [Theo] van Gogh's murder, but was largely silent on the 2009 murder of a Muslim woman—dubbed "the veil martyr"—and shooting of her husband in a German courtroom."[20]

Compounding the problems is the low birthrate among nonimmigrant Europeans. Many European countries' populations will, as a result, shrink by 25 percent at the end of this century.

Writer Christopher Caldwell also points out that that the heavy concentration of Muslim populations in European cities has the potential to multiply their influence. A million Muslims now live in London, where they make up an eighth of the population. In Amsterdam, Muslims account for more than a third of religious believers, outnumbering Catholics, as well as all the Protestant orders combined. In fact, Caldwell's research shows that Muslims now dominate or vie for domination of numerous important European cities: Amsterdam and Rotterdam in the Netherlands; Strasbourg and Marseille (and many of the Paris suburbs) in France; Duisburg, Cologne, and the Berlin neighborhoods of Kreuzberg and Neukölln in Germany; and Blackburn, Bradford, Dewsbury, Leicester, East London, and the periphery of Manchester in England. "Such places may, as immigration continues and the voting power and political savvy of the Muslims already there increases, take on an increasingly Muslim character," Caldwell concludes.[21]

It is a conclusion with which Valenzuela agrees. "Ultimately political structures have to correspond with the society they serve, and that means, in the case of Europe in thirty years or so, politics will have to reflect much more the Muslim population," he told me. "Politicians will have acknowledge these [Islamic] constituencies and take them into their own political calculations."

This observation emphasizes the point I want to make: over the next decade or two, European politicians will have to pay increasing attention to Europe's Muslim community to get elected. After all, they are already 10 percent of the population and represent a far greater percentage in major European cities. While such percentages may not overly impress American pollsters, 10 percent is a significant factor in Europe, where parties rarely win by margins that allow one party to govern by itself. Most European governments are formed of coalitions, and a 10 percent swing vote is very meaningful.So how will this new reality affect NATO? Afghanistan offers one glimpse into the future.

The Turkish military contributes only seventeen hundred troops to NATO's Afghan mission. All are deployed in the city of Kabul, and none of them can be used in combat. In December 2009, the United States, NATO's leader, announced it would be sending thirty thousand additional troops to Afghanistan and asked its NATO allies to also increase their commitments. The response from Turkey was swift and unequivocal. Prime Minister Recep Tayyip Erdogan, on his way to a meeting with President Obama in Washington, ruled out sending any more troops to Afghanistan. "Turkey has already contributed the 'necessary number' of troops," he said.[22]

Graham Fuller puts Turkey's troop contribution to NATO's Afghan mission in context:

> With some 515,000 troops, the Turkish army constitutes the second largest standing force in NATO after the United States. Furthermore, according to the Stockholm International Peace Research Institute (SIPRI), Turkey ranked fourteenth in the world in military expenditures in 2004—with a $10.1 billion defense budget, second only to Israel in the Middle East. . . .
>
> Turkey's intense program of military modernization that began in 1996 . . . will ultimately allocate some $150 billion over a thirty-year period. . . .
>
> . . . Turkey no longer confronts any serious regional military power. . . .
>
> All of these factors taken together have overwhelmingly transformed Turkey into the most important military power in the Middle East after Israel.[23]

Soner Cagapty was even more emphatic when we discussed this point. "If NATO is operating in or against a Muslim country, Turkey will opt out of NATO," he told me. "That will mean two things: a decrease in NATO's military capacity, because Turkey has NATO's second-largest military, but also a decrease in NATO's legitimacy, because NATO's only real Muslim-majority country will have opted out of this operation, and that will make the operation look like one that excludes Muslims and is therefore anti-Islamic."

But will the impact of the growing Muslim community in Europe actually be hostile to a Western security agenda? Will Muslims in Europe necessarily follow the divisive agenda that the right-of-center, xenophobic politicians in Europe and American neo-conservatives expect them to pursue?[24] Shada Islam is not so sure.

"The reality of Europe is one where the majority of Muslims are actually very much engaged as European citizens," Islam told me. "They are entrepreneurs, they're in political mainstream parties, they're in communal parties, they're slowly moving into the European parliament. They are increasingly in the services sector. They are the backbone of the services sector, in fact."

This account is a wholly different narrative from what one sees in the media about the Muslims in Europe. There are tensions in European society, Islam says, but she adds many of them exist because there is no counter narrative to the simple, attractive, but false version that the extremist elements in European society have circulated. For instance, they say all Muslims in Europe are so culturally different from Europeans that it will not be possible for them to live in mainstream European society. To the contrary, Islam says, "we are living through a period of transition, but there is real integration taking place."

As the Muslims in Europe become more integrated, more educated, and more successful, is there not a chance they will follow the path that immigrants in the United States have? Hispanic Americans have filled senior ranks in the administrations of both U.S. political parties for many years, but the broad thrust of American foreign policy has not changed and become more Mexican or Latin or Central American centric. Why should that not be the case in Europe?

There are multiple moving pieces in this chapter, but they intersect at the crossroads between the European Union and NATO. The future of Turkey's membership; the impact of Europe's growing Muslim population on decisions to participate in or support the American-led ongoing wars, and wars yet to come, in Muslim countries; and the direction that the future growth of Islam will take in the European Union are all difficult questions that policymakers will confront in the next decade. Managing these issues toward a successful conclusion is another reason why both NATO and the European Union must work together.

We will not know the answers to all these questions for a while, but of one thing we may be quite sure: NATO will not be in quite such a hurry to select its next secretary-general as it was with Rasmussen. It will have to keep its Muslim constituents in mind. Much as Rasmussen himself did during the fall of 2010, when confronted with an American preacher's threat to stage a public burning of the Koran.

As Andrea Stone, senior Washington correspondent for *AOL News*, put it, "NATO Secretary General Anders Fogh Rasmussen, who once defended the publication of cartoons mocking the Prophet Muhammad, is condemning a Florida pastor's plan to burn Qurans on the ninth anniversary of 9/11, saying it could 'have a negative impact on the security for our troops' fighting in Afghanistan."[25]

CHAPTER SEVEN

To NATO 2.0

If we get the capabilities, NATO, along with the European Union, can do amazing things.

—*Lord Robertson, NATO secretary-general, 1999–2003*

Whoever invented the expression "iron fist in a velvet glove" must have had U.S. secretary of defense Robert Gates in mind. The secretary's soft voice and low-key manner belie a record of getting tough things done in Washington, D.C., a record that has few equals. He delivers speeches with a deadpan expression and little inflection in his voice. It often takes a few moments after he has said something profound to fully grasp the gravity of what one has just heard.

I had firsthand exposure to Gates's way of delivering brutally honest messages at NATO's New Strategic Concept conference, held in Washington, D.C., on February 23, 2010. It was the final conference in a series of four to determine what NATO's mission would be during the next decade.

The auditorium of Washington's National Defense University was packed with three- and four-star generals, ambassadors, and key government officials from all twenty-eight NATO member nations. Anders Fogh Rasmussen, the Danish secretary-general of NATO was there, as was Vice Adm. Ann Rondeau (USN), the president of the National Defense University. She and Gen. Stéphane Abrial, NATO's Supreme Allied Commander

Transformation, were cohosts of the proceedings. (General Abrial would use his notes to write and present a superb summary of the day's proceedings after the conference, vividly demonstrating that the former head of the French air force can still roll up his sleeves and get the job done.) A few seats away from Abrial and watching impassively was the tall and burly NATO chief of staff, German Army Gen. Klaus-Heinz Lather. There was a palpable sense among the audience that Gates's speech would be a critically important one for the future of NATO. In this respect, the secretary would not disappoint his listeners.

A little before 9 a.m., the welcoming remarks concluded, and the secretary of defense mounted the podium and began to speak. He had been asked to open this conference and set the stage for an off-the-record examination of NATO for the rest of the day. He did, but perhaps not in the manner the organizers had thought he would.

After reiterating the continuing importance of NATO, underscoring its accomplishments, and pointing out that at that very moment NATO-led troops were engaged in ferocious combat on the Afghan battlefields, his speech reached the message he had really come to deliver. Calmly, without changing volume or pitch, Gates drove home the need for structural improvements in the alliance. How, he asked, could it be that in the second month of the fiscal year, NATO's budget was already millions of euros in the red? Then he made it clear that NATO had to face up to its obsolete and costly Cold War infrastructure.

Gates underscored the perennial inability of European governments to meet NATO's agreed defense funding level of 2 percent of their GDP. He reminded his overwhelmingly European audience—twenty-six of the twenty-eight NATO members are from Europe—that only five of the NATO members achieved this target after repeatedly pledging to do so.

Then, with the briefest of pauses, Gates dropped the hammer. He warned,

> These budget limitations relate to a larger cultural and political trend affecting the alliance. One of the triumphs of the last century was the pacification of Europe after ages of ruinous warfare. But, as I've said before, I believe we have reached an inflection point, where much of

the continent has gone too far in the other direction. *The demilitariza-tion of Europe—where large swaths of the general public and political class are averse to military force and the risks that go with it—has gone from a blessing in the twentieth century to an impediment to achieving real security and last-ing peace in the twenty-first.* (emphasis added)

It took a few seconds for me, and I suspect for many others who were there, to absorb the gravity of what the secretary had just said. Gates had literally taken Europe's unprecedented success story of the last century—that is, the creation of the European Union—and turned it on its head. Were I a European, I would have heard this message: The Europeans achieved an impossible mission after World War II. They found a way to transform centuries-old antagonists into peaceful nations and in the pro-cess created a prosperous and peaceful new Europe of integrated national states—the European Union. The union was built bit by bit with painstak-ing negotiations and treaties. Proud, ancient nations learned the art of trading parts of their national sovereignty for the common good. And the results were there for all to see. For the first time in centuries, Europeans have lived in peace for sixty years. A Europe whole and free, prosperous and proud had emerged from the ruins of the Second World War.[1]

But, Gates warned his NATO audience, the very traits that had brought peace—negotiations and the art of compromise—and replaced ultima-tums and war, admirable though they were in the twentieth century, had become liabilities in the twenty-first. New threats required new defenses. New defenses required the expenditure of more money than the Europe-ans were willing to contribute, even after repeated promises.

So, the American secretary of defense informed his transfixed audi-ence, the very legacy of creating the European Union had now converted the Europeans into a liability for Western security. It was a mistake to think that Europe's success could be extrapolated to the rest of the world, which was still a dangerous place full of dangerous people who had no use for compromise and negotiations. For all these reasons it was increasingly dif-ficult for NATO to operate and fight as an alliance. The bottom line was that America's European allies were no longer considered reliable NATO partners.

The implication of Gates's message was clear: if the Europeans did not change their lackluster support of NATO, the alliance would continue its slide into irrelevance.

Taking it all in from her seat in the front row was the former U.S. secretary of state Madeleine Albright. As mentioned in chapter 4, Albright chaired NATO's new strategic concept's task force, charged with making recommendations to Secretary-General Rasmussen about redefining the alliance's mission for the twenty-first century.

Her politically loaded task had just been brought into sharp focus by Gates's message. Unless Europeans changed their attitude toward defense and security and proved their conversion to true believers through increased defense investment and willingness to put European lives on the line, as a military alliance NATO would have minimal value to the United States. Thus Albright's task force would have to address NATO's structural deficiencies, such as the inexplicable lack of a chief financial officer in the alliance's multibillion-dollar operation, a plethora of commands and bases, and a bureaucracy comprising hundreds of committees with overlapping jurisdictions. But at the end of day, the task force would have to address America's perception that the Europeans are simply not as committed to NATO as America is. Besides jolting his audience to attention, Gates had made Albright's already tough job even harder.

Gates was not alone in placing NATO at an existential crossroad at the conference. Secretary of State Hillary Clinton delivered the same message in remarks that were carefully orchestrated with Gates's speech, leaving no doubt of American feelings that NATO was in need of major surgery, the Europeans in need of a reality check, and the time for action was now. The Europeans had now to decide whether they valued the sixty-year-old alliance as much as they said they did.

The trouble is, as Albright must have found out, the Europeans simply do not agree with the commonly held American perception, reflected in Gates's remarks, that they have become soft, compromise-seeking peaceniks. Far from it. Instead, rather than relying on NATO's Cold War–vintage solutions, they have been busy building a holistic approach to crisis management that is being chiseled into the European Union's own military arm, its Common Security and Defense Policy. Whatever the United States may think of it, the European Union, through its CSDP, has already established itself as a powerful force to promote European influence abroad. Unlike NATO, it has no American vote in its councils, and as NATO's effectiveness has withered, that of the CSDP has steadily grown. In fact, when they believe it is in the Europeans' interest to do so, they will put their lives on the line. They did so during the European Union's military mission to Chad and the Central African Republic. "Where the Europeans find their interest involved, they are probably more warlike than most other societies," General Scowcroft told me when I was researching my earlier book on transatlantic relations.[2]

It is the need to reconcile the dramatically different perspectives on either side of the Atlantic, the growing maturity of Europe's defense and security policy, together with the structural problems within NATO, that mades Albright's task so difficult. Her recommendations had to bridge the divide between NATO and the CSDP and reconcile the strategic visions of the United States and Europe, visions that have increasingly diverged over the last decade. I'm afraid her recommendations did not do that.

The Europeans' unwillingness to commit additional resources toward defense is generally ascribed in the United States to Europe's transformation into a culture that can no longer tolerate wars and their costs in both blood and money. Secretary Gates's speech in Washington underscores this sentiment. But this simplistic analysis, in my opinion, is just not true.

I would argue instead that the Europeans seem to understand the nuances and complexities of today's threats to the West's security and to its economies more accurately than their American allies do. And the Europeans have begun to leverage both their sharper understanding of today's threats and the European Union's built-in strengths to create a security and defense structure that is more appropriate for meeting the majority of today's threats than is the existing Euro-Atlantic solution, NATO.

Contrary to popular belief, most wars are not fought between countries. This basic principle drives the European defense and security strategy. "Large-scale aggression against any Member State is now improbable. Instead, Europe faces new threats which are more diverse, less visible, and less predictable," notes the European Security Strategy, the document that provides the intellectual underpinning to the CSDP (see appendix D).[3]

"Of some 467 wars that were fought over 200 years, only around 67 have been between states, the rest were between people," David Kilcullen, a counterinsurgency expert and former adviser to the U.S. Department of State told a conference on security strategy that I attended in the spring of 2010. State on-state conflicts have not and will not be the norm, he explains; instead, it is the wars between people—civil wars over food, water, mineral resources, and religious/ethnic conflicts—that have accounted for most of the devastation of the last two centuries. "Forty million people were killed in these people on people wars during the second half of the twentieth century, which is twice the number of Russians killed in the Second World War," Kilcullen said. "The greatest threat facing humanity today is not terrorism or nuclear annihilation but global instability caused by the disproportionate distribution of resources," Senator Hagel said.[4] It is this competition for scarce resources that fuels the intrastate feuds, both Hagel and Kilcullen warn.

So, if history is any guide, the classic state-on-state wars are not going to be the primary threats facing the Euro-Atlantic community. Rather, the escalation of local tensions, the potential for regional instability from people-to-people wars, and the need to control crises before they explode out of control will increasingly determine the security of the Euro-Atlantic nations and their economies. NATO is not yet prepared to meet these types of quasi-military threats. It intends to create the capabilities to handle such crises over the next decade, according to the recently adopted new strategic concept. According to Article 25 of that document, "To be effective across the crisis management spectrum, we will . . . form an appropriate but modest civilian crisis management capability . . . enhance civilian-military planning throughout the crisis spectrum" (see appendix E).

"The risk of a military attack, in the conventional sense, while not totally inconsequential, is going south all the time," Lt. Gen. David Leakey, director general of the European Union's Military Staff, told me. "What is much more pertinent is the protection and promotion of our interests." And this task, Leakey points out, the European Union is singularly equipped to do with its Common Security and Defense Policy.

"Finland did not get rich by cutting down its trees and exporting wood. It got rich by leveraging technical innovations, for example, mobile phone technology exports by companies such as Nokia. Nokia, or any other corporation for that matter, continues to grow by expanding its markets and increasing market share," Leakey said. But "you can only make a market when there is stability. For stability Finland needs an organization that can stabilize, improve, and secure."

The requirements for stepping into a potentially unstable situation and changing it into a safer and more stable environment before it degenerates into conflict are far more complex and nuanced than are the requirements for simply waging war. "With the threat of conventional war diminishing rapidly, Russia is not the biggest threat to Finland," Leakey said. "The threat is that the markets it is in, and the new markets it needs to expand into, will become unstable. Finland needs much more than a military to defend its interests."

It is precisely this kind of situation that the European Union's Common Security and Foreign Policy, with it operational arm, the European Union's Common Security and Defense Policy, is designed to address.

The European Union's size and political weight are already impressive, to say the least. It has a population of over five hundred million people and represents over a quarter of the world's GDP. The European Union distributes around $49 billion in development aid either through its executive arm, the European Commission, or from donations by individual member nations.[5] This amount is over half of the entire world's development aid and dwarfs what anyone else does, including the United States. The European Union also contributes a fifth of worldwide imports and exports, making it an important player in global markets.[6]

With this kind of clout, it would be surprising if the European Union had no global aspirations, with regional and global security interests and responsibilities to match. In fact, the European Union now plays an increasingly more powerful role throughout the world. Chapter 5 addressed examples of its active involvement off the coast of Somalia and in Chad. The European Union also plays a part in the Middle East peace process, in the international community's diplomatic engagement with Iran, and in the western Balkans, including Kosovo. Through its CSDP, European troops, police, and judges are helping to save lives and stabilize countries and regions after conflicts across the globe. The European Union provides emergency relief to countries stricken with natural disasters and facilitates the entry of UN peacekeepers.[7]

The European Union's ability to undertake these crisis prevention missions is fairly new. When conflict erupted in Kosovo during the late 1990s, all the Europeans could do was stand and watch until the United States and NATO came to their aid. The European reaction to this feeling of helplessness jump-started the development of the CSDP. It became the European Union's toolbox of institutions to build political consensus, plan crisis management missions including military interventions, and then to take action by deploying troops under an integrated European military structure.

So well has the European Union done its job in creating these structures to support European military missions that when war broke out between Georgia and Russia in 2007, it was the European Union that negotiated an end to the war. For the first time, the United States was neither necessary nor involved in ending a European conflict. It was quite a change from the Kosovo experience.

"We learned from the hard school of failure during the Balkans crisis in the 1990s," says Javier Solana, who played an instrumental role in creating the CSDP and served as its first head. "We saw, when the Balkans descended into violence that we did not have the instruments to react. . . . The handling of our periphery is essential for our credibility in international politics. We have to be able to stabilize our own neighborhood."

In 2007, during the Georgia-Russia conflict, the European Union had the tools that it had lacked during its Balkan crises, and they proved to be powerful ones indeed. The European Union's Common Security and Defense Policy is the operational arm of a far more encompassing group of policies and instruments that fall under the European Union's Common Foreign and Security Policy. (It is confusing that the Europeans have chosen these terms to mean both a set of policies and the governmental institutions through which to execute them.) The CSFP provides the European Union with a streamlined structure to control its worldwide diplomatic missions, its military arm, its development aid budget, and its responsibility to mesh the foreign policies of its twenty-seven members into one coherent policy. (To appreciate the CSFP's futuristic vision, think about combining the U.S. Defense and State Departments and replacing the two secretaries with one.) The Lisbon Treaty was a milestone in the development of the European Union.

The entire CSFP is now the responsibility of one person, the high representative of the European Union for Common Security and Foreign Policy. The European Council, the European Union's highest political decision-making body, comprised of the elected heads of all twenty-seven EU nations, appoints the high representative for the CSFP.

The bureaucratic changes made by the Lisbon Treaty have, understandably, generated ferocious turf wars that will keep the European Union preoccupied for a while. But when the dust settles and the CSFP begins to function smoothly, the European Union will be able to deploy unified crisis management missions using all the civil, political, economic, and military tools available to it. To some extent it does so now by using those tools that are within different silos of the European Union's bureaucracy. When the new structure kicks in, the silos will be eliminated, and the EU will become a powerhouse in global security and stability operations.

That the CSDP can undertake combined civil, military, development, and governance missions on behalf of the European Union is the reason why it is much more suited than NATO is to respond to the kinds of conflicts that Kilcullen says will dominate many of the world's trouble spots. The advantages of CSFP operations in managing crises have already been demonstrated through the European Union's deployment of twenty-seven civilian and military missions over three continents in just the first decade of its existence from 1999 to 2009 (see table 5 in chapter 5). In fact, during 2009, the CSDP was operating twelve missions concurrently, all over the world, from Kabul, Afghanistan, to Pristina, Kosovo, and from Ramallah in the West Bank to Kinshasa in the Democratic Republic of the Congo. This range is an impressive accomplishment by any standard and especially so for a relatively young organization.[8]

As noted in chapter 5, the CSDP's multiple strengths were evident in the planning, logistics, and execution of the European Union's 3,700-person military mission in Chad and are every day on display in the European Union's first naval mission off Somalia. It should also be noted that the missions deployed during the CSDP's first decade preceded passage of the Lisbon Treaty in 2009, which meant civil-military coordination in the mission had to be accomplished through multiple EU departments. The CSFP will bring all the pieces together and place them under one official, the high representative, which can only make the deployment of future CSDP missions even more efficient.

To be sure, the CSDP is still a relatively small organization. Indeed, the entire EU Military Staff has two hundred people compared to some fourteen thousand in NATO. (I recognize this comparison is far from perfect, and the NATO headcount is about to be slashed by at least a third during 2011.) As a result, the CSDP can only take on a limited number of missions. The European Union has built the CSDP's foundation carefully, however, with the potential to scale up in size and capability.

It is also true that most CSDP missions, unlike the one to Chad, have been small operations. But "once you have the command structure to handle military missions, there is not much difference from sending out a mission of a few hundred or a few thousand," Gen. Håkan Syren, chairman of the European Union's Military Committee, told me.

In his message celebrating the CSDP's first ten years, the EU High Representative for the Common Foreign and Security Policy Javier Solana said,

> We were ahead of our time in 1999. The comprehensive, multi-faceted nature of our approach was novel. And the EU is still the only organization that can call on a whole range of stabilization instruments, both to pre-empt or prevent a crisis, and to restore peace and rebuild institutions after a conflict…We can combine humanitarian aid and support for institution-building and good governance in developing countries with crisis-management capacities and technical and financial assistance, as well as the more specifically diplomatic tools, such as political dialogue and mediation.[9]

The decade that saw the CSDP emerge as a player on the world's geopolitical stage also witnessed NATO still searching for a role to replace its Cold War functions. As discussed in chapter 3, NATO finally got its chance to prove that it can be an effective global player when it assumed command of the International Security and Assistance Force in Afghanistan. But in this role it has performed poorly.

Instead of an alliance that used to be a model of solidarity, NATO's mission in Afghanistan has been riddled by weakness as some of the allies simply refuse to fight. "For our allies to tell us that they will contribute troops to the war, but not participate in it, is a crisis for the alliance," Nick Burns, the former American NATO ambassador, said to me. "You cannot sweep it aside." After nine years of war in Afghanistan, the alliance is close to splitting ranks. Many of the NATO allies that actually participate on the battlefield with the U.S. forces have left or are preparing to remove their forces in the next two years.

The experience of 9/11 shook NATO's confidence as its leader, the United States, sidelined the alliance and fought the 2001 war in Afghanistan by itself. This stance was in spite of NATO invoking Article 5 for the first time and expecting that its assistance would be gratefully accepted by America.

Hard on the heels of the 9/11 experience, the United States struck another blow at the core of NATO. Knowing the alliance would not approve an invasion of Iraq, but convinced of the rightness of its cause, America simply ignored the opinion of some of its biggest NATO allies and launched the invasion with those allies who chose to accompany it. This action was a double blow for NATO. Not only had the United States caused a split in the alliance but America had also ignored the UN Security Council, which had refused to support the American-led invasion of Iraq. Not only does NATO get its legitimacy from the Charter of the United Nations, but the Europeans consider the United Nations to be at the center of global governance. For the Europeans, America's unilateral decision to invade a sovereign country called into question America's belief in the core principles around which the alliance was created.

Worse, NATO is now an organization with built-in political dissonance that can be leveraged for political reasons as a force for instability. It happened when Georgia decided to go to war against Russia in the hopes that NATO's cavalry, or at least the U.S. cavalry, would come to its rescue. And NATO creates a false sense of security by implying that it is ready, willing, and able to play its historical role of defending its members against aggression. The alliance's continuing inability to defend its members against cyber and space warfare has shown that is not the case, and its disparate membership calls the alliance's core mission of territorial defense into question.

As NATO has expanded from a tight-knit group of Western European allies to a collection of twenty-eight members whose security interests are not always aligned, NATO has lost the political cohesion that is essential to successful alliances. While NATO's eastern European members still have nightmares about Russia's intentions against them, Western European members happily do business with a Russia they do not consider to be much of a threat. Witness France's sale in February 2010 of one of its most sophisticated warships to Russia. This weapon, called the Mistral, will make it significantly easier for Russia to invade Georgia again, should it want to do so. "Everything that we did in the space of 26 hours at the time [Russia's occupation of Georgia's naval facilities], this ship will do within 40 minutes," Russia's naval chief, Adm. Vladimir S. Vysotsky, was quoted as saying.[10] The multimillion-euro Mistral sale has been viewed by alarm by NATO members that are Russia's neighbors, because "France may have pioneered the way for othr Western countries to sell Russia whatever they have to offer . . . "[11]

The return from Afghanistan might well pose the biggest challenge yet to NATO's future. Absent a political turnaround in the attitude of member countries, which is highly unlikely, when NATO returns from that mission, it will be seen in America as a weakened military alliance that cannot be trusted to defend the West's interests, as America sees them, or its members in a war.

Ambassador Burns was scathing in his comments about the alliance when I asked him about some of the largest European countries' unwillingness to fight along with their NATO allies in Afghanistan. "I think it is . . . against the NATO ethic, which is one for all and all for one. We're supposed to be fighting these, confronting these threats together, on an equal basis, and that's not the case in Afghanistan."

Col. Charles Van Bebber, who heads up the European studies program at the elite U.S. Army War College, is convinced Afghanistan is an existential threat for NATO. He tells his students the British Army in Afghanistan is the bellwether for the future of NATO in that war.

Britain has probably the best-resourced and best-funded military in the European Union, "but look at what has been happening to the British Army in Afghanistan," he says. "Look at the conflicts they are having about being under-resourced, their inability to adapt to what they used to do well—counterinsurgency. There was that embarrassing incident in which Britain's chief of defense staff went to Afghanistan, and he had to get the Americans to ferry him around. There just were not enough British helicopters." If the British cannot sustain their NATO fighting force in Afghanistan, what hope is there for the other NATO countries? I spoke to Colonel van Bebber before the current economic crisis had forced Britain to slash its defense budget even further, so the situation is far worse today.

Canadian defense minister Peter MacKay, like Van Bebber, a strong NATO supporter, also believes Afghanistan poses an existential threat to NATO. "We need to have a frank discussion about the future of NATO," MacKay told the Royal Institute of International Affairs, also known as Chatham House, on February 16, 2009.[12] "Afghanistan tests the ability of the alliance to execute its most basic mission in the twenty-first century and in a global context," he said. "*If NATO cannot deter or defeat the real physical threat facing alliance members*, and indeed contribute to the building of security for the larger international community, then we have to ask ourselves, what is NATO for?"

"Present-day NATO is a shadow of what it once was. Calling it a successful alliance today is the equivalent of calling General Motors a successful car company—it privileges nostalgia over self-awareness," according to Andrew Bacevich.[13]

With all of these fault lines stretching its credibility and cohesion, and with the CSDP increasingly taking center stage in Europe's crisis management strategy, the question that must now be asked is, wither NATO?

Some, including NATO secretary-general Anders Fogh Rasmussen and former U.S. national security adviser Zbigniew Brzezinski, continue to argue for an expanded NATO. "To live up to its potential, the alliance should become the hub of a globe-spanning web or regional cooperative security undertaking," Brzezinski says.[14] Rasmussen's vision (adopted as a NATO priority at the November 2010 NATO Summit in Lisbon) is equally expansive. He would like to see NATO and Russia together deploy a gigantic missile defense shield, so that "people from Vancouver to Vladivostok would know that they were part of one community. One community, sharing real security, against a real threat, using real technologies."[15]

Its recent performance alone would make this idea a very hard sell. On Friday, February 5, 2010, NATO acknowledged that after seven years in Afghanistan it still lacked twenty-five hundred trainers, almost half the number its European members had promised years ago "to help build up the army and police in Afghanistan."[16] If NATO's European members cannot deliver a thousand or so trainers from a population of five hundred million people, the idea that they will provide the resources to deploy a missile shield from Vancouver to Vladivostok borders on the absurd.

NATO maintains the massive anti-ballistic missile shield will cost around $200 million over ten years. When I asked Dmitry Rogozin, the Russian ambassador to NATO, what he thought about this price tag, his answer was quite revealing: "Perhaps you could make a movie about missile defense in this budget." It is this gap between what NATO wants to do and its ability to find the resources to make its visions a reality that has accounted for NATO's increasing irrelevance since the end of the Cold War.

The former SACEUR Gen. John Craddock made this point forcefully when he testified before the U.S. Senate Committee on Foreign Relations on October 22, 2009. The committee held hearings on NATO's plans for the next ten years, or the so-called new strategic concept. "The challenge . . . is not in the development of what NATO wants to do, should do, or feels compelled to do," Craddock told the committee. "The challenge for NATO is *matching its level of ambition with its political will* to resource the means to accomplish its ambitions."[17] (emphasis added)

Finally, besides misfiring badly in Afghanistan, there is also the fact that NATO is widely perceived as a front for the United States. Because the United States is no longer welcome in many parts of the world, NATO is also persona non grata in these countries. Why would countries around the world want such a NATO to serve as a global security hub?

Besides virtually the entire Islamic world, these sentiments against the deployment of U.S. and NATO forces are evident in many other areas as well. Take Africa, for instance, the resource-rich continent that is being courted by America, Europe, and China for its mineral wealth and potential markets. Maintaining stability and promoting goodwill in Africa are key Western objectives and the reasons why the Pentagon set up its Africa Command (AFRICOM).

But AFRICOM is not located anywhere in Africa. Instead, its headquarters is thousands of miles from Africa, in Stuttgart, Germany, because "no African country wanted to host an American military headquarters," a senior European military officer told me. "The Americans tried for three years to set up in Africa and finally gave up." In March 2010, *Stars and Stripes* reported that AFRICOM might soon move even farther away from its theater, all the way to Florida.[18]

When Chad agreed to receive a military mission from the West, under UN auspices, it made sure the United Nations understood it did not want an American or NATO presence. "I was a member of the team that received this message from the prime minister of Chad," a senior EU official who was involved in negotiating the mission's composition told me. "The prime minister was quite clear that the while the European Union could be an acceptable partner, NATO would not."

The same situation occurred during the Georgia-Russia conflict. "Russia made it clear it did not want to see NATO anywhere near its borders," a senior EU diplomat told me. "The reason President Sarkozy of France was successful in being able to quickly arrange a cease-fire between Georgia and Russia during their 2008 war was because France then held the rotating European Union presidency. This meant that the president of France could fly to Georgia and Russia as the president of the European Union, negotiate a cease-fire, and then count on CSDP to deploy an unarmed monitoring mission to oversee the cease-fire's terms. CSDP showed its capabilities by deploying over 340 monitors from twenty-four European Union countries to Georgia, almost as soon as the cease-fire was signed.

"Russia would never have allowed NATO to perform this function," the diplomat told me.

But here is the paradox. Even though it increasingly appears a misfit in today's geopolitical environment, because of is size and maturity, NATO is still in many ways an exemplary military alliance. After sixty years of developing common standards, policies, weapons, and tactics, most NATO countries can operate on battlefields, on the oceans, and in the air together with a high degree of precision, or interoperability in military jargon. Even in Afghanistan, this capability is plain to see among the nations that are willing to fight on the battlefield. Interoperability lets troops from Denmark, Canada, Britain, Netherlands, and the United States, for example, fight in integrated formations.

It is also true that no one I talked to, European or American, at any level can imagine a time without NATO. It is still considered to be that ultimate guarantee against the unknown. Europeans have long memories and know how quickly political events can intrude on a time of bliss. General Lather summed up this European sentiment for me: "Don't forget, it was only ten years from the time the Nazis were elected to office that Hitler took Germany to war."

NATO's continued viability is equally in America's national interest. After all, NATO has never been just a military alliance. Dean Acheson, U.S. secretary of state from 1949 to 1953 and one of NATO's key architects, said the treaty "sought to add the power of the United States to create a stabilizing and preventive force. The treaty was more than a purely military treaty. It was a means and a vehicle for closer political, economic and security cooperation with Western Europe."[19]

As unimaginable as it might be, for all the reasons I have presented in this book, NATO's future, as a military alliance, is for the first time, uncertain. To continue being a viable alliance, NATO must be transformed into an organization that properly reflects not just the threats but the economic and political realities of the new century. Arguably, the most important geopolitical development of recent times has been the creation of the European Union with its Common Security and Defense Policy. This development is why, I believe, it is meaningless to draft a future for NATO that is independent of the European Union's CSDP.

Both NATO and the CSDP are primarily European organizations, with significantly overlapping memberships and decision-making structures.

- Twenty-one European states are members both of the European Union and NATO (see table 6). Far more significant than the cross-membership is the fact that the six countries that account for around 80 percent of the EU's defense spending—the United Kingdom, France, Germany, Italy, the Netherlands, and Spain—are members of both groups.[20]

Table 6. Membership Overlap between the European Union and NATO

COUNTRY	EUROPEAN UNION	NATO
Belgium	—	—
Bulgaria	—	—
Czech Republic	—	—
Denmark	—	—
Estonia	—	—
France	—	—
Germany	—	—
Greece	—	—
Hungary	—	—
Italy	—	—
Latvia	—	—
Lithuania	—	—
Luxembourg	—	—
Netherlands	—	—
Poland	—	—
Portugal	—	—
Romania	—	—
Slovakia	—	—
Slovenia	—	—
Spain	—	—
United Kingdom	—	—
Albania		—
Canada		—
Croatia		—
Iceland		—
Norway		—
Turkey		—
United States		—
Austria	—	
Cyprus	—	
Finland	—	
Ireland	—	
Malta	—	
Sweden	—	

Note: NATO (twenty-eight members) and the European Union (twenty-seven members) have twenty-one members in common. Table by author.

- The "boards of directors" of the two organizations, the North Atlantic Council (NATO) and the Political and Security Committee (CSDP), are appointed by the same heads of state.
- Both the NAC and the PSC rely on the recommendation of their respective Military Committee, probably the most influential group in both organizations. Both committees are composed of the defense chiefs of member nations; thus the European Union and NATO share twenty-one committee members.

The most important fact of all is often overlooked. Both NATO and the CSDP rely on the same pool of European military assets (see table 7). When serving with NATO's naval force off Somalia, a German frigate flies the NATO flag, but when assigned to the CSDP, the same German frigate will fly the European Union's flag. Further, the strengths and weaknesses of Europe's military forces equally influence NATO's capabilities and those of the CSDP. For instance, fully 70 percent of Europe's land forces remain unusable outside national territory.[21] A serious handicap for today's military requirements, this status is an equally negative factor for both NATO and the CSDP.

It is also the case that the European Union intends to transform its military capabilities along the same lines as the United States—that is, adopt small, mobile forces that can be airlifted to trouble spots and supported by technology-driven weaponry. As the EU Institute for Security Studies has pointed out: "The good news is that in the coming years, based on their current procurement plans, EU countries should have a number of new strategic capabilities such as . . . transport planes; . . . air tankers; . . . Joint-Strike-Fighter jets. . . . EU defence ministries will be able to use Galileo—a [European] satellite navigation system—to guide their equipment and define their positions. All this equipment will greatly add to the military prowess of Europe's [national] armies in the future."[22] The military transformations will benefit NATO as much as the European Union's CSDP.

Last but not least, taxes from the same citizens from each of the twenty-one overlapping countries pay for operating the permanent staff and functions of each organization. As table 7 shows, European taxpayers are

Table 7. ESDP Military Capabilities 1999–2009*

	1999: EU15	*1999: EU27*	*2009: EU27*	change '99–'09
Defence Expenditure**				
Total Expenditure (1997/2007)	€156.2 Bn	€162.9 Bn	€209.7 Bn	+ 29%
Expenditure / GDP (1997/2007)	2.1 %	2.1 %	1.7 %	- 19%
Budget / GDP(1998/2008)	1.7 %	1.8 %	1.4 %	- 22%
Armed Forces				
Total Active Military***	1,789,868	2,508,908	2,013,990	- 20%
Army	1,125,718	1,516,378	996,234	- 34%
Navy	281,450	327,400	222,313	- 32%
Air Force	381,605	538,925	345,153	- 36%
Conscripts	669,770	1,131,020	212,785	- 81%
Equipment				
LAND				
Main Battle Tanks	10,827	17,814	9,823	- 45%
Armoured Fighting Vehicles	6,851	10,622	7,951	- 25%
Armoured Personnel Carriers	19,751	26,311	22,844	- 13%
AVIATION				
Fixed Wing Aircraft	5,600	7,453	5,401	- 28%
Fighter Jets	2,684	3,835	2,410	- 37%
Transport (incl. tankers)	439	612	898	+ 47%
Helicopters	3,515	4,732	3,573	- 24%
Attack	1,000	1,312	826	- 37%
Combat Support	969	1,305	849	- 35%
Utility (incl. transport)	445	584	1,076	+ 84%
NAVAL				
Aircraft Carriers	6	6	7	+ 17%
Destroyers	29	31	26	- 16%
Frigates	145	155	108	- 30%
Patrol and Coastal	314	521	811	+ 56%
Mine Warfare	208	296	243	- 18%
Amphibious	267	274	494	+ 80%

* The estimates in this table above are taken from The Military Balance 1999–2000 and The Military Balance 2009, both published by the International Institute for Strategic Studies (IISS). The 1999–2000 edition uses figures from November 1998, including for defence budgets—the exception is defence expenditure estimates which date from 1997. The 2009 edition uses figures from 2008, except for defence expenditure figures which date from 2007.
** To calculate defence expenditure in euro, the 1997 total defence expenditure figures were calculated using the European Central Bank (ECB) fixed rates to the euro in 1999 where possible, or the earliest available annual average exchange rate provided by the ECB. For 2007 figures, where necessary, the European Central Bank annual average exchange rates of the national currency to the euro were used.
*** This figure also includes military police and paramilitary forces such as Gendarmerie, Carabinieiri etc. as well as army, navy and air force estimates. The editors wish to thank Charlotte Blommestijn sincerely for her research assistance in compiling this table.

Source: Daniel Keohane and Charlotte Blommestijn, "Strength in numbers? Comparing EU military capabilities in 2009 with 1999," *Policy Brief* 05 (EU Institute for Security Studies: Paris, December 2009), http://www.iss.europa.eu/uploads/media/PolicyBrief-05.pdf.

in no mood to spend an ever-increasing amount on their militaries: combined military expenditures of the European Union nations have dropped from 2.1 percent of their GDP in 1999 to 1.7 percent of their GDP in 2009. This drop in military expenditures is what was on Defense Secretary Gates's mind when he spoke at the NATO conference. But if he thinks the Europeans will change tack, Gates is in for a long wait.

"Don't expect the European Union's defense budgets as a percentage of GDP to rise again," General Syren told me unequivocally. He believes the answer is for the EU states to work smarter and make better use of their defense assets.

They had already begun to make this change, albeit at a snail's pace, until 2010 when the continuing global economic crisis dramatically changed Europe's military landscape. According to the *New York Times*, "Britain and France signed defense agreements on Tuesday that promised cooperation far beyond anything achieved previously in 60 years of NATO cooperation, including the creation of a joint expeditionary force, shared use of aircraft carriers and combined efforts to improve the safety and effectiveness of their nuclear weapons."[23]

"Meanwhile, in Germany, Chancellor Angela Merkel called for $10.5 billion in cuts by 2014. German Defense Minister Karl-Theodor zu Guttenberg said he plans to cut the size of the country's standing army from 250,000 to 165,000 . . . ," as stated by the *Fiscal Times*.[24]

More cuts and EU-wide pooling of military assets and capabilities is sure to follow. "If we do not take care of the economic issue, Mother Nature will," General Syren told me, with "Mother Nature" being the taxpayer.

Lieutenant General Leakey had the same reaction as General Syren when I asked him about the probability of increased defense spending in Europe. "If the Europeans did not increase their spending as a percent of GDP during the Cold War, they certainly aren't going to do it now," he told me. Besides Leakey reminded me, the European Union does not rely on military means alone to manage crisis, and there is significant spending under the CSDP in the nonmilitary areas.

The United States, NATO's largest benefactor, has also begun to feel the impact of the economic crisis, and as the year 2010 was ending the alliance moved into American lawmakers' cross-hairs. On December 29, 2010, a leading member of the U.S. House of Representatives, Barney Franks, told the *Huffington Post* that the United States should cut NATO spending. "NATO serves no strategic purpose," he said. In the same article, Lawrence J. Korb, a senior fellow at the Center for American Progress, was quoted as saying, "Barney Frank has a good point...we ought to rethink the whole idea of NATO."[25] With increasing calls, on both the Republican and Democrat side of the aisle to cut the American defense budget, it will not take too long for a lawmaker to ask whether Euro-Atlantic security requires both CSDP and NATO.

I raised this question with a number of Europeans, both civilian and military. In slightly different ways, they reiterated what Shada Islam, from the European Policy Centre, told me when I asked her why we need both NATO and the CSDP.

> For me it just seems very obvious, because I was brought into the entire argument ages ago. In the post–Second World War psyche of Europe, America is the protector. It's the protector of *European defense.* It is the godfather, NATO is. Europe's defense organization, CSDP, *is a projection of Europe's security identity and military identity interests with regard to the outside world.* It [CSDP] is Europe using its security and military institutions outside Europe. CSDP is not supposed to be something that protects Europe from outside invaders . . . It is Europe dispatching people to Congo to supervise elections; it's going to Chad; it's going to Sudan to train; it's going to the seas [off Somalia]. *It's not about protecting Europe from outside threats.* It's about Europe going out, reaching out and trying to resolve global flashpoints. . . . *NATO is defense. CSDP is security.*

But, I pointed out, the European security strategy explicitly lays out the threats that Europe faces today: proliferation of weapons of mass destruction, regional conflicts, state failure, and organized crime. Taking these different elements together—terrorism committed with maximum violence, the availability of WMD, organized crime, the weakening of the state system, the privatization of force—Europe could be confronted with a very radical threat, indeed, says this key document. If the CSDP is meant to forestall these threats, is it not then a defense mechanism also?

No, I was told over and over again. When and if Europe is threatened from the outside, for its defense it will look to NATO. But for everything else it will use the same forces, remove the NATO shoulder patches, slap on the EU patches, paint new logos on the tanks and aircraft, and deploy under CSDP auspices to manage crises around the corner or on the other side of the world. That action will not count as defense but the projection of Europe's gravitas to the outside world.

I confessed it did not make too much sense to me. "I know," Islam exclaimed. "It is not easy to be a European!"

But this explanation of what CSDP is—crisis management operations outside Europe but not for the defense of Europe, is simply not a reflection of where the European Union aims to take the CSDP in the future. In fact, the CSDP's trajectory is already destined to intersect that of NATO's.

Article 42 (Provisions on the Common Security and Defence Policy), Paragraph 2, of the Treaty of the European Union (TEU) makes this quite clear: "The common security and defence policy shall include the progressive framing of a common Union defence policy. This will lead to a common defence, when the European Council, acting unanimously, so decides."

The TEU is the legal basis on which the entire European Union structure is built. Article 42, paragraph 2, is unambiguous: the CSDP can serve the European Union's defense mechanism whenever the Europeans believe it is appropriate to do so. Going further, Article 42, paragraph 7, adds a mutual defense clause to the treaty: "If a Member State is the victim of armed aggression on its territory, the other Member States shall have towards it an obligation of aid and assistance by all means in their power."

Lest there be any doubt, Article 43 of the treaty specifies that the tasks CSDP may be used for include "joint disarmament operations, humanitarian and rescue tasks, military advice and assistance tasks, conflict prevention and peace-keeping tasks, tasks of combat forces in crisis management, including peace-making and post-conflict stabilization."

It seems to me all that is left before the Europeans are ready to take over a large part of their own defense is for the CSDP to grow and mature. The armed forces of the EU member nations also need to modernize and transform themselves, as they are on track to doing.

There is today no doubt that the Europeans can handle future crises similar to what occurred in Bosnia and Kosovo, in their own backyard, with the CSDP. General Nash, who led the EUFOR TChad/RCA, assured me of that with one proviso, "if they have the will." In fact, few Europeans, military or civilian, doubted the EU's ability to defend Europe's security, if the will to do so existed. Almost none of my European interlocutors believed Europe would ever develop the capability for waging a major war on the other side of the world, a massive force projection capability that differentiates the United States from any other country in the world. But neither did these interlocutors feel doing so was a European national interest.

The overarching question is how far and how fast do the Europeans want to take the CSDP. Does Europe want or need to create the expensive, integrated military structures that will be needed before the CSDP can handle the military operations in support of its mutual defense clause that NATO is able to conduct today? Or are the Battle Groups already formed within the CSDP framework sufficient to support the EU's plans?

Meanwhile, NATO does not have the expertise to deploy the multidimensional missions that future crises will require or the type of missions the European Union has deployed successfully twenty-seven times over the last decade. It may, in fact, never be able to deploy CSDP-type missions because NATO is a military alliance and not the military arm of a governmental entity (the European Union) with a full array of civil, legal, and military tools at its disposal. These tools provide an expertise that is at the core of the CSDP.

"We would like nothing better than to take all the nonmilitary functions and give them to the European Union," the military representative of a large NATO member country told me. "And that includes the naval mission off Somalia," he said, recognizing the civil, legal, and military components that have made the European Union's naval force off the Horn of Africa so successful.

Given that the CSDP already has the proven expertise to handle an entire spectrum of military and civilian missions and that its crisis management missions have the clout of the European Union's array of nonmilitary functions—which NATO, a military alliance, could never hope to duplicate—why would the Euro-Atlantic allies want to face the far more complex threats of the twenty-first century using a tool of the twentieth century, NATO? Conversely, why would NATO want to go to the expense of adding a civilian-military component to its capabilities, as the new strategic concept states it wants to do, when the CSDP already has this capability, proven and ready to use? Compared to the largely one-dimensional NATO, in today's globalized world, the CSDP has real utility. "It is like walking out for a game of golf," General Leakey told me. "Why carry three clubs, when one can carry fourteen?"

I do not think NATO by itself is the right crisis management instrument for the future, and transforming it without linking it to the CSDP makes little sense. My recommendation is that the United States, as NATO's leader, should initiate a discussion, perhaps at the level of Secretary of State, and the European Union's high representative for Common Security and Foreign Policy and the Canadian foreign minister, to begin work on bridging NATO and the CSDP. As a prelude to this discussion, the United States ought to make it clear that it expects the EU to be responsible for its own security within a reasonably short period of time, say, three to five years.

These discussions are also timely for the United States, which is facing its own budgetary constraints on military expenditures. The European Union's assumption of the costs and responsibilities for a large part of its own defense, under an arrangement that continues America's (and Canada's) traditional involvement in European security is, it seems to me, in the long-term interest of the entire Euro-Atlantic community.

But there is a far more strategic reason for bridging NATO and the CSDP. In the process of working through the project, both the United States and the European Union will be forced to confront and then agree on a common global vision regarding the use of force.

If one thinks about NATO's ineffective performance in Afghanistan, it has little to do with the bravery of European soldiers. In fact, some of the European countries have suffered casualties at a higher rate than American troops have. What then is the cause of NATO's lackluster performance? I believe it has to do with NATO getting European troops involved in a war on the other side of the world without the full support of most of the European countries whose troops are deployed in Afghanistan. The findings of the annual barometer of transatlantic relations, the German Marshall Fund's *Transatlantic Trends 2009*, bear this out.

"In 2009, Afghanistan was an alliance sore point, since most Americans supported the war and many Europeans opposed it," according to the report for 2009.[26] Of the European countries that the fund polled for its report, most wanted to see the number of their troops reduced or their forces totally withdrawn. Fifty-one percent of the Poles (who are hugely pro-American) and 41 percent of the Germans and British backed complete troop removal. More than half of the West Europeans (55 percent) and two-thirds of East Europeans (69 percent) wanted to reduce or remove their soldiers from Afghanistan.

The poll results remind me of a conversation I had with Peter Jay, a former British ambassador to the United States, a few years ago. "Until we, the United States and Europe, sort out agreed basic premises about the rules of the global game, it will become increasingly difficult to resolve, or even indefinitely to fudge the day to day issues that confront us," he warned.[27] Peter Jay was prescient in his observation.

The military compact between America and Europe that had been steadily eroding over the last two decades broke apart during the lead-up to the American-led invasion of Iraq. This divide has never been fully repaired and cannot be until the two sides agree to a new set of rules about the use of force. The project to bridge NATO and the CSDP will force the two sides to reach an agreement on when force should be used and how it should be used in the context of the transatlantic alliance.

An initiative along the lines of my recommendation will also recognize the European Union's growing role in handling Europe's foreign and security policy. By passing the Lisbon Treaty, the Europeans have placed High Representative not just in charge of the CSDP but also in command of some six thousand European diplomats and 136 delegations, a foreign service that equals that of Germany.[28] Add to these two roles the power of billions of euros in development funds, and one starts to feel the potential power that the European Union can flex to manage crises around the world. It is this structure that NATO must both recognize and to which it must adapt.

While creating a bridge between the two organizations is by far the most logical thing to do, the animosity between Cyprus and Turkey will make any such linking or collaboration between NATO and the CSDP extremely difficult.

"The essence of the blockage [NATO-CSDP collaboration] is the result of a political problem and can be unblocked only by a political decision," says Leakey, director general of the European Union's Military Staff. Turkey will not let any meetings be held between the European Union and NATO if Cyprus is present, and the European Union cannot do anything unless all twenty-seven of its members are present. If Turkey tries to sneak through the back door into the EU by membership into the European Defense Agency (a common procurement cooperative that Turkey feels it should belong to given that it is the largest European military force), Greece will veto it on behalf of Cyprus.

The day I visited Leakey in Brussels, he told me his e-mail had already included four instances in which a serious block on information-sharing between the CSDP and NATO had occurred because of the Cyprus-Turkey issue. "And it is only Tuesday," he said wearily.

So sensitive and widely known is this problem that civilian and military officials do not need to mention the two countries anymore during conversations. They simply say, "But we all know what the problem really is."

Soldiers in the field will always find a way to make things work out despite the political blockages, but as Leakey and every other political and military leader I met with told me, the politicians still have to step up to the plate and resolve the Cyprus-Turkish issue. This one issue, I repeatedly heard, is holding up the transformation of the transatlantic defense and security agenda.

But even if the Cyprus-Turkey issue is resolved, "we are likely to find the problem is really like an onion, with multiple layers," a senior military official in Brussels said. And the other layers involve Greece.

"If we can solve the Turkey-Cyprus issue, it will be the first skin on the onion," the official said, "then my fear is another layer will open up. This will be the Greek-Turkish issue." As improbable as it sounds given the huge difference in size between the two countries, Greece is convinced Turkey intends to invade it. "Consequently, if you go to Greece and visit their army barracks, most of their military faces Turkey." A way must be found to neutralize this perceived threat of invasion.

Finally, he told me, after resolving the second issue, "we are left with one more skin on the onion, the question of Turkey's membership into the European Union."

I have explored the complexities of this issue in chapter 6, but this conversation underscores my point that the problem of linking NATO and the CSDP is a top-level political one. It must be addressed at the highest political level if the United States, the European Union, and Canada are serious about pumping new life into NATO. Not putting the Turkey-Cyprus-Greece political impasse at the top of the agenda at the November 2010 NATO Summit in Lisbon was, I feel, a major strategic error for the future of Euro-Atlantic security.

Turkey's membership in the European Union is an internal EU issue, but it has enormous ramifications for the Euro-Atlantic alliance and for broader relations between the West and Muslim countries. Almost every American interlocutor for this book made it clear that they would like the Europeans to approve Turkey's membership. But I found a distinct division among the Europeans I consulted. I am not confident the membership issue will be resolved in the near term, but top-level pressure to manage, if not end, the Turk-Cypriot-Greek impasse will do a great deal to move the Euro-Atlantic security negotiations to a fruitful completion. And here the United States can play a uniquely helpful role in its position as a strong supporter of both Turkey and Greece.

At the end of the day, the prize is a vibrant Euro-Atlantic relationship in all its dimensions. It is much too important for Americans and Europeans, and I believe for the wider world, to let the alliance's intensity be diminished. Will the relationship remain if NATO were weakened, became irrelevant, or just faded away? Of course it would. But would it be as vibrant, as tightly linked? With the power to inspire and influence the peaceful emergence of a host of new global power centers? I do not believe it would. For this reason the time to bridge NATO and the CSDP is now. As one of the most gifted of NATO's secretary-generals, Lord Robertson, said, "NATO, along with the European Union, can do amazing things."

The North Atlantic Treaty (1949)

Washington, D.C.—April 4, 1949:

The Parties to this Treaty reaffirm their faith in the purposes and principles of the Charter of the United Nations and their desire to live in peace with all peoples and all governments.

They are determined to safeguard the freedom, common heritage and civilisation of their peoples, founded on the principles of democracy, individual liberty and the rule of law. They seek to promote stability and well-being in the North Atlantic area.

They are resolved to unite their efforts for collective defence and for the preservation of peace and security. They therefore agree to this North Atlantic Treaty:

ARTICLE 1

The Parties undertake, as set forth in the Charter of the United Nations, to settle any international dispute in which they may be involved by peaceful means in such a manner that international peace and security and justice are not endangered, and to refrain in their international relations from the threat or use of force in any manner inconsistent with the purposes of the United Nations.

ARTICLE 2

The Parties will contribute toward the further development of peaceful and friendly international relations by strengthening their free institutions, by bringing about a better understanding of the principles upon which these institutions are founded, and by promoting conditions of stability and well-being. They will seek to eliminate conflict in their international economic policies and will encourage economic collaboration between any or all of them.

ARTICLE 3

In order more effectively to achieve the objectives of this Treaty, the Parties, separately and jointly, by means of continuous and effective self-help and mutual aid, will maintain and develop their individual and collective capacity to resist armed attack.

ARTICLE 4

The Parties will consult together whenever, in the opinion of any of them, the territorial integrity, political independence or security of any of the Parties is threatened.

ARTICLE 5

The Parties agree that an armed attack against one or more of them in Europe or North America shall be considered an attack against them all and consequently they agree that, if such an armed attack occurs, each of them, in exercise of the right of individual or collective self-defence recognised by Article 51 of the Charter of the United Nations, will assist the Party or Parties so attacked by taking forthwith, individually and in concert with the other Parties, such action as it deems necessary, including the use of armed force, to restore and maintain the security of the North Atlantic area.

Any such armed attack and all measures taken as a result thereof shall immediately be reported to the Security Council. Such measures shall be terminated when the Security Council has taken the measures necessary to restore and maintain international peace and security.

ARTICLE 6[1]

For the purpose of Article 5, an armed attack on one or more of the Parties is deemed to include an armed attack:

- on the territory of any of the Parties in Europe or North America, on the Algerian Departments of France[2], on the territory of or on the Islands under the jurisdiction of any of the Parties in the North Atlantic area north of the Tropic of Cancer;
- on the forces, vessels, or aircraft of any of the Parties, when in or over these territories or any other area in Europe in which occupation forces of any of the Parties were stationed on the date when the Treaty entered into force or the Mediterranean Sea or the North Atlantic area north of the Tropic of Cancer.

ARTICLE 7

This Treaty does not affect, and shall not be interpreted as affecting in any way the rights and obligations under the Charter of the Parties which are members of the United Nations, or the primary responsibility of the Security Council for the maintenance of international peace and security.

ARTICLE 8

Each Party declares that none of the international engagements now in force between it and any other of the Parties or any third State is in conflict with the provisions of this Treaty, and undertakes not to enter into any international engagement in conflict with this Treaty.

ARTICLE 9

The Parties hereby establish a Council, on which each of them shall be represented, to consider matters concerning the implementation of this Treaty. The Council shall be so organised as to be able to meet promptly at any time. The Council shall set up such subsidiary bodies as may be necessary; in particular it shall establish immediately a defence committee which shall recommend measures for the implementation of Articles 3 and 5.

ARTICLE 10

The Parties may, by unanimous agreement, invite any other European State in a position to further the principles of this Treaty and to contribute to the security of the North Atlantic area to accede to this Treaty. Any State so invited may become a Party to the Treaty by depositing its instrument of accession with the Government of the United States of America. The Government of the United States of America will inform each of the Parties of the deposit of each such instrument of accession.

ARTICLE 11

This Treaty shall be ratified and its provisions carried out by the Parties in accordance with their respective constitutional processes. The instruments of ratification shall be deposited as soon as possible with the Government of the United States of America, which will notify all the other signatories of each deposit. The Treaty shall enter into force between the States which have ratified it as soon as the ratifications of the majority of the signatories, including the ratifications of Belgium, Canada, France, Luxembourg, the Netherlands, the United Kingdom and the United States, have been deposited and shall come into effect with respect to other States on the date of the deposit of their ratifications.[3]

ARTICLE 12

After the Treaty has been in force for ten years, or at any time thereafter, the Parties shall, if any of them so requests, consult together for the purpose of reviewing the Treaty, having regard for the factors then affecting peace and security in the North Atlantic area, including the development of universal as well as regional arrangements under the Charter of the United Nations for the maintenance of international peace and security.

ARTICLE 13

After the Treaty has been in force for twenty years, any Party may cease to be a Party one year after its notice of denunciation has been given to the Government of the United States of America, which will inform the Governments of the other Parties of the deposit of each notice of denunciation.

ARTICLE 14

This Treaty, of which the English and French texts are equally authentic, shall be deposited in the archives of the Government of the United States of America. Duly certified copies will be transmitted by that Government to the Governments of other signatories.

---

1. The definition of the territories to which Article 5 applies was revised by Article 2 of the Protocol to the North Atlantic Treaty on the accession of Greece and Turkey signed on October 22, 1951.
2. On January 16, 1963, the North Atlantic Council noted that insofar as the former Algerian Departments of France were concerned, the relevant clauses of this Treaty had become inapplicable as from July 3, 1962.
3. The Treaty came into force on August 24, 1949, after the deposition of the ratifications of all signatory states.

Source: NATO, last updated December 9, 2008, http://www.nato.int/cps/en/nato-live/official_texts_17120.htm.

The Alliance's Strategic Concept (1999)

Approved by the Heads of State and Government participating in the meeting of the North Atlantic Council in Washington, D.C., April 24, 1999

INTRODUCTION

1. At their Summit meeting in Washington in April 1999, NATO Heads of State and Government approved the Alliance's new Strategic Concept.

2. NATO has successfully ensured the freedom of its members and prevented war in Europe during the 40 years of the Cold War. By combining defence with dialogue, it played an indispensable role in bringing East-West confrontation to a peaceful end. The dramatic changes in the Euro-Atlantic strategic landscape brought by the end of the Cold War were reflected in the Alliance's 1991 Strategic Concept. There have, however, been further profound political and security developments since then.

3. The dangers of the Cold War have given way to more promising, but also challenging prospects, to new opportunities and risks. A new Europe of greater integration is emerging, and a Euro-Atlantic security structure is evolving in which NATO plays a central part. The Alliance has been at the heart of efforts to establish new patterns of cooperation and mutual understanding across the Euro-Atlantic region and has committed itself to essential new activities in the interest of a wider stability. It has shown the depth of that commitment in its efforts to

put an end to the immense human suffering created by conflict in the Balkans. The years since the end of the Cold War have also witnessed important developments in arms control, a process to which the Alliance is fully committed. The Alliance's role in these positive developments has been underpinned by the comprehensive adaptation of its approach to security and of its procedures and structures. The last ten years have also seen, however, the appearance of complex new risks to Euro-Atlantic peace and stability, including oppression, ethnic conflict, economic distress, the collapse of political order, and the proliferation of weapons of mass destruction.

4. The Alliance has an indispensable role to play in consolidating and preserving the positive changes of the recent past, and in meeting current and future security challenges. It has, therefore, a demanding agenda. It must safeguard common security interests in an environment of further, often unpredictable change. It must maintain collective defence and reinforce the transatlantic link and ensure a balance that allows the European Allies to assume greater responsibility. It must deepen its relations with its partners and prepare for the accession of new members. It must, above all, maintain the political will and the military means required by the entire range of its missions.

5. This new Strategic Concept will guide the Alliance as it pursues this agenda. It expresses NATO's enduring purpose and nature and its fundamental security tasks, identifies the central features of the new security environment, specifies the elements of the Alliance's broad approach to security, and provides guidelines for the further adaptation of its military forces.

PART I. THE PURPOSE AND TASKS OF THE ALLIANCE

6. NATO's essential and enduring purpose, set out in the Washington Treaty, is to safeguard the freedom and security of all its members by political and military means. Based on common values of democracy, human rights and the rule of law, the Alliance has striven since its inception to secure a just and lasting peaceful order in Europe. It will continue to do so. The achievement of this aim can be put at risk by crisis and conflict affecting the security of the Euro-Atlantic area. The

Alliance therefore not only ensures the defence of its members but contributes to peace and stability in this region.

7. The Alliance embodies the transatlantic link by which the security of North America is permanently tied to the security of Europe. It is the practical expression of effective collective effort among its members in support of their common interests.

8. The fundamental guiding principle by which the Alliance works is that of common commitment and mutual co-operation among sovereign states in support of the indivisibility of security for all of its members. Solidarity and cohesion within the Alliance, through daily cooperation in both the political and military spheres, ensure that no single Ally is forced to rely upon its own national efforts alone in dealing with basic security challenges. Without depriving member states of their right and duty to assume their sovereign responsibilities in the field of defence, the Alliance enables them through collective effort to realise their essential national security objectives.

9. The resulting sense of equal security among the members of the Alliance, regardless of differences in their circumstances or in their national military capabilities, contributes to stability in the Euro-Atlantic area. The Alliance does not seek these benefits for its members alone, but is committed to the creation of conditions conducive to increased partnership, cooperation, and dialogue with others who share its broad political objectives.

10. To achieve its essential purpose, as an Alliance of nations committed to the Washington Treaty and the United Nations Charter, the Alliance performs the following fundamental security tasks:

Security: To provide one of the indispensable foundations for a stable Euro-Atlantic security environment, based on the growth of democratic institutions and commitment to the peaceful resolution of disputes, in which no country would be able to intimidate or coerce any other through the threat or use of force.

Consultation: To serve, as provided for in Article 4 of the Washington Treaty, as an essential transatlantic forum for Allied consultations on any issues that affect their vital interests, including possible developments posing risks for members' security, and for appropriate co-ordination of their efforts in fields of common concern.

Deterrence and Defence: To deter and defend against any threat of aggression against any NATO member state as provided for in Articles 5 and 6 of the Washington Treaty.

And in order to enhance the security and stability of the Euro-Atlantic area:

Crisis Management: To stand ready, case-by-case and by consensus, in conformity with Article 7 of the Washington Treaty, to contribute to effective conflict prevention and to engage actively in crisis management, including crisis response operations.

Partnership: To promote wide-ranging partnership, cooperation, and dialogue with other countries in the Euro-Atlantic area, with the aim of increasing transparency, mutual confidence and the capacity for joint action with the Alliance.

11. In fulfilling its purpose and fundamental security tasks, the Alliance will continue to respect the legitimate security interests of others, and seek the peaceful resolution of disputes as set out in the Charter of the United Nations. The Alliance will promote peaceful and friendly international relations and support democratic institutions. The Alliance does not consider itself to be any country's adversary.

PART II. STRATEGIC PERSPECTIVES

The Evolving Strategic Environment

12. The Alliance operates in an environment of continuing change. Developments in recent years have been generally positive, but uncertainties and risks remain which can develop into acute crises. Within this evolving context, NATO has played an essential part in strengthening Euro-Atlantic security since the end of the Cold War. Its growing political role; its increased political and military partnership, cooperation and dialogue with other states, including with Russia, Ukraine and Mediterranean Dialogue countries; its continuing openness to the accession of new members; its collaboration with other international

organisations; its commitment, exemplified in the Balkans, to conflict prevention and crisis management, including through peace support operations: all reflect its determination to shape its security environment and enhance the peace and stability of the Euro-Atlantic area.

13. In parallel, NATO has successfully adapted to enhance its ability to contribute to Euro-Atlantic peace and stability. Internal reform has included a new command structure, including the Combined Joint Task Force (CJTF) concept, the creation of arrangements to permit the rapid deployment of forces for the full range of the Alliance's missions, and the building of the European Security and Defence Identity (ESDI) within the Alliance.

14. The United Nations (UN), the Organisation for Security and Cooperation in Europe (OSCE), the European Union (EU), and the Western European Union (WEU) have made distinctive contributions to Euro-Atlantic security and stability. Mutually reinforcing organisations have become a central feature of the security environment.

15. The United Nations Security Council has the primary responsibility for the maintenance of international peace and security and, as such, plays a crucial role in contributing to security and stability in the Euro-Atlantic area.

16. The OSCE, as a regional arrangement, is the most inclusive security organisation in Europe, which also includes Canada and the United States, and plays an essential role in promoting peace and stability, enhancing cooperative security, and advancing democracy and human rights in Europe. The OSCE is particularly active in the fields of preventive diplomacy, conflict prevention, crisis management, and post-conflict rehabilitation. NATO and the OSCE have developed close practical cooperation, especially with regard to the international effort to bring peace to the former Yugoslavia.

17. The European Union has taken important decisions and given a further impetus to its efforts to strengthen its security and defence dimension. This process will have implications for the entire Alliance, and all European Allies should be involved in it, building on arrangements developed by NATO and the WEU. The development of a common foreign and security policy (CFSP) includes the progressive framing of a common defence policy. Such a policy, as called for in the Am-

sterdam Treaty, would be compatible with the common security and defence policy established within the framework of the Washington Treaty. Important steps taken in this context include the incorporation of the WEU's Petersberg tasks into the Treaty on European Union and the development of closer institutional relations with the WEU.

18. As stated in the 1994 Summit declaration and reaffirmed in Berlin in 1996, the Alliance fully supports the development of the European Security and Defence Identity within the Alliance by making available its assets and capabilities for WEU-led operations. To this end, the Alliance and the WEU have developed a close relationship and put into place key elements of the ESDI as agreed in Berlin. In order to enhance peace and stability in Europe and more widely, the European Allies are strengthening their capacity for action, including by increasing their military capabilities. The increase of the responsibilities and capacities of the European Allies with respect to security and defence enhances the security environment of the Alliance.

19. The stability, transparency, predictability, lower levels of armaments, and verification which can be provided by arms control and non-proliferation agreements support NATO's political and military efforts to achieve its strategic objectives. The Allies have played a major part in the significant achievements in this field. These include the enhanced stability produced by the CFE Treaty, the deep reductions in nuclear weapons provided for in the START treaties; the signature of the Comprehensive Test Ban Treaty, the indefinite and unconditional extension of the Nuclear Non-Proliferation Treaty, the accession to it of Belarus, Kazakhstan, and Ukraine as non-nuclear weapons states, and the entry into force of the Chemical Weapons Convention. The Ottawa Convention to ban anti-personnel landmines and similar agreements make an important contribution to alleviating human suffering. There are welcome prospects for further advances in arms control in conventional weapons and with respect to nuclear, chemical, and biological (NBC) weapons.

Security Challenges and Risks

20. Notwithstanding positive developments in the strategic environment and the fact that large-scale conventional aggression against the Alli-

ance is highly unlikely, the possibility of such a threat emerging over the longer term exists. The security of the Alliance remains subject to a wide variety of military and non-military risks which are multi-directional and often difficult to predict. These risks include uncertainty and instability in and around the Euro-Atlantic area and the possibility of regional crises at the periphery of the Alliance, which could evolve rapidly. Some countries in and around the Euro-Atlantic area face serious economic, social and political difficulties. Ethnic and religious rivalries, territorial disputes, inadequate or failed efforts at reform, the abuse of human rights, and the dissolution of states can lead to local and even regional instability. The resulting tensions could lead to crises affecting Euro-Atlantic stability, to human suffering, and to armed conflicts. Such conflicts could affect the security of the Alliance by spilling over into neighbouring countries, including NATO countries, or in other ways, and could also affect the security of other states.

21. The existence of powerful nuclear forces outside the Alliance also constitutes a significant factor which the Alliance has to take into account if security and stability in the Euro-Atlantic area are to be maintained.

22. The proliferation of NBC weapons and their means of delivery remains a matter of serious concern. In spite of welcome progress in strengthening international non-proliferation regimes, major challenges with respect to proliferation remain. The Alliance recognises that proliferation can occur despite efforts to prevent it and can pose a direct military threat to the Allies' populations, territory, and forces. Some states, including on NATO's periphery and in other regions, sell or acquire or try to acquire NBC weapons and delivery means. Commodities and technology that could be used to build these weapons of mass destruction and their delivery means are becoming more common, while detection and prevention of illicit trade in these materials and know-how continues to be difficult. Non-state actors have shown the potential to create and use some of these weapons.

23. The global spread of technology that can be of use in the production of weapons may result in the greater availability of sophisticated military capabilities, permitting adversaries to acquire highly capable offensive and defensive air, land, and sea-borne systems, cruise missiles,

and other advanced weaponry. In addition, state and non-state adversaries may try to exploit the Alliance's growing reliance on information systems through information operations designed to disrupt such systems. They may attempt to use strategies of this kind to counter NATO's superiority in traditional weaponry.

24. Any armed attack on the territory of the Allies, from whatever direction, would be covered by Articles 5 and 6 of the Washington Treaty. However, Alliance security must also take account of the global context. Alliance security interests can be affected by other risks of a wider nature, including acts of terrorism, sabotage and organised crime, and by the disruption of the flow of vital resources. The uncontrolled movement of large numbers of people, particularly as a consequence of armed conflicts, can also pose problems for security and stability affecting the Alliance. Arrangements exist within the Alliance for consultation among the Allies under Article 4 of the Washington Treaty and, where appropriate, co-ordination of their efforts including their responses to risks of this kind.

Part III. The Approach to Security in the 21st Century

25. The Alliance is committed to a broad approach to security, which recognises the importance of political, economic, social and environmental factors in addition to the indispensable defence dimension. This broad approach forms the basis for the Alliance to accomplish its fundamental security tasks effectively, and its increasing effort to develop effective cooperation with other European and Euro-Atlantic organisations as well as the United Nations. Our collective aim is to build a European security architecture in which the Alliance's contribution to the security and stability of the Euro-Atlantic area and the contribution of these other international organisations are complementary and mutually reinforcing, both in deepening relations among Euro-Atlantic countries and in managing crises. NATO remains the essential forum for consultation among the Allies and the forum for agreement on policies bearing on the security and defence commitments of its members under the Washington Treaty.

26. The Alliance seeks to preserve peace and to reinforce Euro-Atlantic

security and stability by: the preservation of the transatlantic link; the maintenance of effective military capabilities sufficient for deterrence and defence and to fulfil the full range of its missions; the development of the European Security and Defence Identity within the Alliance; an overall capability to manage crises successfully; its continued openness to new members; and the continued pursuit of partnership, cooperation, and dialogue with other nations as part of its co-operative approach to Euro-Atlantic security, including in the field of arms control and disarmament.

The Transatlantic Link

27. NATO is committed to a strong and dynamic partnership between Europe and North America in support of the values and interests they share. The security of Europe and that of North America are indivisible. Thus the Alliance's commitment to the indispensable transatlantic link and the collective defence of its members is fundamental to its credibility and to the security and stability of the Euro-Atlantic area.

The Maintenance of Alliance Military Capabilities

28. The maintenance of an adequate military capability and clear preparedness to act collectively in the common defence remain central to the Alliance's security objectives. Such a capability, together with political solidarity, remains at the core of the Alliance's ability to prevent any attempt at coercion or intimidation, and to guarantee that military aggression directed against the Alliance can never be perceived as an option with any prospect of success.

29. Military capabilities effective under the full range of foreseeable circumstances are also the basis of the Alliance's ability to contribute to conflict prevention and crisis management through non-Article 5 crisis response operations. These missions can be highly demanding and can place a premium on the same political and military qualities, such as cohesion, multinational training, and extensive prior planning, that would be essential in an Article 5 situation. Accordingly, while they may pose special requirements, they will be handled through a common set of Alliance structures and procedures.

The European Security and Defence Identity

30. The Alliance, which is the foundation of the collective defence of its members and through which common security objectives will be pursued wherever possible, remains committed to a balanced and dynamic transatlantic partnership. The European Allies have taken decisions to enable them to assume greater responsibilities in the security and defence field in order to enhance the peace and stability of the Euro-Atlantic area and thus the security of all Allies. On the basis of decisions taken by the Alliance, in Berlin in 1996 and subsequently, the European Security and Defence Identity will continue to be developed within NATO. This process will require close cooperation between NATO, the WEU and, if and when appropriate, the European Union. It will enable all European Allies to make a more coherent and effective contribution to the missions and activities of the Alliance as an expression of our shared responsibilities; it will reinforce the transatlantic partnership; and it will assist the European Allies to act by themselves as required through the readiness of the Alliance, on a case-by-case basis and by consensus, to make its assets and capabilities available for operations in which the Alliance is not engaged militarily under the political control and strategic direction either of the WEU or as otherwise agreed, taking into account the full participation of all European Allies if they were so to choose.

Conflict Prevention and Crisis Management

31. In pursuit of its policy of preserving peace, preventing war, and enhancing security and stability and as set out in the fundamental security tasks, NATO will seek, in cooperation with other organisations, to prevent conflict, or, should a crisis arise, to contribute to its effective management, consistent with international law, including through the possibility of conducting non-Article 5 crisis response operations. The Alliance's preparedness to carry out such operations supports the broader objective of reinforcing and extending stability and often involves the participation of NATO's Partners. NATO recalls its offer, made in Brussels in 1994, to support on a case-by-case basis in accordance with its own procedures, peacekeeping and other operations

under the authority of the UN Security Council or the responsibility of the OSCE, including by making available Alliance resources and expertise. In this context NATO recalls its subsequent decisions with respect to crisis response operations in the Balkans. Taking into account the necessity for Alliance solidarity and cohesion, participation in any such operation or mission will remain subject to decisions of member states in accordance with national constitutions.

32. NATO will make full use of partnership, cooperation and dialogue and its links to other organisations to contribute to preventing crises and, should they arise, defusing them at an early stage. A coherent approach to crisis management, as in any use of force by the Alliance, will require the Alliance's political authorities to choose and co-ordinate appropriate responses from a range of both political and military measures and to exercise close political control at all stages.

Partnership, Cooperation, and Dialogue

33. Through its active pursuit of partnership, cooperation, and dialogue, the Alliance is a positive force in promoting security and stability throughout the Euro-Atlantic area. Through outreach and openness, the Alliance seeks to preserve peace, support and promote democracy, contribute to prosperity and progress, and foster genuine partnership with and among all democratic Euro-Atlantic countries. This aims at enhancing the security of all, excludes nobody, and helps to overcome divisions and disagreements that could lead to instability and conflict.

34. The Euro-Atlantic Partnership Council (EAPC) will remain the overarching framework for all aspects of NATO's cooperation with its Partners. It offers an expanded political dimension for both consultation and cooperation. EAPC consultations build increased transparency and confidence among its members on security issues, contribute to conflict prevention and crisis management, and develop practical cooperation activities, including in civil emergency planning, and scientific and environmental affairs.

35. The Partnership for Peace is the principal mechanism for forging practical security links between the Alliance and its Partners and for enhancing interoperability between Partners and NATO. Through

detailed programmes that reflect individual Partners' capacities and interests, Allies and Partners work towards transparency in national defence planning and budgeting; democratic control of defence forces; preparedness for civil disasters and other emergencies; and the development of the ability to work together, including in NATO-led PfP operations. The Alliance is committed to increasing the role the Partners play in PfP decision-making and planning, and making PfP more operational. NATO has undertaken to consult with any active participant in the Partnership if that Partner perceives a direct threat to its territorial integrity, political independence, or security.

36. Russia plays a unique role in Euro-Atlantic security. Within the framework of the NATO-Russia Founding Act on Mutual Relations, Cooperation and Security, NATO and Russia have committed themselves to developing their relations on the basis of common interest, reciprocity and transparency to achieve a lasting and inclusive peace in the Euro-Atlantic area based on the principles of democracy and co-operative security. NATO and Russia have agreed to give concrete substance to their shared commitment to build a stable, peaceful and undivided Europe. A strong, stable and enduring partnership between NATO and Russia is essential to achieve lasting stability in the Euro-Atlantic area.

37. Ukraine occupies a special place in the Euro-Atlantic security environment and is an important and valuable partner in promoting stability and common democratic values. NATO is committed to further strengthening its distinctive partnership with Ukraine on the basis of the NATO-Ukraine Charter, including political consultations on issues of common concern and a broad range of practical cooperation activities. The Alliance continues to support Ukrainian sovereignty and independence, territorial integrity, democratic development, economic prosperity and its status as a non-nuclear weapons state as key factors of stability and security in central and eastern Europe and in Europe as a whole.

38. The Mediterranean is an area of special interest to the Alliance. Security in Europe is closely linked to security and stability in the Mediterranean. NATO's Mediterranean Dialogue process is an integral part of

NATO's co-operative approach to security. It provides a framework for confidence building, promotes transparency and cooperation in the region, and reinforces and is reinforced by other international efforts. The Alliance is committed to developing progressively the political, civil, and military aspects of the Dialogue with the aim of achieving closer cooperation with, and more active involvement by, countries that are partners in this Dialogue.

Enlargement

39. The Alliance remains open to new members under Article 10 of the Washington Treaty. It expects to extend further invitations in coming years to nations willing and able to assume the responsibilities and obligations of membership, and as NATO determines that the inclusion of these nations would serve the overall political and strategic interests of the Alliance, strengthen its effectiveness and cohesion, and enhance overall European security and stability. To this end, NATO has established a programme of activities to assist aspiring countries in their preparations for possible future membership in the context of its wider relationship with them. No European democratic country whose admission would fulfil the objectives of the Treaty will be excluded from consideration.

Arms Control, Disarmament, and Non-Proliferation

40. The Alliance's policy of support for arms control, disarmament, and non-proliferation will continue to play a major role in the achievement of the Alliance's security objectives. The Allies seek to enhance security and stability at the lowest possible level of forces consistent with the Alliance's ability to provide for collective defence and to fulfil the full range of its missions. The Alliance will continue to ensure that—as an important part of its broad approach to security—defence and arms control, disarmament, and non-proliferation objectives remain in harmony. The Alliance will continue to actively contribute to the development of arms control, disarmament, and non-proliferation agreements as well as to confidence and security building measures. The Allies take seriously their distinctive role in promoting a broader, more

comprehensive and more verifiable international arms control and disarmament process. The Alliance will enhance its political efforts to reduce dangers arising from the proliferation of weapons of mass destruction and their means of delivery. The principal non-proliferation goal of the Alliance and its members is to prevent proliferation from occurring or, should it occur, to reverse it through diplomatic means. The Alliance attaches great importance to the continuing validity and the full implementation by all parties of the CFE Treaty as an essential element in ensuring the stability of the Euro-Atlantic area.

PART IV. GUIDELINES FOR THE ALLIANCE'S FORCES PRINCIPLES OF ALLIANCE STRATEGY

41. The Alliance will maintain the necessary military capabilities to accomplish the full range of NATO's missions. The principles of Allied solidarity and strategic unity remain paramount for all Alliance missions. Alliance forces must safeguard NATO's military effectiveness and freedom of action. The security of all Allies is indivisible: an attack on one is an attack on all. With respect to collective defence under Article 5 of the Washington Treaty, the combined military forces of the Alliance must be capable of deterring any potential aggression against it, of stopping an aggressor's advance as far forward as possible should an attack nevertheless occur, and of ensuring the political independence and territorial integrity of its member states. They must also be prepared to contribute to conflict prevention and to conduct non-Article 5 crisis response operations. The Alliance's forces have essential roles in fostering cooperation and understanding with NATO's Partners and other states, particularly in helping Partners to prepare for potential participation in NATO-led PfP operations. Thus they contribute to the preservation of peace, to the safeguarding of common security interests of Alliance members, and to the maintenance of the security and stability of the Euro-Atlantic area. By deterring the use of NBC weapons, they contribute to Alliance efforts aimed at preventing the proliferation of these weapons and their delivery means.

42. The achievement of the Alliance's aims depends critically on the equitable sharing of the roles, risks and responsibilities, as well as the benefits,

of common defence. The presence of United States conventional and nuclear forces in Europe remains vital to the security of Europe, which is inseparably linked to that of North America. The North American Allies contribute to the Alliance through military forces available for Alliance missions, through their broader contribution to international peace and security, and through the provision of unique training facilities on the North American continent. The European Allies also make wide-ranging and substantial contributions. As the process of developing the ESDI within the Alliance progresses, the European Allies will further enhance their contribution to the common defence and to international peace and stability including through multinational formations.

43. The principle of collective effort in Alliance defence is embodied in practical arrangements that enable the Allies to enjoy the crucial political, military and resource advantages of collective defence, and prevent the renationalisation of defence policies, without depriving the Allies of their sovereignty. These arrangements also enable NATO's forces to carry out non-Article 5 crisis response operations and constitute a prerequisite for a coherent Alliance response to all possible contingencies. They are based on procedures for consultation, an integrated military structure, and on co-operation agreements. Key features include collective force planning; common funding; common operational planning; multinational formations, headquarters and command arrangements; an integrated air defence system; a balance of roles and responsibilities among the Allies; the stationing and deployment of forces outside home territory when required; arrangements, including planning, for crisis management and reinforcement; common standards and procedures for equipment, training and logistics; joint and combined doctrines and exercises when appropriate; and infrastructure, armaments and logistics cooperation. The inclusion of NATO's Partners in such arrangements or the development of similar arrangements for them, in appropriate areas, is also instrumental in enhancing cooperation and common efforts in Euro-Atlantic security matters.

44. Multinational funding, including through the Military Budget and the NATO Security Investment Programme, will continue to play an impor-

tant role in acquiring and maintaining necessary assets and capabilities. The management of resources should be guided by the military requirements of the Alliance as they evolve.

45. The Alliance supports the further development of the ESDI within the Alliance, including by being prepared to make available assets and capabilities for operations under the political control and strategic direction either of the WEU or as otherwise agreed.

46. To protect peace and to prevent war or any kind of coercion, the Alliance will maintain for the foreseeable future an appropriate mix of nuclear and conventional forces based in Europe and kept up to date where necessary, although at a minimum sufficient level. Taking into account the diversity of risks with which the Alliance could be faced, it must maintain the forces necessary to ensure credible deterrence and to provide a wide range of conventional response options. But the Alliance's conventional forces alone cannot ensure credible deterrence. Nuclear weapons make a unique contribution in rendering the risks of aggression against the Alliance incalculable and unacceptable. Thus, they remain essential to preserve peace.

The Alliance's Force Posture

The Missions of Alliance Military Forces

47. The primary role of Alliance military forces is to protect peace and to guarantee the territorial integrity, political independence and security of member states. The Alliance's forces must therefore be able to deter and defend effectively, to maintain or restore the territorial integrity of Allied nations and—in case of conflict—to terminate war rapidly by making an aggressor reconsider his decision, cease his attack and withdraw. NATO forces must maintain the ability to provide for collective defence while conducting effective non-Article 5 crisis response operations.

48. The maintenance of the security and stability of the Euro-Atlantic area is of key importance. An important aim of the Alliance and its forces is to keep risks at a distance by dealing with potential crises at an early stage. In the event of crises which jeopardise Euro-Atlantic stability and could affect the security of Alliance members, the Alliance's mili-

tary forces may be called upon to conduct crisis response operations. They may also be called upon to contribute to the preservation of international peace and security by conducting operations in support of other international organisations, complementing and reinforcing political actions within a broad approach to security.

49. In contributing to the management of crises through military operations, the Alliance's forces will have to deal with a complex and diverse range of actors, risks, situations and demands, including humanitarian emergencies. Some non-Article 5 crisis response operations may be as demanding as some collective defence missions. Well-trained and well-equipped forces at adequate levels of readiness and in sufficient strength to meet the full range of contingencies as well as the appropriate support structures, planning tools and command and control capabilities are essential in providing efficient military contributions. The Alliance should also be prepared to support, on the basis of separable but not separate capabilities, operations under the political control and strategic direction either of the WEU or as otherwise agreed. The potential participation of Partners and other non-NATO nations in NATO-led operations as well as possible operations with Russia would be further valuable elements of NATO's contribution to managing crises that affect Euro-Atlantic security.

50. Alliance military forces also contribute to promoting stability throughout the Euro-Atlantic area by their participation in military-to-military contacts and in other cooperation activities and exercises under the Partnership for Peace as well as those organised to deepen NATO's relationships with Russia, Ukraine and the Mediterranean Dialogue countries. They contribute to stability and understanding by participating in confidence-building activities, including those which enhance transparency and improve communication; as well as in verification of arms control agreements and in humanitarian de-mining. Key areas of consultation and cooperation could include inter alia: training and exercises, interoperability, civil-military relations, concept and doctrine development, defence planning, crisis management, proliferation issues, armaments cooperation as well as participation in operational planning and operations.

Guidelines for the Alliance's Force Posture

51. To implement the Alliance's fundamental security tasks and the principles of its strategy, the forces of the Alliance must continue to be adapted to meet the requirements of the full range of Alliance missions effectively and to respond to future challenges. The posture of Allies' forces, building on the strengths of different national defence structures, will conform to the guidelines developed in the following paragraphs.

52. The size, readiness, availability and deployment of the Alliance's military forces will reflect its commitment to collective defence and to conduct crisis response operations, sometimes at short notice, distant from their home stations, including beyond the Allies' territory. The characteristics of the Alliance's forces will also reflect the provisions of relevant arms control agreements. Alliance forces must be adequate in strength and capabilities to deter and counter aggression against any Ally. They must be interoperable and have appropriate doctrines and technologies. They must be held at the required readiness and deployability, and be capable of military success in a wide range of complex joint and combined operations, which may also include Partners and other non-NATO nations.

53. This means in particular:

    a. that the overall size of the Allies' forces will be kept at the lowest levels consistent with the requirements of collective defence and other Alliance missions; they will be held at appropriate and graduated readiness;

    b. that the peacetime geographical distribution of forces will ensure a sufficient military presence throughout the territory of the Alliance, including the stationing and deployment of forces outside home territory and waters and forward deployment of forces when and where necessary. Regional and, in particular, geostrategic considerations within the Alliance will have to be taken into account, as instabilities on NATO's periphery could lead to crises or conflicts requiring an Alliance military response, potentially with short warning times;

c. that NATO's command structure will be able to undertake command and control of the full range of the Alliance's military missions including through the use of deployable combined and joint HQs, in particular CJTF headquarters, to command and control multinational and multiservice forces. It will also be able to support operations under the political control and strategic direction either of the WEU or as otherwise agreed, thereby contributing to the development of the ESDI within the Alliance, and to conduct NATO-led non-Article 5 crisis response operations in which Partners and other countries may participate;

d. that overall, the Alliance will, in both the near and long term and for the full range of its missions, require essential operational capabilities such as an effective engagement capability; deployability and mobility; survivability of forces and infrastructure; and sustainability, incorporating logistics and force rotation. To develop these capabilities to their full potential for multinational operations, interoperability, including human factors, the use of appropriate advanced technology, the maintenance of information superiority in military operations, and highly qualified personnel with a broad spectrum of skills will be important. Sufficient capabilities in the areas of command, control and communications as well as intelligence and surveillance will serve as necessary force multipliers;

e. that at any time a limited but militarily significant proportion of ground, air and sea forces will be able to react as rapidly as necessary to a wide range of eventualities, including a short-notice attack on any Ally. Greater numbers of force elements will be available at appropriate levels of readiness to sustain prolonged operations, whether within or beyond Alliance territory, including through rotation of deployed forces. Taken together, these forces must also be of sufficient quality, quantity and readiness to contribute to deterrence and to defend against limited attacks on the Alliance;

f. that the Alliance must be able to build up larger forces, both in response to any fundamental changes in the security environment and for limited requirements, by reinforcement, by mobilising reserves, or by reconstituting forces when necessary. This ability must be in proportion to potential threats to Alliance security, including potential long-term developments. It must take into account the possibility of substantial improvements in the readiness and capabilities of military forces on the periphery of the Alliance. Capabilities for timely reinforcement and resupply both within and from Europe and North America will remain of critical importance, with a resulting need for a high degree of deployability, mobility and flexibility;

g. that appropriate force structures and procedures, including those that would provide an ability to build up, deploy and draw down forces quickly and selectively, are necessary to permit measured, flexible and timely responses in order to reduce and defuse tensions. These arrangements must be exercised regularly in peacetime;

h. that the Alliance's defence posture must have the capability to address appropriately and effectively the risks associated with the proliferation of NBC weapons and their means of delivery, which also pose a potential threat to the Allies' populations, territory, and forces. A balanced mix of forces, response capabilities and strengthened defences is needed;

i. that the Alliance's forces and infrastructure must be protected against terrorist attacks.

Characteristics of Conventional Forces

54. It is essential that the Allies' military forces have a credible ability to fulfil the full range of Alliance missions. This requirement has implications for force structures, force and equipment levels; readiness, availability, and sustainability; training and exercises; deployment and employment options; and force build-up and mobilisation capabilities. The aim should be to achieve an optimum balance between high readiness forces capable of beginning rapidly, and immediately as necessary, collective defence or non-Article 5 crisis response operations; forces at different levels of lower readiness to provide the bulk of those

required for collective defence, for rotation of forces to sustain crisis response operations, or for further reinforcement of a particular region; and a longer-term build-up and augmentation capability for the worst case—but very remote—scenario of large scale operations for collective defence. A substantial proportion of Alliance forces will be capable of performing more than one of these roles.

55. Alliance forces will be structured to reflect the multinational and joint nature of Alliance missions. Essential tasks will include controlling, protecting, and defending territory; ensuring the unimpeded use of sea, air, and land lines of communication; sea control and protecting the deployment of the Alliance's sea-based deterrent; conducting independent and combined air operations; ensuring a secure air environment and effective extended air defence; surveillance, intelligence, reconnaissance and electronic warfare; strategic lift; and providing effective and flexible command and control facilities, including deployable combined and joint headquarters.

56. The Alliance's defence posture against the risks and potential threats of the proliferation of NBC weapons and their means of delivery must continue to be improved, including through work on missile defences. As NATO forces may be called upon to operate beyond NATO's borders, capabilities for dealing with proliferation risks must be flexible, mobile, rapidly deployable and sustainable. Doctrines, planning, and training and exercise policies must also prepare the Alliance to deter and defend against the use of NBC weapons. The aim in doing so will be to further reduce operational vulnerabilities of NATO military forces while maintaining their flexibility and effectiveness despite the presence, threat or use of NBC weapons.

57. Alliance strategy does not include a chemical or biological warfare capability. The Allies support universal adherence to the relevant disarmament regimes. But, even if further progress with respect to banning chemical and biological weapons can be achieved, defensive precautions will remain essential.

58. Given reduced overall force levels and constrained resources, the ability to work closely together will remain vital for achieving the Alliance's missions. The Alliance's collective defence arrangements in which, for

those concerned, the integrated military structure plays the key role, are essential in this regard. The various strands of NATO's defence planning need to be effectively coordinated at all levels in order to ensure the preparedness of the forces and supporting structures to carry out the full spectrum of their roles. Exchanges of information among the Allies about their force plans contribute to securing the availability of the capabilities needed for the execution of these roles. Consultations in case of important changes in national defence plans also remain of key importance. Cooperation in the development of new operational concepts will be essential for responding to evolving security challenges. The detailed practical arrangements that have been developed as part of the ESDI within the Alliance contribute to close allied co-operation without unnecessary duplication of assets and capabilities.

59. To be able to respond flexibly to possible contingencies and to permit the effective conduct of Alliance missions, the Alliance requires sufficient logistics capabilities, including transport capacities, medical support and stocks to deploy and sustain all types of forces effectively. Standardisation will foster cooperation and cost-effectiveness in providing logistic support to allied forces. Mounting and sustaining operations outside the Allies' territory, where there may be little or no host-nation support, will pose special logistical challenges. The ability to build-up larger, adequately equipped and trained forces, in a timely manner and to a level able to fulfil the full range of Alliance missions, will also make an essential contribution to crisis management and defence. This will include the ability to reinforce any area at risk and to establish a multinational presence when and where this is needed. Forces of various kinds and at various levels of readiness will be capable of flexible employment in both intra-European and transatlantic reinforcement. This will require control of lines of communication, and appropriate support and exercise arrangements.

60. The interaction between Alliance forces and the civil environment (both governmental and non-governmental) in which they operate is crucial to the success of operations. Civil-military cooperation is interdependent: military means are increasingly requested to assist civil

authorities; at the same time civil support to military operations is important for logistics, communications, medical support, and public affairs. Cooperation between the Alliance's military and civil bodies will accordingly remain essential.

61. The Alliance's ability to accomplish the full range of its missions will rely increasingly on multinational forces, complementing national commitments to NATO for the Allies concerned. Such forces, which are applicable to the full range of Alliance missions, demonstrate the Alliance's resolve to maintain a credible collective defence; enhance Alliance cohesion; and reinforce the transatlantic partnership and strengthen the ESDI within the Alliance. Multinational forces, particularly those capable of deploying rapidly for collective defence or for non-Article 5 crisis response operations, reinforce solidarity. They can also provide a way of deploying more capable formations than might be available purely nationally, thus helping to make more efficient use of scarce defence resources. This may include a highly integrated, multinational approach to specific tasks and functions, an approach which underlies the implementation of the CJTF concept. For peace support operations, effective multinational formations and other arrangements involving Partners will be valuable. In order to exploit fully the potential offered by multinational formations, improving interoperability, inter alia through sufficient training and exercises, is of the highest importance.

Characteristics of Nuclear Forces

62. The fundamental purpose of the nuclear forces of the Allies is political: to preserve peace and prevent coercion and any kind of war. They will continue to fulfil an essential role by ensuring uncertainty in the mind of any aggressor about the nature of the Allies' response to military aggression. They demonstrate that aggression of any kind is not a rational option. The supreme guarantee of the security of the Allies is provided by the strategic nuclear forces of the Alliance, particularly those of the United States; the independent nuclear forces of the United Kingdom and France, which have a deterrent role of their own, contribute to the overall deterrence and security of the Allies.

63. A credible Alliance nuclear posture and the demonstration of Alliance solidarity and common commitment to war prevention continue to require widespread participation by European Allies involved in collective defence planning in nuclear roles, in peacetime basing of nuclear forces on their territory and in command, control and consultation arrangements. Nuclear forces based in Europe and committed to NATO provide an essential political and military link between the European and the North American members of the Alliance. The Alliance will therefore maintain adequate nuclear forces in Europe. These forces need to have the necessary characteristics and appropriate flexibility and survivability, to be perceived as a credible and effective element of the Allies' strategy in preventing war. They will be maintained at the minimum level sufficient to preserve peace and stability.

64. The Allies concerned consider that, with the radical changes in the security situation, including reduced conventional force levels in Europe and increased reaction times, NATO's ability to defuse a crisis through diplomatic and other means or, should it be necessary, to mount a successful conventional defence has significantly improved. The circumstances in which any use of nuclear weapons might have to be contemplated by them are therefore extremely remote. Since 1991, therefore, the Allies have taken a series of steps which reflect the post-Cold War security environment. These include a dramatic reduction of the types and numbers of NATO's sub-strategic forces including the elimination of all nuclear artillery and ground-launched short-range nuclear missiles; a significant relaxation of the readiness criteria for nuclear-roled forces; and the termination of standing peacetime nuclear contingency plans. NATO's nuclear forces no longer target any country. Nonetheless, NATO will maintain, at the minimum level consistent with the prevailing security environment, adequate sub-strategic forces based in Europe which will provide an essential link with strategic nuclear forces, reinforcing the transatlantic link. These will consist of dual capable aircraft and a small number of United Kingdom Trident warheads. Sub-strategic nuclear weapons will, however, not be deployed in normal circumstances on surface vessels and attack submarines.

PART V. CONCLUSION

65. As the North Atlantic Alliance enters its sixth decade, it must be ready to meet the challenges and opportunities of a new century. The Strategic Concept reaffirms the enduring purpose of the Alliance and sets out its fundamental security tasks. It enables a transformed NATO to contribute to the evolving security environment, supporting security and stability with the strength of its shared commitment to democracy and the peaceful resolution of disputes. The Strategic Concept will govern the Alliance's security and defence policy, its operational concepts, its conventional and nuclear force posture and its collective defence arrangements, and will be kept under review in the light of the evolving security environment. In an uncertain world the need for effective defence remains, but in reaffirming this commitment the Alliance will also continue making full use of every opportunity to help build an undivided continent by promoting and fostering the vision of a Europe whole and free.

Source: NATO, last updated June 25, 2009, http://www.nato.int/cps/en/natolive/official_texts_27433.htm.

Franco-British Summit: Joint Declaration on European Defense (1998)

Saint Malo, 4 December 1998

The Heads of State and Government of France and the United Kingdom are agreed that:

1. The European Union needs to be in a position to play its full role on the international stage. This means making a reality of the Treaty of Amsterdam, which will provide the essential basis for action by the Union. It will be important to achieve full and rapid implementation of the Amsterdam provisions on CFSP. This includes the responsibility of the European Council to decide on the progressive framing of a common defence policy in the framework of CFSP. The Council must be able to take decisions on an intergovernmental basis, covering the whole range of activity set out in Title V of the Treaty of European Union.

2. To this end, the Union must have the capacity for autonomous action, backed up by credible military forces, the means to decide to use them and a readiness to do so, in order to respond to international crises.

    In pursuing our objective, the collective defence commitments to which member states subscribe (set out in Article 5 of the Washington Treaty, Article V of the Brussels Treaty) must be maintained. In strengthening the solidarity between the member states of the European Union, in order that Europe can make its voice heard in world affairs, while acting in conformity with our respective obligations in NATO, we are contributing to the vitality of a modernised Atlantic Alliance which is the foundation of the collective defence of its members.

Europeans will operate within the institutional framework of the European Union (European Council, General Affairs Council and meetings of Defence Ministers).

The reinforcement of European solidarity must take into account the various positions of European states.

The different situations of countries in relation to NATO must be respected.

3. In order for the European Union to take decisions and approve military action where the Alliance as a whole is not engaged, the Union must be given appropriate structures and a capacity for analysis of situations, sources of intelligence and a capability for relevant strategic planning, without unnecessary duplication, taking account of the existing assets of the WEU and the evolution of its relations with the EU. In this regard, the European Union will also need to have recourse to suitable military means (European capabilities pre-designated within NATO's European pillar or national or multinational European means outside the NATO framework).

4. Europe needs strengthened armed forces that can react rapidly to the new risks, and which are supported by a strong and competitive European defence industry and technology.

5. We are determined to unite in our efforts to enable the European Union to give concrete expression to these objectives.

Source: Atlantic Community Initiative, http://www.atlanticcommunity.org/Saint-Malo%20Declaration%20Text.html.

A Secure Europe in a Better World: European Security Strategy (2003)

Brussels, 12 December 2003

INTRODUCTION

Europe has never been so prosperous, so secure nor so free. The violence of the first half of the 20th Century has given way to a period of peace and stability unprecedented in European history.

The creation of the European Union has been central to this development. It has transformed the relations between our states, and the lives of our citizens. European countries are committed to dealing peacefully with disputes and to co-operating through common institutions. Over this period, the progressive spread of the rule of law and democracy has seen authoritarian regimes change into secure, stable and dynamic democracies. Successive enlargements are making a reality of the vision of a united and peaceful continent.

The United States has played a critical role in European integration and European security, in particular through NATO. The end of the Cold War has left the United States in a dominant position as a military actor. However, no single country is able to tackle today's complex problems on its own.

Europe still faces security threats and challenges. The outbreak of conflict in the Balkans was a reminder that war has not disappeared from our continent. Over the last decade, no region of the world has been untouched by armed conflict. Most of these conflicts have been within rather than between states, and most of the victims have been civilians.

As a union of 25 states with over 450 million people producing a quarter of the world's Gross National Product (GNP), and with a wide range of instruments at its disposal, the European Union is inevitably a global player. In the last decade European forces have been deployed abroad to places as distant as Afghanistan, East Timor and the DRC [Democratic Republic of the Congo]. The increasing convergence of European interests and the strengthening of mutual solidarity of the EU makes us a more credible and effective actor. Europe should be ready to share in the responsibility for global security and in building a better world.

I. THE SECURITY ENVIRONMENT: GLOBAL CHALLENGES AND KEY THREATS

Global Challenges

The post Cold War environment is one of increasingly open borders in which the internal and external aspects of security are indissolubly linked. Flows of trade and investment, the development of technology and the spread of democracy have brought freedom and prosperity to many people. Others have perceived globalisation as a cause of frustration and injustice. These developments have also increased the scope for non-state groups to play a part in international affairs. And they have increased European dependence—and so vulnerability—on an interconnected infrastructure in transport, energy, information and other fields.

Since 1990, almost 4 million people have died in wars, 90% of them civilians. Over 18 million people world-wide have left their homes as a result of conflict.

In much of the developing world, poverty and disease cause untold suffering and give rise to pressing security concerns. Almost 3 billion people, half the world's population, live on less than 2 Euros a day. 45 million die every year of hunger and malnutrition. AIDS is now one of the most devastating pandemics in human history and contributes to the breakdown of societies. New diseases can spread rapidly and become global threats. Sub-Saharan Africa is poorer now than it was 10 years ago. In many cases, economic failure is linked to political problems and violent conflict.

Security is a precondition of development. Conflict not only destroys infrastructure, including social infrastructure; it also encourages criminality, deters investment and makes normal economic activity impossible. A number of countries and regions are caught in a cycle of conflict, insecurity and poverty.

Competition for natural resources—notably water—which will be aggravated by global warming over the next decades, is likely to create further turbulence and migratory movements in various regions.

Energy dependence is a special concern for Europe. Europe is the world's largest importer of oil and gas. Imports account for about 50% of energy consumption today. This will rise to 70% in 2030. Most energy imports come from the Gulf, Russia and North Africa.

Key Threats

Large-scale aggression against any Member State is now improbable. Instead, Europe faces new threats which are more diverse, less visible and less predictable.

Terrorism: Terrorism puts lives at risk; it imposes large costs; it seeks to undermine the openness and tolerance of our societies, and it poses a growing strategic threat to the whole of Europe. Increasingly, terrorist movements are well-resourced, connected by electronic networks, and are willing to use unlimited violence to cause massive casualties.

The most recent wave of terrorism is global in its scope and is linked to violent religious extremism. It arises out of complex causes. These include the pressures of modernisation, cultural, social and political crises, and the alienation of young people living in foreign societies. This phenomenon is also a part of our own society.

Europe is both a target and a base for such terrorism: European countries are targets and have been attacked. Logistical bases for Al Qaeda cells have been uncovered in the UK, Italy, Germany, Spain and Belgium. Concerted European action is indispensable.

Proliferation of Weapons of Mass Destruction is potentially the greatest threat to our security. The international treaty regimes and export control arrangements have slowed the spread of WMD and delivery systems. We are now, however, entering a new and dangerous period that raises the possibility of a WMD arms race, especially in the Middle East. Advances in the biological sciences may increase the potency of biological weapons in the coming years; attacks with chemical and radiological materials are also a serious possibility. The spread of missile technology adds a further element of instability and could put Europe at increasing risk.

The most frightening scenario is one in which terrorist groups acquire weapons of mass destruction. In this event, a small group would be able to inflict damage on a scale previously possible only for States and armies.

Regional Conflicts: Problems such as those in Kashmir, the Great Lakes Region and the Korean Peninsula impact on European interests directly and indirectly, as do conflicts nearer to home, above all in the Middle East. Violent or frozen conflicts, which also persist on our borders, threaten regional stability. They destroy human lives and social and physical infrastructures; they threaten minorities, fundamental freedoms and human rights. Conflict can lead to extremism, terrorism and state failure; it provides opportunities for organised crime. Regional insecurity can fuel the demand for WMD. The most practical way to tackle the often elusive new threats will sometimes be to deal with the older problems of regional conflict.

State Failure: Bad governance—corruption, abuse of power, weak institutions and lack of accountability—and civil conflict corrode States from within. In some cases, this has brought about the collapse of State institutions. Somalia, Liberia and Afghanistan under the Taliban are the best known recent examples. Collapse of the State can be associated with obvious threats, such as organised crime or terrorism. State failure is an alarming phenomenon, that undermines global governance, and adds to regional instability.

Organised Crime: Europe is a prime target for organised crime. This internal threat to our security has an important external dimension: cross-border trafficking in drugs, women, illegal migrants and weapons accounts for a large part of the activities of criminal gangs. It can have links with terrorism.

Such criminal activities are often associated with weak or failing states. Revenues from drugs have fuelled the weakening of state structures in several drug-producing countries. Revenues from trade in gemstones, timber and small arms, fuel conflict in other parts of the world. All these activities undermine both the rule of law and social order itself. In extreme cases, organised crime can come to dominate the state. 90% of the heroin in Europe comes from poppies grown in Afghanistan—where the drugs trade pays for private armies. Most of it is distributed through Balkan criminal networks which are also responsible for some 200,000 of the 700,000 women victims of the sex trade world wide. A new dimension to organised crime which will merit further attention is the growth in maritime piracy.

Taking these different elements together—terrorism committed to maximum violence, the availability of weapons of mass destruction, organised crime, the weakening of the state system and the privatisation of force—we could be confronted with a very radical threat indeed.

II. STRATEGIC OBJECTIVES

We live in a world that holds brighter prospects but also greater threats than we have known. The future will depend partly on our actions. We need both to think globally and to act locally. To defend its security and to promote its values, the EU has three strategic objectives:

Addressing the Threats

The European Union has been active in tackling the key threats.

- It has responded after 11 September with measures that included the adoption of a European Arrest Warrant, steps to attack terrorist financing and an agreement on mutual legal assistance with the U.S.A. The EU continues to develop cooperation in this area and to improve its defences.
- It has pursued policies against proliferation over many years. The Union has just agreed a further programme of action which foresees steps to strengthen the International Atomic Energy Agency, measures to tighten export controls and to deal with illegal shipments and illicit procurement. The EU is committed to achieving

universal adherence to multilateral treaty regimes, as well as to
strengthening the treaties and their verification provisions.

- The European Union and Member States have intervened to help
deal with regional conflicts and to put failed states back on their
feet, including in the Balkans, Afghanistan, and in the DRC. Restoring good government to the Balkans, fostering democracy
and enabling the authorities there to tackle organised crime is
one of the most effective ways of dealing with organised crime
within the EU.

In an era of globalisation, distant threats may be as much a concern
as those that are near at hand. Nuclear activities in North Korea, nuclear
risks in South Asia, and proliferation in the Middle East are all of concern
to Europe.

Terrorists and criminals are now able to operate world-wide: their
activities in central or south-east Asia may be a threat to European countries or their citizens. Meanwhile, global communication increases awareness in Europe of regional conflicts or humanitarian tragedies anywhere
in the world.

Our traditional concept of self-defence—up to and including the
Cold War—was based on the threat of invasion. With the new threats, the
first line of defence will often be abroad. The new threats are dynamic.
The risks of proliferation grow over time; left alone, terrorist networks will
become ever more dangerous. State failure and organised crime spread
if they are neglected—as we have seen in West Africa. This implies that
we should be ready to act before a crisis occurs. Conflict prevention and
threat prevention cannot start too early.

In contrast to the massive visible threat in the Cold War, none of the
new threats is purely military; nor can any be tackled by purely military
means. Each requires a mixture of instruments. Proliferation may be contained through export controls and attacked through political, economic
and other pressures while the underlying political causes are also tackled.
Dealing with terrorism may require a mixture of intelligence, police, judi-
cial, military and other means. In failed states, military instruments may
be needed to restore order, humanitarian means to tackle the immediate
crisis. Regional conflicts need political solutions but military assets and
effective policing may be needed in the post conflict phase. Economic

instruments serve reconstruction, and civilian crisis management helps restore civil government. The European Union is particularly well equipped to respond to such multi-faceted situations.

Building Security in our Neighbourhood

Even in an era of globalisation, geography is still important. It is in the European interest that countries on our borders are well-governed. Neighbours who are engaged in violent conflict, weak states where organised crime flourishes, dysfunctional societies or exploding population growth on its borders all pose problems for Europe.

The integration of acceding states increases our security but also brings the EU closer to troubled areas. Our task is to promote a ring of well governed countries to the East of the European Union and on the borders of the Mediterranean with whom we can enjoy close and cooperative relations.

The importance of this is best illustrated in the Balkans. Through our concerted efforts with the US, Russia, NATO and other international partners, the stability of the region is no longer threatened by the outbreak of major conflict. The credibility of our foreign policy depends on the consolidation of our achievements there. The European perspective offers both a strategic objective and an incentive for reform.

It is not in our interest that enlargement should create new dividing lines in Europe. We need to extend the benefits of economic and political cooperation to our neighbours in the East while tackling political problems there. We should now take a stronger and more active interest in the problems of the Southern Caucasus, which will in due course also be a neighbouring region.

Resolution of the Arab/Israeli conflict is a strategic priority for Europe. Without this, there will be little chance of dealing with other problems in the Middle East. The European Union must remain engaged and ready to commit resources to the problem until it is solved. The two state solution—which Europe has long supported—is now widely accepted. Implementing it will require a united and cooperative effort by the European Union, the United States, the United Nations and Russia, and the countries of the region, but above all by the Israelis and the Palestinians themselves.

The Mediterranean area generally continues to undergo serious problems of economic stagnation, social unrest and unresolved conflicts. The European Union's interests require a continued engagement with Mediterranean partners, through more effective economic, security and cultural cooperation in the framework of the Barcelona Process. A broader engagement with the Arab World should also be considered.

An International Order Based on Effective Multilateralism

In a world of global threats, global markets and global media, our security and prosperity increasingly depend on an effective multilateral system. The development of a stronger international society, well functioning international institutions and a rule-based international order is our objective.

We are committed to upholding and developing International Law. The fundamental framework for international relations is the United Nations Charter. The United Nations Security Council has the primary responsibility for the maintenance of international peace and security. Strengthening the United Nations, equipping it to fulfil its responsibilities and to act effectively, is a European priority.

We want international organisations, regimes and treaties to be effective in confronting threats to international peace and security, and must therefore be ready to act when their rules are broken.

Key institutions in the international system, such as the World Trade Organisation (WTO) and the International Financial Institutions, have extended their membership. China has joined the WTO and Russia is negotiating its entry. It should be an objective for us to widen the membership of such bodies while maintaining their high standards.

One of the core elements of the international system is the transatlantic relationship. This is not only in our bilateral interest but strengthens the international community as a whole. NATO is an important expression of this relationship.

Regional organisations also strengthen global governance. For the European Union, the strength and effectiveness of the OSCE [Organization for Security and Cooperation in Europe] and the Council of Europe has a particular significance. Other regional organisations such as ASEAN [Association of Southeast Asian Nations], MERCOSUR [Southern Common Market] and the African Union make an important contribution to a more orderly world.

It is a condition of a rule-based international order that law evolves in response to developments such as proliferation, terrorism and global warming. We have an interest in further developing existing institutions such as the World Trade Organisation and in supporting new ones such as the International Criminal Court. Our own experience in Europe demonstrates that security can be increased through confidence building and arms control regimes. Such instruments can also make an important contribution to security and stability in our neighbourhood and beyond.

The quality of international society depends on the quality of the governments that are its foundation. The best protection for our security is a world of well-governed democratic states. Spreading good governance, supporting social and political reform, dealing with corruption and abuse of power, establishing the rule of law and protecting human rights are the best means of strengthening the international order.

Trade and development policies can be powerful tools for promoting reform. As the world's largest provider of official assistance and its largest trading entity, the European Union and its Member States are well placed to pursue these goals.

Contributing to better governance through assistance programmes, conditionality and targeted trade measures remains an important feature in our policy that we should further reinforce. A world seen as offering justice and opportunity for everyone will be more secure for the European Union and its citizens.

A number of countries have placed themselves outside the bounds of international society. Some have sought isolation; others persistently violate international norms. It is desirable that such countries should rejoin the international community, and the EU should be ready to provide assistance. Those who are unwilling to do so should understand that there is a price to be paid, including in their relationship with the European Union.

III. POLICY IMPLICATIONS FOR EUROPE

The European Union has made progress towards a coherent foreign policy and effective crisis management. We have instruments in place that can be used effectively, as we have demonstrated in the Balkans and beyond.

But if we are to make a contribution that matches our potential, we need to be more active, more coherent and more capable. And we need to work with others.

More active in pursuing our strategic objectives. This applies to the full spectrum of instruments for crisis management and conflict prevention at our disposal, including political, diplomatic, military and civilian, trade and development activities. Active policies are needed to counter the new dynamic threats. We need to develop a strategic culture that fosters early, rapid, and when necessary, robust intervention.

As a Union of 25 members, spending more than 160 billion Euros on defence, we should be able to sustain several operations simultaneously. We could add particular value by developing operations involving both military and civilian capabilities.

The EU should support the United Nations as it responds to threats to international peace and security. The EU is committed to reinforcing its cooperation with the UN to assist countries emerging from conflicts, and to enhancing its support for the UN in short-term crisis management situations.

We need to be able to act before countries around us deteriorate, when signs of proliferation are detected, and before humanitarian emergencies arise. Preventive engagement can avoid more serious problems in the future. A European Union which takes greater responsibility and which is more active will be one which carries greater political weight.

More Capable. A more capable Europe is within our grasp, though it will take time to realise our full potential. Actions underway—notably the establishment of a defence agency—take us in the right direction.

To transform our militaries into more flexible, mobile forces, and to enable them to address the new threats, more resources for defence and more effective use of resources are necessary.

Systematic use of pooled and shared assets would reduce duplications, overheads and, in the medium-term, increase capabilities.

In almost every major intervention, military efficiency has been followed by civilian chaos. We need greater capacity to bring all necessary civilian resources to bear in crisis and post crisis situations.

Stronger diplomatic capability: we need a system that combines the resources of Member States with those of EU institutions. Dealing with problems that are more distant and more foreign requires better understanding and communication.

Common threat assessments are the best basis for common actions. This requires improved sharing of intelligence among Member States and with partners.

As we increase capabilities in the different areas, we should think in terms of a wider spectrum of missions. This might include joint disarmament operations, support for third countries in combating terrorism and security sector reform. The last of these would be part of broader institution building.

The EU-NATO permanent arrangements, in particular Berlin Plus, enhance the operational capability of the EU and provide the framework for the strategic partnership between the two organisations in crisis management. This reflects our common determination to tackle the challenges of the new century.

More Coherent. The point of the Common Foreign and Security Policy and European Security and Defence Policy is that we are stronger when we act together. Over recent years we have created a number of different instruments, each of which has its own structure and rationale.

The challenge now is to bring together the different instruments and capabilities: European assistance programmes and the European Development Fund, military and civilian capabilities from Member States and other instruments. All of these can have an impact on our security and on that of third countries. Security is the first condition for development.

Diplomatic efforts, development, trade and environmental policies, should follow the same agenda. In a crisis there is no substitute for unity of command.

Better co-ordination between external action and Justice and Home Affairs policies is crucial in the fight both against terrorism and organised crime.

Greater coherence is needed not only among EU instruments but also embracing the external activities of the individual member states.

Coherent policies are also needed regionally, especially in dealing with conflict. Problems are rarely solved on a single country basis, or without regional support, as in different ways experience in both the Balkans and West Africa shows.

Working with Partners. There are few if any problems we can deal with on our own. The threats described above are common threats, shared with all our closest partners. International cooperation is a necessity. We need to pursue our objectives both through multilateral cooperation in international organisations and through partnerships with key actors.

The transatlantic relationship is irreplaceable. Acting together, the European Union and the United States can be a formidable force for good in the world. Our aim should be an effective and balanced partnership with the USA. This is an additional reason for the EU to build up further its capabilities and increase its coherence.

We should continue to work for closer relations with Russia, a major factor in our security and prosperity. Respect for common values will reinforce progress towards a strategic partnership.

Our history, geography and cultural ties give us links with every part of the world: our neighbours in the Middle East, our partners in Africa, in Latin America, and in Asia. These relationships are an important asset to build on. In particular we should look to develop strategic partnerships, with Japan, China, Canada and India as well as with all those who share our goals and values, and are prepared to act in their support.

CONCLUSION

This is a world of new dangers but also of new opportunities. The European Union has the potential to make a major contribution, both in dealing with the threats and in helping realise the opportunities. An active and capable European Union would make an impact on a global scale. In doing so, it would contribute to an effective multilateral system leading to a fairer, safer and more united world.

Source: European Union External Action, http://www.consilium.europa.eu/show Page.aspx?id=266&lang=EN.

The Alliance's Strategic Concept: Active Engagement, Modern Defence (2010)

Strategic Concept for the Defence and Security of the Members of the North Atlantic Treaty Organisation
Adopted by Heads of State and Government in Lisbon

PREFACE

We, the Heads of State and Government of the NATO nations, are determined that NATO will continue to play its unique and essential role in ensuring our common defence and security. This Strategic Concept will guide the next phase in NATO's evolution, so that it continues to be effective in a changing world, against new threats, with new capabilities and new partners:

- It reconfirms the bond between our nations to defend one another against attack, including against new threats to the safety of our citizens.
- It commits the Alliance to prevent crises, manage conflicts and stabilize post-conflict situations, including by working more closely with our international partners, most importantly the United Nations and the European Union.
- It offers our partners around the globe more political engagement with the Alliance, and a substantial role in shaping the NATO-led operations to which they contribute.

- It commits NATO to the goal of creating the conditions for a world without nuclear weapons—but reconfirms that, as long as there are nuclear weapons in the world, NATO will remain a nuclear Alliance.
- It restates our firm commitment to keep the door to NATO open to all European democracies that meet the standards of membership, because enlargement contributes to our goal of a Europe whole, free and at peace.
- It commits NATO to continuous reform towards a more effective, efficient and flexible Alliance, so that our taxpayers get the most security for the money they invest in defence.

The citizens of our countries rely on NATO to defend Allied nations, to deploy robust military forces where and when required for our security, and to help promote common security with our partners around the globe. While the world is changing, NATO's essential mission will remain the same: to ensure that the Alliance remains an unparalleled community of freedom, peace, security and shared values.

CORE TASKS AND PRINCIPLES

1. NATO's fundamental and enduring purpose is to safeguard the freedom and security of all its members by political and military means. Today, the Alliance remains an essential source of stability in an unpredictable world.

2. NATO member states form a unique community of values, committed to the principles of individual liberty, democracy, human rights and the rule of law. The Alliance is firmly committed to the purposes and principles of the Charter of the United Nations, and to the Washington Treaty, which affirms the primary responsibility of the Security Council for the maintenance of international peace and security.

3. The political and military bonds between Europe and North America have been forged in NATO since the Alliance was founded in 1949; the transatlantic link remains as strong, and as important to the preservation of Euro-Atlantic peace and security, as ever. The security of NATO members on both sides of the Atlantic is indivisible. We will

continue to defend it together, on the basis of solidarity, shared purpose and fair burden-sharing.

4. The modern security environment contains a broad and evolving set of challenges to the security of NATO's territory and populations. In order to assure their security, the Alliance must and will continue fulfilling effectively three essential core tasks, all of which contribute to safeguarding Alliance members, and always in accordance with international law:

    A. **Collective defence.** NATO members will always assist each other against attack, in accordance with Article 5 of the Washington Treaty. That commitment remains firm and binding. NATO will deter and defend against any threat of aggression, and against emerging security challenges where they threaten the fundamental security of individual Allies or the Alliance as a whole.

    B. **Crisis management.** NATO has a unique and robust set of political and military capabilities to address the full spectrum of crises—before, during and after conflicts. NATO will actively employ an appropriate mix of those political and military tools to help manage developing crises that have the potential to affect Alliance security, before they escalate into conflicts; to stop ongoing conflicts where they affect Alliance security; and to help consolidate stability in post-conflict situations where that contributes to Euro-Atlantic security.

    C. **Cooperative security.** The Alliance is affected by, and can affect, political and security developments beyond its borders. The Alliance will engage actively to enhance international security, through partnership with relevant countries and other international organisations; by contributing actively to arms control, non-proliferation and disarmament; and by keeping the door to membership in the Alliance open to all European democracies that meet NATO's standards.

5. NATO remains the unique and essential transatlantic forum for consultations on all matters that affect the territorial integrity, political

independence and security of its members, as set out in Article 4 of the Washington Treaty. Any security issue of interest to any Ally can be brought to the NATO table, to share information, exchange views and, where appropriate, forge common approaches.

6. In order to carry out the full range of NATO missions as effectively and efficiently as possible, Allies will engage in a continuous process of reform, modernisation and transformation.

THE SECURITY ENVIRONMENT

7. Today, the Euro-Atlantic area is at peace and the threat of a conventional attack against NATO territory is low. That is an historic success for the policies of robust defence, Euro-Atlantic integration and active partnership that have guided NATO for more than half a century.

8. However, the conventional threat cannot be ignored. Many regions and countries around the world are witnessing the acquisition of substantial, modern military capabilities with consequences for international stability and Euro-Atlantic security that are difficult to predict. This includes the proliferation of ballistic missiles, which poses a real and growing threat to the Euro-Atlantic area.

9. The proliferation of nuclear weapons and other weapons of mass destruction, and their means of delivery, threatens incalculable consequences for global stability and prosperity. During the next decade, proliferation will be most acute in some of the world's most volatile regions.

10. Terrorism poses a direct threat to the security of the citizens of NATO countries, and to international stability and prosperity more broadly. Extremist groups continue to spread to, and in, areas of strategic importance to the Alliance, and modern technology increases the threat and potential impact of terrorist attacks, in particular if terrorists were to acquire nuclear, chemical, biological or radiological capabilities.

11. Instability or conflict beyond NATO borders can directly threaten Alliance security, including by fostering extremism, terrorism, and transnational illegal activities such as trafficking in arms, narcotics and people.

12. Cyber attacks are becoming more frequent, more organised and more costly in the damage that they inflict on government administrations,

businesses, economies and potentially also transportation and supply networks and other critical infrastructure; they can reach a threshold that threatens national and Euro-Atlantic prosperity, security and stability. Foreign militaries and intelligence services, organised criminals, terrorist and/or extremist groups can each be the source of such attacks.

13. All countries are increasingly reliant on the vital communication, transport and transit routes on which international trade, energy security and prosperity depend. They require greater international efforts to ensure their resilience against attack or disruption. Some NATO countries will become more dependent on foreign energy suppliers and in some cases, on foreign energy supply and distribution networks for their energy needs. As a larger share of world consumption is transported across the globe, energy supplies are increasingly exposed to disruption.

14. A number of significant technology-related trends—including the development of laser weapons, electronic warfare and technologies that impede access to space—appear poised to have major global effects that will impact on NATO military planning and operations.

15. Key environmental and resource constraints, including health risks, climate change, water scarcity and increasing energy needs will further shape the future security environment in areas of concern to NATO and have the potential to significantly affect NATO planning and operations.

DEFENCE AND DETERRENCE

16. The greatest responsibility of the Alliance is to protect and defend our territory and our populations against attack, as set out in Article 5 of the Washington Treaty. The Alliance does not consider any country to be its adversary. However, no one should doubt NATO's resolve if the security of any of its members were to be threatened.

17. Deterrence, based on an appropriate mix of nuclear and conventional capabilities, remains a core element of our overall strategy. The circumstances in which any use of nuclear weapons might have to be contemplated are extremely remote. As long as nuclear weapons exist, NATO will remain a nuclear alliance.

18. The supreme guarantee of the security of the Allies is provided by the strategic nuclear forces of the Alliance, particularly those of the United States; the independent strategic nuclear forces of the United Kingdom and France, which have a deterrent role of their own, contribute to the overall deterrence and security of the Allies.

19. We will ensure that NATO has the full range of capabilities necessary to deter and defend against any threat to the safety and security of our populations. Therefore, we will:

- maintain an appropriate mix of nuclear and conventional forces;
- maintain the ability to sustain concurrent major joint operations and several smaller operations for collective defence and crisis response, including at strategic distance;
- develop and maintain robust, mobile and deployable conventional forces to carry out both our Article 5 responsibilities and the Alliance's expeditionary operations, including with the NATO Response Force;
- carry out the necessary training, exercises, contingency planning and information exchange for assuring our defence against the full range of conventional and emerging security challenges, and provide appropriate visible assurance and reinforcement for all Allies;
- ensure the broadest possible participation of Allies in collective defence planning on nuclear roles, in peacetime basing of nuclear forces, and in command, control and consultation arrangements;
- develop the capability to defend our populations and territories against ballistic missile attack as a core element of our collective defence, which contributes to the indivisible security of the Alliance. We will actively seek cooperation on missile defence with Russia and other Euro-Atlantic partners;
- further develop NATO's capacity to defend against the threat of chemical, biological, radiological and nuclear weapons of mass destruction;
- develop further our ability to prevent, detect, defend against and recover from cyber-attacks, including by using the NATO planning process to enhance and coordinate national cyber-defence

capabilities, bringing all NATO bodies under centralized cyber protection, and better integrating NATO cyber awareness, warning and response with member nations;

- enhance the capacity to detect and defend against international terrorism, including through enhanced analysis of the threat, more consultations with our partners, and the development of appropriate military capabilities, including to help train local forces to fight terrorism themselves;

- develop the capacity to contribute to energy security, including protection of critical energy infrastructure and transit areas and lines, cooperation with partners, and consultations among Allies on the basis of strategic assessments and contingency planning;

- ensure that the Alliance is at the front edge in assessing the security impact of emerging technologies, and that military planning takes the potential threats into account;

- sustain the necessary levels of defence spending, so that our armed forces are sufficiently resourced;

- continue to review NATO's overall posture in deterring and defending against the full range of threats to the Alliance, taking into account changes to the evolving international security environment.

SECURITY THROUGH CRISIS MANAGEMENT

20. Crises and conflicts beyond NATO's borders can pose a direct threat to the security of Alliance territory and populations. NATO will therefore engage, where possible and when necessary, to prevent crises, manage crises, stabilize post-conflict situations and support reconstruction.

21. The lessons learned from NATO operations, in particular in Afghanistan and the Western Balkans, make it clear that a comprehensive political, civilian and military approach is necessary for effective crisis management. The Alliance will engage actively with other international actors before, during and after crises to encourage collaborative analysis, planning and conduct of activities on the ground, in order to maximise coherence and effectiveness of the overall international effort.

22. The best way to manage conflicts is to prevent them from happening. NATO will continually monitor and analyse the international environment to anticipate crises and, where appropriate, take active steps to prevent them from becoming larger conflicts.

23. Where conflict prevention proves unsuccessful, NATO will be prepared and capable to manage ongoing hostilities. NATO has unique conflict management capacities, including the unparalleled capability to deploy and sustain robust military forces in the field. NATO-led operations have demonstrated the indispensable contribution the Alliance can make to international conflict management efforts.

24. Even when conflict comes to an end, the international community must often provide continued support, to create the conditions for lasting stability. NATO will be prepared and capable to contribute to stabilisation and reconstruction, in close cooperation and consultation wherever possible with other relevant international actors.

25. To be effective across the crisis management spectrum, we will:

- enhance intelligence sharing within NATO, to better predict when crises might occur, and how they can best be prevented;
- further develop doctrine and military capabilities for expeditionary operations, including counterinsurgency, stabilization and reconstruction operations;
- form an appropriate but modest civilian crisis management capability to interface more effectively with civilian partners, building on the lessons learned from NATO-led operations. This capability may also be used to plan, employ and coordinate civilian activities until conditions allow for the transfer of those responsibilities and tasks to other actors;
- enhance integrated civilian-military planning throughout the crisis spectrum;
- develop the capability to train and develop local forces in crisis zones, so that local authorities are able, as quickly as possible, to maintain security without international assistance;
- identify and train civilian specialists from member states, made available for rapid deployment by Allies for selected missions, able

to work alongside our military personnel and civilian specialists from partner countries and institutions;

- broaden and intensify the political consultations among Allies, and with partners, both on a regular basis and in dealing with all stages of a crisis—before, during and after.

PROMOTING INTERNATIONAL SECURITY THROUGH COOPERATION

Arms Control, Disarmament, and Non-Proliferation

26. NATO seeks its security at the lowest possible level of forces. Arms control, disarmament and non-proliferation contribute to peace, security and stability, and should ensure undiminished security for all Alliance members. We will continue to play our part in reinforcing arms control and in promoting disarmament of both conventional weapons and weapons of mass destruction, as well as non-proliferation efforts:

- We are resolved to seek a safer world for all and to create the conditions for a world without nuclear weapons in accordance with the goals of the Nuclear Non-Proliferation Treaty, in a way that promotes international stability, and is based on the principle of undiminished security for all.
- With the changes in the security environment since the end of the Cold War, we have dramatically reduced the number of nuclear weapons stationed in Europe and our reliance on nuclear weapons in NATO strategy. We will seek to create the conditions for further reductions in the future.
- In any future reductions, our aim should be to seek Russian agreement to increase transparency on its nuclear weapons in Europe and relocate these weapons away from the territory of NATO members. Any further steps must take into account the disparity with the greater Russian stockpiles of short-range nuclear weapons.
- We are committed to conventional arms control, which provides predictability, transparency and a means to keep armaments at the lowest possible level for stability. We will work to strengthen the conventional arms control regime in Europe on the basis of reciprocity, transparency and host-nation consent.

- We will explore ways for our political means and military capabilities to contribute to international efforts to fight proliferation.
- National decisions regarding arms control and disarmament may have an impact on the security of all Alliance members. We are committed to maintain, and develop as necessary, appropriate consultations among Allies on these issues.

Open Door

27. NATO's enlargement has contributed substantially to the security of Allies; the prospect of further enlargement and the spirit of cooperative security have advanced stability in Europe more broadly. Our goal of a Europe whole and free, and sharing common values, would be best served by the eventual integration of all European countries that so desire into Euro-Atlantic structures.

- The door to NATO membership remains fully open to all European democracies which share the values of our Alliance, which are willing and able to assume the responsibilities and obligations of membership, and whose inclusion can contribute to common security and stability.

Partnerships

28. The promotion of Euro-Atlantic security is best assured through a wide network of partner relationships with countries and organisations around the globe. These partnerships make a concrete and valued contribution to the success of NATO's fundamental tasks.

29. Dialogue and cooperation with partners can make a concrete contribution to enhancing international security, to defending the values on which our Alliance is based, to NATO's operations, and to preparing interested nations for membership of NATO. These relationships will be based on reciprocity, mutual benefit and mutual respect.

30. We will enhance our partnerships through flexible formats that bring NATO and partners together—across and beyond existing frameworks:

- We are prepared to develop political dialogue and practical cooperation with any nations and relevant organisations across the globe that share our interest in peaceful international relations.

- We will be open to consultation with any partner country on security issues of common concern.
- We will give our operational partners a structural role in shaping strategy and decisions on NATO-led missions to which they contribute.
- We will further develop our existing partnerships while preserving their specificity.

31. Cooperation between NATO and the United Nations continues to make a substantial contribution to security in operations around the world. The Alliance aims to deepen political dialogue and practical cooperation with the UN, as set out in the UN-NATO Declaration signed in 2008, including through:

- enhanced liaison between the two Headquarters;
- more regular political consultation; and
- enhanced practical cooperation in managing crises where both organisations are engaged.

32. An active and effective European Union contributes to the overall security of the Euro-Atlantic area. Therefore the EU is a unique and essential partner for NATO. The two organisations share a majority of members, and all members of both organisations share common values. NATO recognizes the importance of a stronger and more capable European defence. We welcome the entry into force of the Lisbon Treaty, which provides a framework for strengthening the EU's capacities to address common security challenges. Non-EU Allies make a significant contribution to these efforts. For the strategic partnership between NATO and the EU, their fullest involvement in these efforts is essential. NATO and the EU can and should play complementary and mutually reinforcing roles in supporting international peace and security. We are determined to make our contribution to create more favourable circumstances through which we will:

- fully strengthen the strategic partnership with the EU, in the spirit of full mutual openness, transparency, complementarity and respect for the autonomy and institutional integrity of both organisations;

- enhance our practical cooperation in operations throughout the crisis spectrum, from coordinated planning to mutual support in the field;

- broaden our political consultations to include all issues of common concern, in order to share assessments and perspectives;

- cooperate more fully in capability development, to minimise duplication and maximise cost-effectiveness.

33. NATO-Russia cooperation is of strategic importance as it contributes to creating a common space of peace, stability and security. NATO poses no threat to Russia. On the contrary: we want to see a true strategic partnership between NATO and Russia, and we will act accordingly, with the expectation of reciprocity from Russia.

34. The NATO-Russia relationship is based upon the goals, principles and commitments of the NATO-Russia Founding Act and the Rome Declaration, especially regarding the respect of democratic principles and the sovereignty, independence and territorial integrity of all states in the Euro-Atlantic area. Notwithstanding differences on particular issues, we remain convinced that the security of NATO and Russia is intertwined and that a strong and constructive partnership based on mutual confidence, transparency and predictability can best serve our security. We are determined to:

- enhance the political consultations and practical cooperation with Russia in areas of shared interests, including missile defence, counter-terrorism, counter-narcotics, counter-piracy and the promotion of wider international security;

- use the full potential of the NATO-Russia Council for dialogue and joint action with Russia.

35. The Euro-Atlantic Partnership Council and Partnership for Peace are central to our vision of Europe whole, free and in peace. We are firmly committed to the development of friendly and cooperative relations with all countries of the Mediterranean, and we intend to further de-

velop the Mediterranean Dialogue in the coming years. We attach great importance to peace and stability in the Gulf region, and we intend to strengthen our cooperation in the Istanbul Cooperation Initiative. We will aim to:

- enhance consultations and practical military cooperation with our partners in the Euro-Atlantic Partnership Council;
- continue and develop the partnerships with Ukraine and Georgia within the NATO-Ukraine and NATO-Georgia Commissions, based on the NATO decision at the Bucharest summit 2008, and taking into account the Euro-Atlantic orientation or aspiration of each of the countries;
- facilitate the Euro-Atlantic integration of the Western Balkans, with the aim to ensure lasting peace and stability based on democratic values, regional cooperation and good neighbourly relations;
- deepen the cooperation with current members of the Mediterranean Dialogue and be open to the inclusion in the Mediterranean Dialogue of other countries of the region;
- develop a deeper security partnership with our Gulf partners and remain ready to welcome new partners in the Istanbul Cooperation Initiative.

Reform and Transformation

36. Unique in history, NATO is a security Alliance that fields military forces able to operate together in any environment; that can control operations anywhere through its integrated military command structure; and that has at its disposal core capabilities that few Allies could afford individually.

37. NATO must have sufficient resources—financial, military and human— to carry out its missions, which are essential to the security of Alliance populations and territory. Those resources must, however, be used in the most efficient and effective way possible. We will:

- maximise the deployability of our forces, and their capacity to sustain operations in the field, including by undertaking focused efforts to meet NATO's usability targets;

- ensure the maximum coherence in defence planning, to reduce unnecessary duplication, and to focus our capability development on modern requirements;
- develop and operate capabilities jointly, for reasons of cost-effectiveness and as a manifestation of solidarity;
- preserve and strengthen the common capabilities, standards, structures and funding that bind us together;
- engage in a process of continual reform, to streamline structures, improve working methods and maximise efficiency.

An Alliance for the 21st Century

38. We, the political leaders of NATO, are determined to continue renewal of our Alliance so that it is fit for purpose in addressing the 21st Century security challenges. We are firmly committed to preserve its effectiveness as the globe's most successful political-military Alliance. Our Alliance thrives as a source of hope because it is based on common values of individual liberty, democracy, human rights and the rule of law, and because our common essential and enduring purpose is to safeguard the freedom and security of its members. These values and objectives are universal and perpetual, and we are determined to defend them through unity, solidarity, strength and resolve.

Source: NATO, last updated December 8, 2010, http://www.nato.int/cps/en/SID-B6AD47CE-76D72559/natolive/official_texts_68580.htm?.

Notes

Introduction

1. Praveen Swami, "Full cost of European missile defence could run to billions," *The Telegraph*, November 24, 2010, http://www.telegraph.co.uk/news/newstopics/politics/defence/8157772/Full-cost-of-European-missile-defence-could-run-to-billions.html.

Chapter 1. Fault Lines

1. Statement by the North Atlantic Council, September 12, 2001, http://www.nato.int/docu/pr/2001/p01-124e.htm.
2. Ibid.
3. Don Murray, "Article 5 and 9/11," broadcast September 13, 2001, CBC Digital Archives, http://archives.cbc.ca/war_conflict/defence/clips/10402/.
4. Ibid.
5. Statement by NATO secretary-general Lord Robertson, October 2, 2001, http://www.nato.int/docu/speech/2001/s011002a.htm.
6. "NATO Airborne Early Warning Aircraft Begin Deploying to the United States," NATO/SHAPE News Release, SHAPE Headquarters, Casteau, Belgium, October 10, 2001, http://www.nato.int/docu/update/2001/1008/e1009b.htm.
7. "NATO Naval Force Deploys to Eastern Mediterranean," AFSouth Press Release, October 9, 2001, http://www.nato.int/docu/update/2001/1008/e1009a.htm.
8. Jean-Marie Colombani, "We Are All Americans," *Le Monde*, September 12, 2001, as cited in *World Press Review* 48, no. 11 (November 2001), http://www.worldpress.org/1101we_are_all_americans.htm.
9. Graham E. Fuller, *The New Turkish Republic: Turkey as a Pivotal State in the Muslim World* (Washington, DC: United States Institute for Peace Press, 2008).

219

10. "Turkey's EU Bid Overshadows Angela Merkel Visit," BBC News, March 29, 2010, http://news.bbc.co.uk/2/hi/europe/8592170.stm.

11. Ural Manço, "Turks in Europe: From a Garbled Image to the Complexity of Migrant Social Reality," CIE, Brussels, October 2004, http://www.flwi.ugent.be/cie/umanco/umanco5.htm.

12. Steven Erlanger, "Europeans Woo U.S., Promising Relevance," *New York Times*, March 28, 2010, http://www.nytimes.com/2010/03/29/world/europe/29europe.html.

13. "Germany Asks NATO Allies to Stay Silent on Afghanistan Airstrike," *Deutsche Welle*, November 9, 2009, http://www.dw-world.de/dw/article/0,,4678671,00.html.

14. Erlanger, "Europeans Woo U.S."

15. John R. Schmidt, "Last Alliance Standing? NATO after 9/11," *Washington Quarterly*, Winter 2006–7.

16. Andrew J. Bacevich, *The Limits of Power: The End of American Eceptionalism* (New York: Metropolitan Books, 2008).

17. "Full Transcript: President Obama's Speech on Afghanistan," ABC News/Politics, December 1, 2009, http://abcnews.go.com/Politics/full-transcript-president-obamas-speech-afghanistan-delivered-west/story?id=9220661&page=3.

18. "Pakistan Earthquake Relief Operation: Who Participated?," Topics: NATO, http://www.nato.int/issues/pakistan_earthquake/participation.html.

19. *Transatlantic Trends 2010*, German Marshall Fund.

20. "Speech by German Chancellor Merkel on Receiving the Eric M. Warburg Award in Washington," July 15, 2009, eGov Monitor, London, http://www.egovmonitor.com/node/26349.

Chapter 2. NATO: The Nuts and Bolts

1. Stephen Castle, "NATO Hires a Coke Executive to Retool Its Brand," *New York Times*, July 16, 2008, http://www.nytimes.com/2008/07/16/world/europe/16nato.html?_r=1.

2. Winston S. Churchill, "Iron Curtain Speech," March 5, 1946, delivered at Westminster College, Fulton, MO, http://www.fordham.edu/halsall/mod/churchill-iron.html.

3. Gordon Rayner, "Iraq Inquiry: War 'Not Legitimate,' Sir Jeremy Greenstock Tells Inquiry," *Telegraph*, November 27, 2009, http://www.telegraph.co.uk/news/worldnews/middleeast/iraq/6669634/Iraq-inquiry-war-not-legitimate-Sir-Jeremy-Greenstock-tells-inquiry.html.

4. NATO savvy readers will point out here that NATO went to war in Kosovo without a UN mandate. While true, this stratagem is unlikely to be repeated, and it was a special circumstance. For more discussion of this matter, see chapter 4.

5. James Chace, *Acheson: The Secretary of State Who Created the American World* (New York: Simon & Schuster, 1998), 324.

6. This theme and history of U.S.-EU competition is the subject of chapter 5 in the author's previous book, *America and Europe After 9/11 and Iraq: The Great Divide*, rev. ed. (Washington, DC: Potomac Books, 2008).

7. Secretary of State Dean Acheson and President Truman had played key roles in the creation of the European Coal and Steel Community, the progenitor of the European Union. For those interested in a nontechnical account of the union's creation, read the author's last book (ibid.).

8. Kevin Dougherty, "20 Years after the Berlin Wall: In Europe, U.S. Military Remains Committed to Ensuring Stability while Taking on New Threats," *Stars and Stripes*, November 9, 2009.

9. Frederick Kempe, "Brent Scowcroft on the Fall of the Berlin Wall," New Atlanticist Policy and Analysis Blog, Atlantic Council, February 2, 2009, http://www.acus.org/new_atlanticist/brent-scowcroft-fall-berlin-wall.

10. Zbigniew Brzezinski, "An Agenda for NATO: Toward a Global Security Web," *Foreign Affairs* (September/October 2009): 2.

11. Kempe, "Brent Scowcroft."

12. Secretary of Defense Robert M. Gates, remarks at the NATO Strategic Concept Seminar (Future of NATO), National Defense University, Washington, DC, February 23, 2010, http://www.defense.gov/speeches/speech.aspx?speechid=1423.

13. The 1999 Strategic Concept is reproduced in appendix B. It makes for daunting reading that only the brave will traverse, but the document will serve as the point of departure for the next Strategic Concept, which was adopted in November 2010. The original document is available at NATO's website at http://www.nato.int/cps/en/natolive/official_texts_27433.htm.

14. Hearing of the Senate Committee on Foreign Relations, October 22, 2009, on the development of NATO's new strategic concept.

15. Castle, "NATO Hires a Coke Executive."

16. Partnership for Peace (PfP) and the NATO-Russia Council are not central to this book's narrative. I have included summary information on the Council in chapter 2.

17. *NATO Handbook*, NATO Publications, June 17, 2004, http://www.nato.int/docu/handbook/2001/index.htm.

18. Paul C. Strickland, "USAF Aerospace-Power Doctrine," *Aerospace Power Journal*, Fall 2000, http://www.airpower.maxwell.af.mil/airchronicles/apj/apj00/fal00/strickland.htm.

19. Associated Press, "Allies Block NATO Aid to Turkey," *Global Policy Forum*, February 10, 2003, http://www.globalpolicy.org/component/content/article/167/35198.html.

20. The organization chart is from the NATO website; for the latest chart, see http://www.nato.int/cps/en/natolive/structure.htm. My main references for the description are the website and the *NATO Handbook*.

21. The estimate of NATO's budget comes from a number of conversations with NATO officials. After repeated attempts to meet the chief financial officer (CFO) of NATO, I gave up. Then I found out during my visit to NATO headquarters in Brussels that the multibillion-dollar organization has not had a CFO for quite a while.

22. The early warning AWACS airplanes are an exception to this rule. But the size of this commitment is small relative to the alliance's overall size.

23. Associated Press, "Poland: Afghan Costs Crimping Force Modernization, Leader Says," *New York Times*, September 1, 2010.

24. Carl Ek, "NATO Common Funds Burdensharing: Background and Current Issues," Congressional Research Service Report, RL 30150, January 27, 2009.

25. Ibid.

26. Ibid.

27. Ibid.

28. Ibid.

29. I have calculated the total common funds budget for the alliance by using the total allocation for the United States, $720 million (see ibid., xviii), and each country's allocation ratio from Table 1: NATO Common Budgets Contributions and Cost Shares, 2008/2009.

30. Amy Belasco, "The Cost of Iraq, Afghanistan, and Other Global War on Terror Operations Since 9/11," Congressional Research Service Report, RL 33110 (Washington, DC: CRS, September 28, 2009), http://www.fas.org/sgp/crs/natsec/RL33110.pdf.

Chapter 3. One for All, All for One

1. In fairness I would like to point out that Estonia was vulnerable to this form of attack because it had become one of the most wired countries in Europe. By being so cyber savvy, Estonians were also able to roll with the cyber punches, so to speak. And after the initial, understandable burst of panic and sense of siege, within of days they were able to partially restore many of their Internet services to at least a minimal state of operation.

2. Ian Traynor, "Russia Accused of Unleashing Cyberwar to Disable Estonia," *Guardian*, May 17, 2007, http://www.guardian.co.uk/world/2007/may/17/topstories3.russia.

3. Ibid.

4. Ibid.

5. James Andrew Lewis, *Cyber Attacks Explained* (Washington, DC: Center for Strategic and International Studies, June 15, 2007), http://csis.org/files/media/csis/pubs/070615_cyber_attacks.pdf.

6. Alex Spillius, "Russian Hackers Penetrate Pentagon Computer System in Cyber Attack," *Daily Telegraph*, November 30, 2008, http://www.telegraph.co.uk/news/worldnews/northamerica/usa/3535165/Russian-hackers-penetrate-Pentagon-computer-system-in-cyber-attack.html.

7. Chris Lefkow, "White House, Pentagon Websites Targeted by Cyberattack," *World Military Forum*, July 8, 2009, http://www.armybase.us/2009/07/white-house-pentagon-websites-targeted-by-cyberattack/.

8. NATO, "NATO A–Z: Defending against Cyber Attacks," http://www.nato.int/cps/en/natolive/topics_49193.htm.

9. Gates, remarks at the NATO Strategic Concept Seminar.

10. Chris Lefkow, "US Would Lose Cyberwar: Former Intel Chief," *Agence France-Presse*, February 24, 2010, http://www.google.com/hostednews/afp/article/ALeqM5idcpI-eFNCzvuFP57bK1JztcgIbg.

11. "NATO Agrees Common Approach to Cyber Attack," EurActiv.com, April 4, 2008 (updated January 29, 2010), http://www.euractiv.com/en/infosociety/nato-agrees-common-approach-cyber-defence/article-171377.

12. Marc Kaufman and Dafna Linzer, "China Criticized for Anti-Satellite Missile Test Destruction of an Aging Satellite Illustrates Vulnerability of U.S. Space Assets" *Washington Post*, January 19, 2007.

13. Rob de Wijk, "The Challenge: NATO in the Realm of New Geopolitical Realities," *Issue Brief* (Washington, DC; Atlantic Council of the United States, February 2010).

14. Senator Richard Lugar, "NATO Speech 9/28/2009 Transcript," *Atlantic Council*, Washington, DC, September 28, 2009, http://www.acus.org/event/senator-richard-lugar-congressional-perspective-future-nato/transcript.

15. "Georgia," *Encyclopedia of the Nations*, http://www.nationsencyclopedia.com/economies/Europe/Georgia.html.

16. "Russia," ibid., http://www.nationsencyclopedia.com/economies/Europe/Russia.html.

17. "In his December 2, 1823, address to Congress, President James Monroe articulated United States' policy on the new political order developing in the rest of the Americas and the role of Europe in the Western Hemisphere. The statement, known as the Monroe Doctrine, was little noted by the Great Powers of Europe but eventually became a long-standing tenet of U.S. foreign policy. Monroe and his Secretary of State John Quincy Adams drew upon a foundation of American diplomatic ideals such as disentanglement from European affairs and defense of neutral rights as expressed in Washington's Farewell Address and Madison's stated rationale for waging the War of 1812. The three main concepts of the doctrine—separate spheres of influence for the Americas and Europe, non-colonization, and non-intervention—were designed to signify a clear break between the New World and the autocratic realm of Europe. Monroe's administration forewarned the imperial European powers against interfering in the affairs of the newly independent Latin American states or potential United States territories." More details are available at Office of the Historian, Department of State, "Milestones: 1801–1829—Monroe Doctrine, 1823," http://history.state.gov/milestones/1801-1829/Monroe.

18. Zbigniew Brzezinski and Brent Scowcroft, *America and the World: Conversations on the Future of American Foreign Policy,* moderated by David Ignatius (New York: Basic Books, 2008), 176.
19. "NATO: No MAP for Georgia or Ukraine, but Alliance Vows Membership," Radio Free Europe/Radio Liberty, April 3, 2008, http://www.rferl.org/content/article/1079726.html.
20. Ibid.
21. Michael Schwirtz, Anne Barnard, and C. J. Chivers, "Russia and Georgia Clash over Separatist Region," *New York Times,* August 8, 2008, http://www.nytimes.com/2008/08/09/world/europe/09georgia.html.
22. "Georgia 'Started Unjustified War,'" *BBC News,* September 30, 2009, http://news.bbc.co.uk/2/hi/8281990.stm.
23. "McCain Calls for Russia to Pull Out of Georgia," *Washington Post,* August 8, 2008, http://voices.washingtonpost.com/the-trail/2008/08/08/mccain-calls-for-russia-to-pul.html.
24. "Georgia President Decorates 'Hero' McCain," Agence France-Presse, January 11, 2010.
25. "Rice Criticises 'Isolated' Russia," BBC News, September 18, 2008.
26. "Georgia President Decorates 'Hero' McCain."
27. Edgar Buckley and Ioan Mircea Pascu, "Article 5 and Strategic Reassurance," *Issue Brief* (Washington, DC: Atlantic Council of the United States, February 2010).

Chapter 4. NATO at War

1. "The Powell Doctrine Versus the Albright Doctrine," *The Infamous Brad,* June 17, 2008, http://bradhicks.livejournal.com/398465.html.
2. Madeleine Albright, keynote speech, "NATO Launch of Public Debate on Its New Strategic Concept," Brussels, July 7, 2009, http://www.nato.int/nato_static/assets/audio/audio_2009_07/20090707_090707e-albright.mp3.
3. "Removal of United States Armed Forces from the Federal Republic of Yugoslavia," *Congressional Record: Proceedings and Debates of the 106th Congress, First Session,* April 28, 1999, 7775–96.
4. George Szamuely, "Decline of the West," Antiwar.com, August 10, 2010, http://www.antiwar.com/szamuely/sz081000.html.
5. "Kosovars Flee Region as NATO Strike Enters Day Five," CNN.com, March 28, 1999, http://www.cnn.com/WORLD/europe/9903/28/nato.attack.05/#1.
6. "World: Europe NATO's Bombing Blunders," BBC News, June 1, 1999, http://news.bbc.co.uk/2/hi/340966.stm.
7. Xinhua New Agency, "NATO Chief Sees Possible Withdrawal of Troops from Kosovo in Four Years," China View, August 3, 2009, http://news.xinhuanet.com/english/2009-08/03/content_11820381.htm.
8. Gen. Wesley Clark, USA (Ret.), *Waging Modern War* (New York: PublicAffairs Books, 2001), 43.

9. Ibid., 249.

10. Author's conversation with Gen. Wesley Clark, September 2003.

11. Wikipedia, s.v. "The Bosnian War," last modified November 21, 2010, *http://en.wikipedia.org/wiki/Bosnian_War.*

12. Jorri Duursma, "Justifying NATO's Use of Force in Kosovo?" *Leiden Journal of International Law* 12, no. 2 (1999): 287–95.

13. Transcript of BBC program, *Talking Point on Air*, April 20, 1999.

14. Javier Solana, "NATO's Success in Kosovo," *Foreign Affairs*, November/ December 1999, http://www.foreignaffairs.com/articles/55610/javier-solana/natos-success-in-kosovo.

15. The 1999 Alliance's Strategic Concept is reproduced in appendix B. I felt it should be available to the more inquisitive reader.

16. Ibid.

17. International Security Assistance Force: Key Facts and Figures (as of March 3, 2010), http://www.isaf.nato.int/images/stories/File/Placemats/20100303%20Placemat.pdf.

18. Vincent Morelli and Paul Belkin, *NATO in Afghanistan: A Test of the Transatlantic Alliance*, Congressional Research Service Report, RL 33627 (Washington, DC: CRS, July 2009). I've relied on this excellent and well-researched document to illuminate NATO's performance in Afghanistan and to compile my narrative for this section. Where another source is used, it is acknowledged.

19. The German Marshall Fund of the United States, *Transatlantic Trends 2009*, http://www.gmfus.org/trends/doc/2009_English_Key.pdf.

20. Morellit and Belkin, *NATO in Afghanistan*, 1–2.

21. Ibid., 10–11.

22. Ibid., 17.

23. John Brophy and Miloslav Fisera, "'National Caveats' and It's [sic] Impact on the Army of the Czech Republic," http://www.vabo.cz/stranky/fisera/files/National_Caveats_Short_Version_version_V_29%20JULY.pdf.

24. Ibid.

25. "International Security Assistance Force (ISAF): Facts and Figures," NATO, December 14, 2010, and July 23, 2009, http://www.nato.int/isaf/docu/epub/pdf/placemat.html. These webpages are referred to as ISAF placemats.

26. The German Marshall Fund, *Transatlantic Trends 2009*.

27. Daneil Keohane and Charlotte Blommestijn, *Strength in Numbers? Comparing EU Military Capabilities in 2009 and 1999*, ISS Brief (Paris: EU Institute for Security Studies, December 2009).

Chapter 5. At the Crossroads of NATO and the European Union

1. European Council Joint Action 2008/851/CFSP of 10 November 2008, http://eur-lex.europa.eu/LexUriServ/LexUriServ.do?uri=OJ:L:2008:301:0033:0037:EN:PDF.

2. European Union, "EU Naval Operation Against Piracy (EUNAVFOR Somalia–Operation Atalanta), fact sheet, February 2010, http://www.consilium.europa.eu/uedocs/cms_data/docs/missionPress/files/100201%20Factsheet%20EU%20NAVFOR%20Somalia%20-%20version%2014_EN04.pdf.

3. "Operation Atalanta."

4. Ibid.

5. James Blitz and Gideon Rachman, "More Pirate Attacks Feared off Somalia," *Financial Times*, July 19, 2009, http://www.ft.com/cms/s/0/dd91f388-7492-11de-8ad5-00144feabdc0.html.

6. In ESDP protocol, the designator at the beginning of the mission's name reveals the kind of mission it is: EUPT or EUPOL for a police mission; EUJUST for a rule of law mission; EUFOR for a military mission, as the one in Chad; and so on. This mission also impacted the Central African Republic (RCA) but is far more often called the Chad mission, and I have adopted this name in the book.

7. Actually the ESDP, or European Security and Defense Policy. The Lisbon Treaty in 2010 changed the name to CSDP, and for simplicity and consistency I use CSDP in most of this book, except where the use of ESDP is historically required.

8. For the mission description, I relied on Raymond Frenken's article "EU Chad/CAR Force Aims to Enhance Stability and Protection," *European Security and Defence Policy* 6 (July 2008), http://www.consilium.europa.eu/uedocs/cmsUpload/Pages_from_CEU-8-003%20ESDP6.final_version-7-16.pdf.

9. *Operation EUFOR TChad/RCA* (Armées, France: EUFOR OHQ Tchad RCA, Fort du Mont Valérien-BCAC case 80-00450, 2009).

10. "Top General Chides Germany on Afghanistan Strategy," *Deutsche Welle*, January 20, 2010, http://www.dw-world.de/dw/article/0,,5148528,00.html?maca=en-newsletter_en_Newsline-2356-txt-nl.

11. Steven Erlanger, "Europeans Woo U.S., Promising Relevance," *New York Times*, March 28, 2010, http://www.nytimes.com/2010/03/29/world/europe/29europe.html.

12. The phrase "ever closer union" is at the heart of the European Union. It is found in the preamble to the Treaty of Rome, signed by the European Union states on March 25, 2007. See http://www.historiasiglo20.org/europe/traroma.htm.

13. *Columbia Encyclopedia*, 6th ed. (2008), s.v. "European Coal and Steel Community," http://www.encyclopedia.com/topic/European_Coal_and_Steel_Community.aspx.

14. European Union Delegation to the United States, *The European Union: A Guide for Americans* (Washington, DC: Delegation of the European Union to the United States, 2007), 3.

15. David Armitage, "Soft Power in Hard Times: An American Perspective of ESDP after a Decade," paper presented at the European Union Studies Association Conference, April 23–26, 2009, Los Angeles, CA, http://www.unc.edu/euce/eusa2009/papers/armitage_10J.pdf.

16. See the famous Saint-Malo declaration of December 4, 1998, in "Franco-British Summit Joint Declaration on European Defense," Saint-Malo, http://www.atlanticcommunity.org/Saint-Malo%20Declaration%20Text.html.

17. Armitage, "Soft Power in Hard Times."

18. Antonio Missiroli, "ESDP—How It Works," in *EU Security and Defense Policy: The First Five Years (1999–2004)*, ed. Nicole Gnessoto (Paris: EU Institute for Security Studies, 2004), 58–72, http://www.iss.europa.eu/uploads/media/5esdpen.pdf.

19. Council of the European Union, "CSDP Structures and Instruments," http://www.consilium.europa.eu/showPage.aspx?id=279&lang=EN.

20. Ibid.

21. Robert E. Hunter, "The Three Ds—and a Fourth," *The European Security and Defense Policy: NATO's Companion—or Competitor?*, Rand Monograph 1463 (Santa Monica, CA: Rand, 2002), http://www.rand.org/pubs/monograph_reports/MR1463/MR1463.ch6.pdf.

22. "Military Approves EU Chad Mission," BBC News, January 11, 2008, http://news.bbc.co.uk/2/hi/africa/7181907.stm.

Chapter 6. Islam, Turkey, and NATO

1. John Ward Anderson, "Cartoons of Prophet Met with Outrage," *Washington Post,* January 31, 2006, http://www.washingtonpost.com/wp-dyn/content/article/2006/01/30/AR2006013001316.html.

2. Henrik, "Islam vs Freedom Speech: Moslem Ambassadors Are Turned Down," *Viking Observer,* September 28, 2005, http://viking-observer.blogspot.com/2005/10/islam-vs-freedom-of-speech-moslem.html.

3. Erik Bleich, "Free Speech or Hate Speech? The Danish Cartoon Controversy in the European Legal Context," paper presented at Mount Holyoke College, South Hadley, MA, March 5–6, 2010.

4. Ibid.

5. Stephen Kinzer, "Nato Disses the Muslim World: Choosing Controversial Danish PM Rasmussen as Nato Secretary General Would Threaten the Mission in Afghanistan," *Guardian,* March 25, 2009, http://www.guardian.co.uk/commentisfree/cifamerica/2009/mar/24/nato-afghanistan-rasmussen.

6. "Muslim Nations Ask Turkey to Veto Rasmussen," Welt Online, March 28, 2009, http://www.welt.de/english-news/article3459936/Muslim-nations-ask-Turkey-to-veto-Rasmussen.html.

7. The 2009 Heads-of-State Ministerial (as these meetings are labeled) coincided with the fiftieth anniversary of NATO's founding. Germany and France were cohosts, and the meetings spanned the twin cities of Stras-

bourg, France, and Kehl, Germany. The cities are spanned by a new, modern bridge that metaphorically served as a backdrop to one of NATO's great accomplishments—the linking of France and Germany in a perpetual alliance. One of the scheduled events had French prime minister Sarkozy walk from the French side of the bridge to greet German chancellor Merkel, who walked over from the German side. They met in the middle for a celebratory photograph.

8. "NATO Wants Muslim Troop Support in Afghanistant," *The Voice of Russia*, January 9, 2010, http://english.ruvr.ru/2010/01/09/3472985.html.

9. More accurately the southern, Greek-occupied part of the island.

10. "Turkey Country Report," *Global Finance*, http://www.gfmag.com/gdp-data-country-reports/157-turkey-gdp-country-report.html.

11. "A Mediterranean Maelstrom," *The Economist*, December 10, 2009, http://www.economist.com/world/europe/displaystory.cfm?story_id=15065921.

12. Secretary Hillary Rodham Clinton, remarks at the NATO Strategic Concept Seminar, Washington, DC, February 22, 2010, http://georgia.usembassy.gov/latest-news/official-statements-2010/remarks-at-the-nato-strategic-concept-seminar-february-22.html.

13. "Background Note: Turkey," Bureau of European and Eurasian Affairs, U.S. Department of State, March 10, 2010, http://www.state.gov/r/pa/ei/bgn/3432.htm.

14. David Schenker, "A NATO without Turkey?" *Wall Street Journal*, November 5, 2009, http://online.wsj.com/article/SB10001424052748704013004574517210622936876.html.

15. Daniel Pipes, "Does Turkey Still Belong in NATO?" *Philadelphia Bulletin*, April 6, 2009, http://www.danielpipes.org/6269/does-turkey-still-belong-in-nato.

16. Fulya Ozerkan, "Muslim's Election to Lead PACE Important Signal for Europe, FM Says," *Hürriyet Daily News*, January 31, 2010, http://www.hurriyetdailynews.com/n.php?n=muslims-election-for-pace-important-signal-for-europe-fm-2010-01-31.

17. Christine Benlafquih, "American Muslim Statistics: U.S. Muslims Are Middle Class and Mostly Mainstream," Suite 101.com, March 24, 2008, http://americanaffairs.suite101.com/article.cfm/american_muslim_statistics.

18. Toni Johnson, "Europe: Integrating Islam," Council of Foreign Relations, Backgrounder, December 1, 2009, http://www.cfr.org/publication/8252/integrating_islam_in_europe.html.

19. Ibid.

20. Ibid. Theo van Gogh was a great-grandnephew of the famous painter Vincent van Gogh and was killed in 2004 after making a television film critical of some elements of Islam.

21. Christopher Caldwell, *Reflections on the Revolution in Europe: Immigration, Islam, and the West* (New York: Doubleday, 2009).

22. Xinhua News Agency, "Turkey Refuses U.S. Call to Send More Troops in Afghanistan," China View, December 12, 2009, http://news.xinhuanet.com/english/2009-12/07/content_12601617.htm.

23. Fuller, *The New Turkish Republic*.

24. For an analysis of the new security situation in Europe, see Inna Rogatchi, "Europe: A Dangerous Place to Live," http://www.hvk.org/articles/0703/171.html. This piece is just one of numerous such entries that a simple Google search will find.

25. Andrea Stone, "NATO Chief Condemns Planned Koran Burning," AOLNews.com, September 7, 2010, http://www.aolnews.com/2010/09/07/nato-chief-condemns-planned-quran-burning/.

Chapter 7. To NATO 2.0

1. I realize that the wars related to Bosnia and later in the Balkans around the breakup of Yugoslavia might, for some, tarnish this image of a "Europe whole and free." But I consider these conflicts to be more akin to civil conflicts, not the devastating state-on-state wars through which Europeans have slaughtered each other for centuries.

2. General Scowcroft was an interlocutor for my previous book, *America and Europe After 9/11 and Iraq: The Great Divide*, rev. ed. (Washington, DC: Potomac Books, 2008).

3. "A Secure Europe in a Better World: European Security Strategy," December 12, 2003, http://www.consilium.europa.eu/uedocs/cmsUpload/78367.pdf.

4. Jan Sjostrom, "Chuck Hagel says nation's challenges all 'global,'" *Palm Beach Daily News*, March 17, 2010.

5. "Getting the Millennium Development Goals Back on Track: A Twelve Points EU Action Plan," European Commission Development Center, April 21, 2010, http://ec.europa.eu/development/icenter/featured_20100421_en.cfm.

6. *Promoting Peace and Prosperity—the European Union in the World* (Brussels: Council of the European Union, 2008).

7. Ibid.

8. Council of the European Union, ESDP newsletter, special edition *ESDP@10* (Brussels: InfEuropa schuman, October 2009).

9. Ibid.

10. Doreen Carvajal, "French Deal To Sell Ships To Russians Is Criticized," *New York Times*, December 29, 2010.

11. Ibid.

12. Hon. Peter Gordon MacKay, "NATO in Afghanistan: Transatlantic Security and Canadian Defence Strategy," Royal Institute of International Affairs, February 16, 2009, http://www.google.com/search?sourceid=navclient&ie=UTF-8&rlz=1T4GGLJ_enCA227US228&q=chatham+house+mackay+nato.

13. Andrew J. Bacevich, "How Do We Save NATO? We Quit," *Los Angeles Times*, April 2, 2009.

14. Zbigniew Brzezinski, "An Agenda for NATO," *Foreign Affairs* (September/ October 2009): 2.

15. Secretary-General Anders Fogh Rasmussen, speech, "Building a Euro-Atlantic Security Architecture," Brussels, March 27, 2010, http://www.nato.int/cps/en/natolive/opinions_62395.htm.

16. Judy Dempsey, "NATO Falls Far Short of Helping Afghans," *New York Times*, February 4, 2010, http://www.nytimes.com/2010/02/05/world/europe/05iht-nato.html?emc=tnt&tntemail1=y.

17. General Craddock's testimony to the Senate Foreign Relations Committee, October 22, 2009, http://foreign.senate.gov/hearings/hearing/?id=671ad436-dc08-673a-2439-16c9cf63d81f.

18. John Vandiver, "Miami-Dade area woos AFRICOM ahead of move," *Stars and Stripes*, March 26, 2010, http://www.stripes.com/news/miami-dade-area-woos-africom-ahead-of-move-1.100318.

19. Dean Acheson, *Present at the Creation: My Years at the State Department* (New York: W. W. Norton, 1969, reissued 1987), 493.

20. Giovanni Grevi, Damien Helly, and Daniel Keohane, eds., *European Security and Defence Policy: The first 10 Years (1999–2009)*, The European Institute for Security Studies, 2009, Paris, France, http://www.iss.europa.eu/uploads/media/ESDP_10-web.pdf.

21. Keohane and Blommestijn, *Strength in Numbers?*

22. Ibid., 80.

23. John F. Burns, "British Military Expands Links to French Allies," *New York Times*, November 2, 2010, http://www.nytimes.com/2010/11/03/world/europe/03britain.html?_r=2.

24. David Francis, "European Budget Cuts Change Global Defense Strategy," *Fiscal Times*, October 7, 2010, http://www.thefiscaltimes.com/Issues/Budget-Impact/2010/10/07/European-Budget-Cuts-Change-Global-Defense-Strategy.aspx.

25. Amanda Terkel, "Barney Frank: Cut NATO Spending, It 'Serves No Strategic Purpose," *Huffington Post*, December 27, 2010, http://www.huffingtonpost.com/2010/12/27/barney-frank-nato_n_801515.html.

26. German Marshall Fund, *Transatlantic Trends 2009*.

27. Peter Jay was an interlocutor for my previous book, *America and Europe After 9/11 and Iraq*.

28. Fabrizio Tassinari and Julie Herschend Christoffersen, "Hidden Values: The New Diplomatic Service Brings New Opportunities for the EU," *Global Europe*, April 23, 2010. http://www.globeurope.com/standpoint/hidden-values.

Selected Bibliography

I list here only the resources that I used in writing this book. This bibliography is by no means a complete record of all the works and sources I have consulted. It indicates the substance and range of reading upon which I have formed my ideas, and I intend it to serve as a convenience for those who wish to pursue the subject of this book in more detail and to strike off on their own.

Acheson, Dean. *Present at the Creation: My Years at the State Department.* New York: W. W. Norton, 1987. First published in 1969.

Bacevich, Andrew J. *The Limits of Power: The End of American Exceptionalism.* New York: Metropolitan Books, 2008.

Baker, James A., III. *The Politics of Diplomacy: Revolution, War & Peace, 1989–1992.* With Thomas M. DeFrank. New York: G. P. Putnam & Sons, 1995.

Brzezinski, Zbigniew, and Brent Scowcroft. *America and the World: Conversations on the Future of American Foreign Policy.* Moderated by David Ignatius. New York: Basic Books, 2008.

Bush, George, and Brent Scowcroft. *A World Transformed.* New York: Alfred A. Knopf, 1998.

Caldwell, Christopher. *Reflections on the Revolution in Europe: Immigration, Islam, and the West.* New York: Doubleday, 2009.

Chace, James. *Acheson: The Secretary of State Who Created the American World.* New York: Simon & Schuster, 1998.

Clark, Gen. Wesley K., USA (Ret.). *Waging Modern War.* New York: PublicAffairs Books, 2001.

———. *Winning Modern Wars: Iraq, Terrorism, and the American Empire.* New York: PublicAffairs, 2003. European Union Delegation to the United States. *The*

European Union: A Guide for Americans. Washington, DC: Delegation of the European Union to the United States of America, 2007.

Fuller, Graham E. *The New Turkish Republic: Turkey as a Pivotal State in the Muslim World.* Washington, DC: United States Institute of Peace Press, 2008.

Halper, Stefan, and Jonathan Clarke. *America Alone: The Neo-Conservatives and the Global Order.* New York: Cambridge University Press, 2004.

Kagan, Robert. *Of Paradise and Power: America and Europe in the New World Order.* New York: Alfred A. Knopf, 2003.

Kupchan, Charles A. *The End of the American Era: U.S. Foreign Policy and the Geopolitics of the Twenty-First Century.* New York: Alfred A. Knopf, 2002.

National Commission on Terrorist Attacks upon the United States. *The 9/11 Commission Report: Final Report of the National Commission on Terrorist Attacks upon the United States, Authorized Edition.* New York: W. W. Norton, 2004.

North Atlantic Treaty Organization. *NATO Handbook.* Brussels: NATO Publications, 2009.

Nye, Joseph S., Jr. *Soft Power: The Means to Success in World Politics.* New York: Public Affairs, 2004.

Operation EUFOR Tchad/RCA. Armées, France: EUFOR OHQ Tchad RCA, Fort du Mont Valérien-BCAC case 80-00450, 2009.

Patten, Chris. *Cousins and Strangers: America, Britain, and Europe in a New Century.* New York: Times Books, 2006.

Quinlan, Joseph P. *Drifting Apart or Growing Together? The Primacy of the Transatlantic Economy.* Washington, DC: Center for Transatlantic Relations, Johns Hopkins University, 2003.

Reid, T. R. *The United States of Europe: The New Superpower and the End of American Supremacy.* New York: Penguin Press, 2004.

Rodman, Peter. *Drifting Apart? Trends in U.S.-European Relations.* Washington, DC: The Nixon Center, 1999.

Said, Edward W. *Covering Islam: How the Media and the Experts Determine How We See the Rest of the World,* rev. ed. New York: Vintage Books, 1997. First published by Random House, 1981.

Smith, Karen E. *European Union Foreign Policy in a Changing World,* 2nd ed. Cambridge, UK: Polity Press, 2008.

Index

About the Author

Sarwar A. Kashmeri is a senior fellow with the Atlantic Council's International Security Program and a fellow of the Foreign Policy Association. He is a current affairs commentator, author, and strategic communications adviser. He is recognized on both sides of the Atlantic as a specialist on U.S.-European relations and speaks frequently before business, foreign policy, and military audiences. He is the author of *America and Europe after 9/11 and Iraq: The Great Divide* (Potomac Books, 2008).

Kashmeri earned a bachelor's degree in aerospace engineering and a master's degree in engineering, both from Saint Louis University, Saint Louis, Missouri, where he also taught on the faculty. He has written numerous opinion pieces on transatlantic business and foreign policy issues and chaired business and public policy panels. A member of a number of boards, he teaches an annual course on American foreign policy at Dartmouth College's school of continuing education, the Institute for Lifelong Education at Dartmouth (ILEAD).